P9-AEW-471

DATE DUE

Also by T. A. Heppenheimer

Colonies in Space
Toward Distant Suns
The Real Future
The Man-made Sun
The National Aerospace Plane

THE
COMING
QUAKE

THE
COMING
QUAKE

Science and Trembling on the California Earthquake Frontier

JOHN TAGGART HINCKLEY LIBRARY
NORTHWEST COMMUNITY COLLEGE
POWELL, WYOMING 82435
WITHDRAWN

T. A. Heppenheimer

Times BOOKS

B 57
9/89
121.22

Copyright © 1988 by T. A. Heppenheimer

All rights reserved under International and Pan-American Copyright Conventions. Published in the United States by Times Books, a division of Random House, Inc., New York, and simultaneously in Canada by Random House of Canada Limited, Toronto.

Grateful acknowledgment is made to J. Kent Clark for permission to reprint excerpts from the lyrics to "The Richter Scale" by J. Kent Clark, from the California Institute of Technology musical *Lee and Sympathy*, 1966. Music by Elliott Davis.

ISBN: 0-8129-1616-6

Manufactured in the United States of America

9 8 7 6 5 4 3 2

First Edition

Design by Karin Batten

To Don Dixon, Anita Gale, and Dave Ross,
who live near me by the fault line

ACKNOWLEDGMENTS

During 1974 and 1975 I held a fellowship at Caltech, in the Division of Geological and Planetary Sciences. I was in planetary science; the second floor of our building housed the Seismological Laboratory. On the third floor was an office for Charles Richter, inventor of the Richter scale for earthquakes. And down the hall from my own office was a set of three seismographs, tracing out a record of the day's small tremors. I soon formed the habit of examining their seismograms each morning, just to make sure that California was still in place.

This fellowship lasted through late 1975, and I went on to hold another one in Germany, then came back to build a career as a science writer. I kept in close touch with my friends at Caltech, frequently driving up for a seminar.

Then in 1984, as my free-lancing was expanding, I started to do articles for *Mosaic,* a magazine published by the National Science Foundation. I soon was working effectively with the editor, Warren Kornberg, and late in May I told him I wanted to do an article on the prospects for earthquake prediction. Then I went up to Caltech, where I quickly found Kerry Sieh, a young professor who had made quite a name for himself for his work in seismology. Kerry was warmly encouraging, and helped me develop the ideas I needed for a proper proposal for my article. The article, "Earthquakes to Come," reached print during the summer of 1985.

In mid-September I got a phone call from Hugh O'Neill, an editor at Times Books. He and I had been talking during the previous year about my doing a book for him, and now he suggested that I take that article in *Mosaic* and expand it to book length. The idea intrigued me. I was well aware that there wasn't much worthwhile in print about earthquake prediction; all too much of what had appeared was balderdash and the worst kind of sensationalism. And such a project would draw me closer to Caltech.

I owe a considerable debt to a number of people who have helped me in the course of writing this book. Kerry Sieh stands out and deserves first mention. He sat still for interviews that ran to a total of six hours or more. He arranged for me to join groups of his colleagues on two separate field trips, so that I could see the San Andreas Fault, and observe, in actual use, the methods he introduced. He has shared with me his extensive collection of primary historical source material dealing with early California earthquakes, and has steered me to people and reference material that have been valuable in developing a scenario for the coming Big One.

Several other people have also been very helpful. Ernie Blythe, of the University of Tennessee at Martin, took an entire day to lead me through the area of the Mississippi Valley that was shaken in the powerful quakes of 1811–12. It is a part of America that I would not likely have had the chance to see, if not for him. Karen McNally gave me a lengthy interview and shared with me the details of her life to a degree that leads me to thank her for her confidence in me. Allan Lindh also was particularly helpful, open, and candid; I also thank him for steering me to some excellent satellite photos of earthquake zones. Robert Castle gave me an interview and the use of valuable source material. Otto Nuttli did the same, in St. Louis. And in Parkfield, California, particular thanks go to Donalee Thomason and Duane Hamann, who took me in tow for a day-long set of visits and tours. Donalee also shared her personal memoirs with me.

A number of other geologists and seismologists have also given me interviews. These include Clarence Allen, Bill Bakun, Clark Blake, Thom Davis, Jim Dieterich, John Filson, Jack Healy, Hiroo Kanamori, Lane Johnson, Arch Johnston,

Lucile Jones, Tom McEvilly, Amos Nur, Leon Otis, Ben Page, Barry Raleigh, Dave Russ, Chris Scholtz, Paul Segall, Lynn Sykes, Pradeep Talwani, Wayne Thatcher, Steve Wesnousky, and Max Wyss. In addition, three Los Angeles city officials met with me: Richard Clemmer, Earl Schwartz, and Al Bernson, a member of the city council.

Then there are the editors and other professionals who have helped. Thanks go to Pam Weintraub of *Omni* for commissioning a column on earthquake control; to Arthur Fisher of *Popular Science* for assigning me a feature article on earthquake prediction; to Linda Forristal of the *Washington Times* for a feature assignment that gave a general review of earthquakes; and, as mentioned earlier, to Warren Kornberg of *Mosaic* for getting the whole thing started in the first place. These articles allowed me to pursue a number of useful interviews and to develop portions of text that later wound up in this book. Thanks go also to the librarians at the U.S. Geological Survey in Menlo Park, California, for help in photo research and for the loan of negatives and slides. And particular appreciation goes to Paula Hurwitz of the Caltech Archives, for a transcript of a lengthy set of interviews with Charles Richter, made in 1979.

Also, while mentioning Caltech, credit is due for the lyrics to the song "The Richter Scale," which appear near the end of Chapter 1. This song is taken from a revue titled *Lee and Sympathy*, in honor of the university president Lee DuBridge, and was first performed in 1966. Lyrics are by J. Kent Clark; music is by R. Elliot Davis.

A special word of appreciation goes to my literary agent, Robert Weil now a senior editor at St. Martin's Press. He has now been with me through two complete book projects. And when I think of those who have been with me through the long haul, my sweetheart Angela Johnson is high on the list. She has gone Bob one better, for she and I met as my second book was reaching print in 1979. Since then we have been together through all three of my subsequent books. It would thus be quite appropriate to dedicate this one to her. However, I gave her the dedication on my last one.

I will use this opportunity to show my appreciation to three particularly close friends, who have been with me even longer than Angela. Don Dixon is a space artist; he and I have worked together on various projects since 1976. He has always been there when I needed him, and we have shared many good lunches at Coco's.

Anita Gale is an engineer on the space shuttle at Rockwell International. She introduced Angela and me to the pleasures of Renaissance Pleasure Faire, an annual celebration of Elizabethan England, for which alone she would deserve a dedication. And we have shared many pleasant evenings and dinners.

Dave Ross is a vice-president at the Palantir Corporation, a Silicon Valley start-up company. The poet Robert Burns might have been anticipating Dave's eventual appearance when he wrote, "A man's a man for a' that!" Dave and I have shared good cheer and fellowship, celestial mechanics, artificial intelligence, Rudyard Kipling, Republican politics, dinners at The Sizzler, and much more. I salute him as a true and cherished friend.

Thank you, Don, Anita, and Dave, for sharing the road with me during this past decade.

Fountain Valley, California
February 18, 1988

CONTENTS

THE
COMING
QUAKE

1

SAN ANDREAS

It was a quarter of eight in the morning of October 1, 1987, and I had just finished a phone call to the East Coast. I was standing in my office with a piece of paper in my hand when the windows began to rattle sharply. I thought for a moment that it might be the low and deep vibrations from offshore naval gunnery, which we sometimes experience, but the shuddering now was much too intense and prolonged for that. Then I felt the floor shaking, and I knew it was an earthquake.

I stood there next to the desk, with my hand on the typewriter to steady it, and waited. The movement of the floor, the rattling of the windows became more intense. Still I stood there, trying to sense when they would reach a peak, realizing that if it kept on much longer I'd have to run outside rather than ride it out. The peak of the disturbances came some seconds later, and they began to diminish. In half a minute it was over.

It had woken my girlfriend Angela, who was frightened

and worried. She had been eleven years old in the last one, the San Fernando tremor of 1971, which had occurred only a few miles from her home in Glendale. Now she remembered the terror of that other morning, and she wanted to reach her mom and dad. She got through on the phone, and was quite relieved to hear they were okay. Then we went downstairs to see the reports on television. Soon we were seeing panoramic views of Los Angeles, with tall spires of smoke marking the places where fires had broken out.

These reports soon showed that the quake's epicenter, or central point, was about twenty-five miles away, near the town of Whittier. I realized that Anita, one of my good friends, was working not far away, and asked her how it had been. ''I was in the cafeteria, getting hot water for my coffee-pot,'' she told me. ''When the shaking began, the lights went out, and people were screaming.'' When the power was restored, rumors began to fly that the building had shifted off its foundations, in which case it would be necessary to demolish it and build another one. Fortunately, those rumors proved to be unfounded.

Then, about midmorning I got a phone call from another friend, Margaret, who had been driving on the freeway not far from the epicenter when the first shock hit. ''It was like driving over barrels,'' she told me. ''Then all the traffic suddenly came to a halt.'' In only a few seconds that freeway had turned into an enormous parking lot, with no one caring to risk the next overpass. Margaret had gotten out of her car to help another motorist—and had lost her footing and fallen down, perhaps amid an aftershock. She had hurt herself in the fall, and she was sorry but she wouldn't be able to make it to the dinner we'd planned for that evening.

That quake was the worst to hit the Los Angeles area since 1971, yet it was no more than moderate in size. It killed only three people—a very low toll by comparison with the thousands who had died in such major earthquakes as in Mexico City, a year earlier. Yet inevitably this Whittier quake brought to mind the looming threat of the Big One. For a catastrophe is haunting southern California, in the prospect of its coming great earthquake. Within the lifetimes of most of its people, Los Angeles and its communities stand to be ripped apart in the greatest disaster to strike the United States since the Civil War.

It will take place along the San Andreas Fault, a far-reaching gash in the bedrock of California that runs from the Mexican border well to the north of San Francisco. Along the southern portions of this fault, for a length of as much as two hundred miles, deep and extensive masses of rock will suddenly shift and move. Locked in place for a century and even for several centuries, held there by pressure and friction, they will suddenly break loose. Southern California will definitely not fall into the sea; that is a mere fantasy. But the rocks along the fault will shift by fifteen feet or more.

At its closest, the San Andreas is some fifty miles from my doorstep; yet I know what there is to fear. Our windows will break and throw their shards of glass through the interior of the home. The chimney is likely to topple and crash to the ground, perhaps breaking through the roof, the ceiling, and the second-story floor. Then, amid the thick and blinding cloud of brick dust, our kitchen range and refrigerator will do a devil's dance into the middle of that room, perhaps to fall over onto the sink and bring it down as well. Great cracks and gashes will suddenly appear in the walls and ceiling, while the attic insulation pours through the gaps and adds its contribution to the wreckage.

Still the shakings will continue, merciless and prolonged. A powerful and volcano-like spout of mud and sand may break through the very foundation, the concrete slab on which our house rests, erupting within the family room. Other such spouts may surge upward amid the nearby streets and houses. And the soil within the community is likely to turn to a quicksand having the consistency of porridge. Houses then would sink downward, even as they continued to shake violently, or they could list like sinking ships, coming to rest at crazy angles that would leave the interior floors sharply inclined.

There will be no telephone service, no electricity. The gas, water, and sewerage systems will be unusable. A grocery store is within view from my upstairs window, a quarter-mile away, but it too will stand shattered, with police to guard it against looters. If Angela and I try to get away by car, we must expect the roads to be shut down or else snarled with hours-long tie-ups. There is an elementary school close by, and the Red Cross will probably use it as an emergency center. There my neighbors and Angela and I may spend uneasy nights sleeping on cots, wondering what we will do next.

And my home in Fountain Valley is some fifty miles from the fault. There are at least 10 million people who live closer to it.

Yet, until recent years, there was no way to say much about the coming California earthquake. So vast was the ignorance that it was possible for exercises in sensationalism to come forth, such as *The Last Days of the Late Great State of California,* with its premise that Los Angeles would split from the mainland and plunge into the sea. A somewhat similar book, *The Jupiter Effect,* put forth the notion that an alignment of the planets would touch off the next round of earthquakes—in 1982. As recently as May 1988, it was widely reported that the medieval Nostradamus had predicted "trembling in the new city"—which some took to mean an imminent earthquake in Los Angeles.

Yet the true situation is different. A great deal is now known about this coming quake. Some of it has appeared in geological journals, or in specialized government reports. Some of this information has come out in news articles, and there have been a few good examples of coverage in magazines. Much of this material has appeared in hit-and-miss fashion, but still the information is there, if anyone cares to look for it. In writing this book, I have set out to pull this material together, and to present for the first time the tale of the coming earthquake.

Where and when is it likely to strike? Through the work of Kerry Sieh of Caltech, we now have an answer: It is likely to take place along at least one major stretch of the San Andreas, running from the mountains north of Los Angeles to San Bernardino, east of that city. A second such stretch of fault, from San Bernardino southward to the Salton Sea, is also likely to give way, making the quake stronger, more prolonged, and more devastating. There is as much as a 90-percent chance that this will happen within the next fifty years.

How will we know when the date is closer, within months or years rather than decades? Another seismologist, Karen McNally, has done pathbreaking work in studying an important clue: the cessation or stopping of small and moderate-sized tremors, which ordinarily would pop at reasonably frequent intervals along the fault. This is called *seismic quiescence*. It amounts to the calm before the storm, an ominous slowdown in normal seismic activity that has repeatedly foreshadowed a great earthquake.

How can we pin down the prediction more closely? There has been a great deal of confusion on this point. Time and again, experts have come forth, proposing that there exist earthquake precursors, physical phenomena that could be monitored and used to develop increasingly accurate predictions as the date of the quake nears. Such efforts continue to attract attention, and it would be easy to set forth the hope that they will succeed. But it would also be irresponsible. The unfortunate fact is that the search for such precursors has not succeeded. It has merely led a number of reputable scientists into blind alleys, from which they have been surprised repeatedly by the unexpected occurrence of unpredicted quakes.

Yet today a new effort is under way, seeking to lay the foundations for a true science of earthquake prediction. Chastised by the disappointments of recent years, seismologists have set their hopes on a remote valley in central California called Cholame, near a village named Parkfield. Here the San Andreas shows an uncommonly regular behavior, breaking in moderate-size quakes every twenty-two years. With a recurrence expected soon, Parkfield is the place where seismologists are developing ways to peek into the earth, observing the behavior of the fault itself as it gathers strain and prepares to give way in the next quake. In the wake of the work at Parkfield, then, it may indeed be possible to prepare well-founded predictions of the coming Los Angeles earthquake. And today there are detailed scenarios describing what it will be like. They have not been prepared for the general public; these scenarios exist for the use of disaster-planning agencies within the city and state governments. But they are not secret; they are available to those who know what to ask for. Drawing on this work, I have prepared a chapter-long discussion, accompanied by a map, showing what the authors of these scenarios believe will happen.

And beyond the coming California quake there will be others, for it is a surprising and unpleasant fact, appreciated only in recent years, that virtually no part of the United States is safe from great earthquakes. It is only within the past decade that we have come to realize that the greatest earthquake danger lies not in California, but in the Midwest—a region that is no better prepared for earthquakes than California is ready for hurricanes. Moreover, it is only within the present year that seismologists have understood that there is considerable danger to Seattle and the Pacific Northwest. The explosion of Mount St. Helens took that part of the country by surprise in 1980; a great earthquake would be just as unexpected.

What may happen, then, in the future? The means are already at hand for electronic warning systems emplaced along dangerous faults. Their transmitted signals, outracing the shock waves from the quake, could give cities a minute or more of warning, which is enough to save many lives and protect some essential services. True earthquake prediction may emerge from efforts building on the work at Parkfield, which seeks to develop pictures of the working fault as it gathers its stress. And, most startlingly, this stress may be controlled, released in small, frequent tremors. The prospect of earthquake control is a real possibility for the future. For the present, however, I wanted to begin by seeing where the quake itself might take place. Thus, one day late in 1986, I drove out to a site a hundred miles east of Los Angeles, where the San Andreas Fault has been laid open to view. It was a dry November morning, and the place was just north of the town of Indio, a few miles off Interstate 10. There I would join a group of geologists on a tour.

An oldies station was playing the 1965 hit "Goldfinger" as I drove gingerly along the Coachella Canal, with nothing on my right but a steep drop-off into its blue water. I parked with the others and quickly found myself in a crowd of casually dressed young people. One man was wearing a T-shirt with a picture of a flasher opening his coat wide as he stands in front of a volcano; the caption read, EXPOSE YOURSELF TO GEOLOGY.

A brushy plain extended toward a line of hills a mile or two away, deeply gullied, eroded and pockmarked with the floods of thousands of years. Someone picked up a fragment of pottery left by the Coahuilla Indians, most likely before any Europeans ever saw this country. The Indians were long gone, yet it was easy to think that this was still their land. The hand of our civilization had touched it only lightly. There was a long, thin levee a half-mile away; beyond it was the fine tracery of a power line; and that was all. The rest was dun-colored desert and starkly contoured uplands. Within its immensity, the works of humans seemed as evanescent as the sharply drawn vapor trail of an aircraft in the featureless blue sky.

It was the permanence of the land that had drawn us, the unchanging soil and sand of its upper layers, in which great earthquakes had left their marks for thousands of years. Here Kerry Sieh, a professor at Caltech, had dug trenches across the San Andreas, laying bare those layers and uncovering those marks. From them he had shown that very large quakes had occurred here several times during the past thousand years. The last one was several hundred years ago; the next might come at any time. Now he would be leading us on a tour. We would see the formations that could tell of the danger of a new quake at this site, one that would rock all of southern California.

Kerry is a tall, slim man in his mid-thirties, with steel-rimmed glasses and silver-blond hair that partly covers his ears. He was dressed in cutoffs and a light blue pullover, standard attire for a day in the field. He strode forward purposefully and took up a bullhorn. "If you'd been here three hundred years ago," he began, "you'd have been standing on the southernmost tip of a peninsula in Lake Coahuilla." He pointed to a whitish, sparsely vegetated area amid the flat desert wastes. "That was a lagoon in the ancient lake. There are salts in the lagoon sediments." Deftly he sketched the extent of the lake in those days, remarking that the nearby town of Indio would have been "under about forty feet of water."

Lake Coahuilla exists today as a small remnant, the Salton Sea. That saline lake formed early in this century when an irrigation project got out of control. Water from the Colorado River surged into the lowlands, flooding them to a considerable depth. But from time to time during the prior centuries, the Colorado itself had done far more, entirely on its own. Through natural shifts in its course, somewhat like those of the Mississippi, this river had sent its waters into south-central California to form the lake. Then, after decades or centuries, another shift in course would send the Colorado's full flow into the Gulf of California, leaving Lake Coahuilla to dry and evaporate. "It would take about sixty years for the lake to desiccate," Sieh went on.

The lake was important. In its intermittent fillings and evaporations, it had deposited successive beds of sediment that contained bits of charcoal or carbon. These could be dated through a method based on decay of the radioactive isotope carbon 14. That would give the ages of the sediment beds. The major earthquakes, shaking the valley from time to time, had broken those beds, wrenching them abruptly.

Dry creek beds, crossing the fault, had been cut, with their separated lengths of channel sliding sideways, forming what are called *offsets*. The lengths of these offsets could be measured with a steel tape. The ages of the offsets came from studies with carbon 14. The ratio, offset length divided by its age, gave the *slip rate*, the rate at which the fault was building up strain. That rate, in turn, was a few centimeters per year. After a century the accumulating strain would build up to several meters, and the land would be ripe for a great quake.

Getting accurate dates was the key. The essential isotope, carbon 14, forms high in the atmosphere when cosmic rays strike molecules of carbon dioxide gas. These molecules drift to the earth's surface, where living plants, taking up the carbon dioxide in the course of their growth, incorporate small amounts of the isotope within their wood or leaves. After they die, the carbon 14 undergoes radioactive decay and slowly diminishes in quantity, with half of it being gone in 5,770 years. The amount remaining could be measured in a lab, using standard instruments for studying radioactivity. By measuring this remaining amount, one could determine how long ago the plant died, and hence the age of the carbon sample being studied.

Now Sieh recalled the first Spanish expedition to the area, led by the army captain Juan Bautista de Anza in 1775. "Anza, when he came across the valley, saw no lake at all. So the lake must have begun to dry up no later than 1715. Radiocarbon dating of chaparral, of brush that was drowned by the rising lake, gives dates of about 1630 to 1700 A.D. (When Boston and Harvard colleges were founded, this land was a wilderness that would demand the age-dating techniques appropriate to the study of early man.) "Indian legends tell of at least three fillings of the lake, though we don't know how far back they go. At this site we have evidence for eight lakes, five of them within the last thousand years, the other three scattered through the previous 3,500 years."

In the two hundred years since the coming of the Spaniards, however, there had been no major quake in this area. The 1906 San Francisco tremor occurred along the San Andreas, it is true; but the fault extends along hundreds of miles, and it is quite possible for a great earthquake to take place along only part of this length, while leaving the rest entirely undisturbed. The long-standing inactivity of the fault, here near Indio and the Salton Sea, thus had led some geologists to propose that the San Andreas in this area was dormant or inactive. But Sieh had his own conclusions, based on what he had learned from the offsets, the major breaks in the sediments: "The evidence certainly suggests that this section of the fault produces very large earthquakes. It certainly has had very major slippage in the past thousand years." It was far from inactive, and probably overdue for its next great quake.

Sieh led us across the desert floor and into one of his main excavations. He had hired a backhoe operator to dig a set of trenches straddling the San Andreas. Within the trench walls he had carefully sampled the layers of soil and noted their sequence. He had also meticulously searched for bits of plant material mixed thinly with the sands and sediments of these layers. Leaf-litter was best, though it was hard to find; he could send it off to a carbon-14 laboratory and get back dates he could trust. Ancient twigs or bits of wood, charred perhaps from lightning or an Indian fire, were less trustworthy. They might have lain in the ground for a century or two before being swept by a rainstorm into Lake Coahuilla; and that would throw off the dates, make the layer appear older than it actually was.

Now we were making our way across a low sandbar that descended sharply into the cut. Dust was rising; the sun was getting hot, and dozens of us were crowding into this narrow ditch in the desert, either standing on its rim or gathering along its length. Sieh now took up his bullhorn once again and spoke of the succession of lakes. He had designated them by letters. Lake A was the most recent, the one that may have dried up during the eighteenth century; Lakes B, C, and so forth were earlier.

"There was an earthquake during the last lake; I would date it at 1680 A.D., plus or minus forty years, and that was probably a great quake. The offset was about two meters; that's unlikely to be less than magnitude 7.5." (The 1906 San Francisco tremor was 7.9.) "The next event back has a total of three and a half meters of offset; that happened about the year 1500, plus or minus one hundred years. Also, Lake B existed around that time, at 1400 to 1500 A.D. Going back still further,, we find two more lakes, with another major quake around the year 1250. Then there is Lake E, which we date at 1003 A.D., plus or minus twenty-seven years. As Lake E was approaching its highest level, there was another great quake." That meant there was an average of about 250 years between the most severe shakers, which would rend the land with offsets many feet long. The last one had been just around three hundred years ago. Even if one made allowances for smaller quakes, which would relieve some of the stress, the ground we were standing on had accumulated well over two hundred years worth of seismic strain.

The tawny sand in the trench walls had a certain cohesiveness. He pointed to a layer within it: "Here's a clayey bed that represents an old lagoon deposit." That was his Lake E; and just as a scattering of bricks can tell of the life of an ancient city, so this clay hinted at the rich vitality that once had been Lake Coahuilla. The land was fertile; there could be no doubt of that, for the irrigated fields of the Imperial and Coachella valleys, overflowing with fruit and green produce, lay only a few miles to the southeast. The lake must have been a lush wetland in its day, ripe with reeds and tall lakeside grass, silent in the morning mists, full of fish and birds, flourishing with the homes of the Coahuilla people. Now the old lakebed had the brown-grayness of old bones. You could break pieces off with your fingers or crumble them to powder in your hand. This layer of clay had been used by the Indians for pottery. Now it could give one more thing: a warning.

"You can see this same clay bed in other excavations," Sieh went on. "We've traced it to the fault. The fault is right here in front of me, running under that gentleman in the red shirt." He nodded at one of our group who was standing directly on top of it. "You're standing on the main trace of the fault. It's razor-thin here, no thicker than a piece of cardboard. If you dug away, you'd see the fault cutting the various beds. This clay bed has sustained a considerable offset due to earthquakes. The distance is about twenty-four meters. Between 1000 and 1700 A.D., that bed was offset by twenty-four meters in seven hundred years. That gives us a slip rate of—what? Can anyone here divide distance by time to get a slip rate?"

The answer was 3.4 centimeters per year. If the San Andreas could slip easily and steadily, then year by year one would find roads, fences, power lines, and the like all shifting by such a distance: an inch and a third per year, a speed somewhat slower than that at which fingernails grow. But the fault does not slide so easily; it hangs up and locks in place, for centuries at a time, eventually releasing its tension all at once. "We haven't had a major earthquake probably for at least two hundred years. So the adjacent rocks here have six meters or more of accumulated strain."

I looked closely at the fault. There was nothing to see. It existed as a crack in the soil, well covered with dust, and that was all. It was like a far-reaching break running through the foundation of a building, whose weight keeps it tightly closed. If you were to brush away the dust, you would see this flaw, this fissure in the dry sand; yet even then it would appear entirely unimpressive. But this crack ran most of the length of California. Here, east of Los Angeles, its rocks had enough strain to cause its opposite sides to shove and butt their way past each other for twenty feet or more. That would mean a quake as severe as at San Francisco in 1906, for which such motions along the fault had been as much as twenty-one feet.

Sieh now pointed toward a low ridge of hills, deep blue in the haze, ten miles or more in the distance. They were off to the southeast. A slot had formed in their profile, a rectangular cut whose right-hand side was a steep cliff. That cliff was the mark of the San Andreas. The fault had ripped away the sides of mountains, forming a scarp that could be seen for many miles.

He described how the fault had slipped slightly, following minor earthquakes in recent years. For example, in July there had been a moderate quake near Palm Springs, which was not on the San Andreas, but was a few miles away. A few days later, there was a millimeter or two of motion on the main fault. The same thing had happened following other such quakes, within the past decade or so. "Some of us are wondering if perhaps the fault is loaded to the point where it's almost ready to fail. Whenever it gets jostled by a nearby earthquake, it produces a small amount of what we call triggered slip."

He was ready to offer his conclusions: "My hunch is that when a great quake occurs here, we're going to see several meters of offset, and it will be on the order of the same size as the 1857 or 1906 earthquakes." Those were the two largest ever to strike California during its recorded history. "My investigations are leading me to the conclusion that this place is likely to be the location of the next great San Andreas quake."

By now the sun was well up and the day was getting hot. As arranged, a truck pulled up on the canal embankment, loaded with coolers full of cold drinks. There I was joined by Mark Smith, a hearty geologist with a California Angels baseball cap. I asked him how a geologist can see so much detail out in the field.

"It's the training," Mark replied. "You have to be able to distinguish the changes, as the browns turn into the grays, or where you have salt deposits. Color is the key—the weathering, the subtle changes in the bedrock units." Another geologist added, "It takes a lot of common sense—following the beds or deposits, stopping to check them when they break." It was a matter of experience, of drawing on the accumulated wisdom of their science. This had taught them not only what to look for, but why it should be there, as in a quote attributed to some unknown geologist from former days: "I wouldn't have seen it if I didn't believe in it." Like hunters tracking game by its spoor, like surgeons studying internal organs amid what to us would be no more than varying hues of red, these geologists could draw far-reaching conclusions from their modestly varying earth tones. Still, Mark was not inclined to think of it as a special talent: "There are four things a good geologist needs on a trip. His brunten [a combination of compass and level for measuring angle of dip], his pick, and two cans of Coors."

The talk turned to the San Andreas itself. The names of Mason Hill and Tom Dibblee came up, two of the leaders in California geology. Hill and Dibblee, as would later be appreciated, had been among the first to glimpse an understanding of the fault such as we possess today. When they had begun their work, late in the 1940s, there was a controversy as to the most basic questions of its nature. One viewpoint held that the fault was a "contact," or boundary, between rocks of different types. This could be understood if rock masses of various kinds had initially formed along its eventual length, these masses then being broken and shifted by subsequent movements of the fault. That would cause different types of rock to lie next to each other, on opposite sides of the contact.

The rock formations were often miles in extent. If their separated sections had shifted completely past each other, then, the shifts along the fault must have been quite large. A geologist named Noble, writing in the mid-1920s, argued that these shifts amounted to twenty-four miles. As he later wrote, "The profound difference in the rocks on opposite sides of the San Andreas Fault shows that the fault movements have been of great magnitude. . . . Nowhere in the thirty-mile sector [north side of the San Gabriel Mountains] are the rocks on opposite sides of the fault similar."

His view was challenged in 1943 by another geologist, named Taliaferro. He noted that the fault indeed ran through distinctive types of rock. However, he wrote, the fault "is rarely the boundary between these two very diverse types, but usually is wholly within [one or the other]. . . . The horizontal shift [on the San Andreas] has been small, and has not been greater than one mile and probably even less."

Who was right? Noble and Taliaferro both were experienced field workers, accustomed to making valid observations from studies of rocks out in the open. They were practitioners within a very level-headed profession that avoided speculation and emphasized hard facts, as in a tale of two such men who saw a cow: "There's a brown cow over there," said one geologist. "It's brown on this side, at least," replied the other. But in this world where nothing could be taken for granted, Noble and Taliaferro could not resolve their disagreement.

Along came Hill and Dibblee, a few years later. They published a map showing some of the rocks along the San Andreas. In central California, on the western edge of the fault, was a deposit of shale known as the Pancho Rico formation. Well to the southeast, on the fault's eastern edge, was another shale formation, called Santa Margarita. Hill and Dibblee argued that they had once been part of a single formation, 10 million years ago. Motions along the fault then had caused them to separate during this time by sixty-five miles, the distance from the Pancho Rico to the Santa Margarita shales. In similar fashion, Dibblee and Hill compared other rock deposits along the fault, and proposed that they had shifted by 175 miles in 25 million years, and by 225 miles in the past 40 million years.

Hill and Dibblee thus came down strongly on the side of Noble; indeed, they went several steps further. It was as much as to say that Taliaferro had based his conclusions on rocks of recent age, which had not shifted much, and that the older the rocks, the larger the shift. Yet there was simply no way to understand how such major displacements could

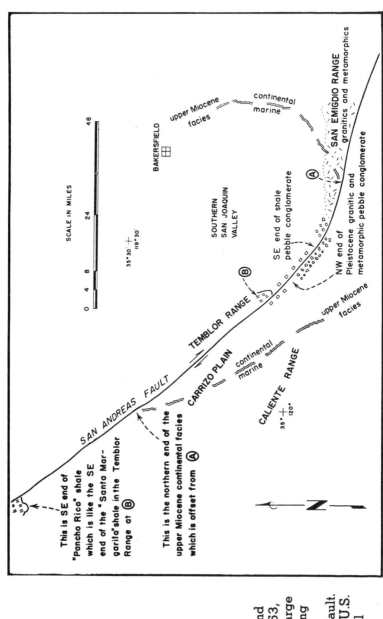

SCALE IN MILES

0   4   8   24   48

35°30'
119°30'

upper Miocene facies

continental marine

BAKERSFIELD

SAN EMIGDIO RANGE
granitics and metamorphics

SE end of shale pebble conglomerate

Ⓐ

SOUTHERN SAN JOAQUIN VALLEY

NW end of Pleistocene granitic and metamorphic pebble conglomerate

Ⓑ

TEMBLOR RANGE

CARRIZO PLAIN

continental marine

upper Miocene facies

CALIENTE RANGE

35°
120°

SAN ANDREAS FAULT

This is the SE end of "Pancho Rico" shale which is like the SE end of the "Santa Margarita" shale in the Temblor Range at Ⓑ

This is the northern end of the upper Miocene continental facies which is offset from Ⓐ

N

Map by Dibblee and Hill in 1953, showing large offsets along the San Andreas Fault. (Courtesy U.S. Geological Survey) take place. At the time Hill and Dibblee wrote their paper, in 1953, there was a well-established view of the earth's history that had prevailed for a century. And this view completely ruled out such large-scale motions. Geologists believed that our planet had formed as a molten ball, which quickly cooled on the outside to form a solid crust. Then, cooling further, it had solidified on the inside to increasingly great depths. As it did so, it contracted and shrunk, following the rule that hot objects expand and cold ones contract. The shrinkage wasn't much, a few tens of miles, perhaps, with the earth being 25,000 miles in circumference. But it was enough to crease the crust into folds and wrinkles—the world's mountain ranges.

In their college courses, young geologists were told that the world was like a baking apple, with its crust resembling the apple's skin. Successive periods of cooling and shrinkage had caused the inner parts to pull away from that outer surface, producing successive intervals of wrinkling or mountain-building. That was why mountains could thrust for miles into the sky. But this viewpoint allowed only for vertical motions in the earth, associated with this wrinkling process. There was no convincing way to propose that there had been large horizontal earth movements. Taliaferro's view, that there had been a mile or less of shift along the San Andreas, was squarely within the prevailing opinions of his day. Noble, proposing a shift of twenty-four miles, was already going too far, according to standard views. Yet here were Hill and Dibblee, proposing motions not of tens but of hundreds of miles.

They were right, and the prevailing opinion of the day was wrong. During the 1960s it became evident that prior views of the earth had been biased through being based on studies of the land. That was understandable; it was what geologists could see and study. But over two-thirds of the earth is covered by ocean, and with the development of methods for the study of the ocean floor, it became apparent that the seabed was where the real story of the earth would be found. It was a story that indeed told of major horizontal motions, in which entire continents had shifted by thousands of miles. Compared to this, Hill and Dibblee's hundreds were almost trivial.

Mariners had been exploring the seas since Prince Henry the Navigator in 1460; they had done so with reasonably good scientific methods since Captain Cook in the late 1760s. But what made the difference was the development of echo-sounding sonar. These instruments, which came into widespread use during World War II, sent out pulses of sound that reflected like radar from the seafloor, to show the distance to the bottom. The routine voyages of ships thus equipped, during the postwar years, then gradually traced out a highly detailed map of the world's seafloors. By the late 1950s it was evident that the seabed was dominated by a single and continuous feature: a world-circling range of mountains lying far beneath the ocean, much vaster in extent than the Alps or Himalayas. These mountains ranged for hundreds of miles, even for more than a thousand. But the ocean's mountains extended unbroken for 40,000 miles.

At the same time, other geophysicists were showing that the earth's interior was not a simple mass of solid rock. It contained uranium and other radioactive elements; these were releasing energy to keep that interior hot. The deep subsurface rock, reaching downward for hundreds of miles, thus had some softness to it, and could flow slowly—it would resemble thick molasses stirring within a heated pot—but the motions of those deep rocks would amount to no more than a few inches per year. Yet that would be enough.

It was found that the earth's crust was divided into extensive plates, as if that crust were a globe of glass that had shattered and then been reassembled. These plates rode and slowly shifted on the backs of the deep currents of flowing rock. Where the plates separated, owing to this motion, new lava welled up from below, cooling to form basalt. This recently formed basalt made up the mountains of the deep oceanic range, and this range marked the boundaries between these plates.

And if new seafloor was being formed at these boundaries, where the plates were pulling apart, then old seafloor had to go somewhere, on the plates' opposite sides where they were pushing together. Where this seafloor went was downward, into the earth, to depths of hundreds of miles. Oceanographers had long been puzzled by the ocean's deepest regions, known as trenches, which were up to seven miles deep. Seismologists had noted that many of the world's greatest earthquakes took place close to these trenches. Now it developed that these were the areas where dense and heavy slabs of basalt from the seafloor, perhaps a thousand miles across and up to a hundred miles thick, were being pushed downward because of the motions of the plates and the slowly flowing deep rock. These slabs did not go willingly to their fate; they usually locked themselves in place due to friction. Only the continuing buildup of stress from the deep subsurface motions would break this lock; and then the slab would plunge downward another few meters, releasing its strain in another major quake.

There were no such trenches off the California coast, but the San Andreas proved to be part of this system. There was a short spur off the world-circling range of deep mountains, which ran up the Gulf of California. It was slowly spreading, as the gulf widened, with its opposite sides—Mexico and Baja California—pulling apart. Off the Pacific Northwest was another short length of plate boundary, an arc of undersea mountains running from northern California to a spot north of Vancouver Island. Between these lengths of boundary the San Andreas Fault existed as a crack in the earth's crust, running from the head of the Gulf to California's Cape Mendocino. To its east lay North America, shifting slowly westward. To its west lay the Pacific Ocean, its offshore regions underlain by its own plate, which was moving to the northwest. Coastal California thus was a mere sliver of land trapped as part of this Pacific Plate, with the combination of plate motions welding it tightly to the rest of the continent like a ship forced by a current against its pier.

The geologist Jason Morgan of Princeton University gave

the name *plate tectonics* to this set of concepts, tectonics being the study of the earth's motions. It pictured the continents riding passively atop the moving plates, almost in the manner that the ancient Egyptians pictured the entire world as a disk riding on the back of an elephant. Because the continents themselves were rarely influenced by these motions, plate tectonics had failed to emerge from what geologists knew from their work on the land. Only when that science had gone to sea could the new theory take shape. But once it had been well developed, plate tectonics gave a strong underpinning to the view of the San Andreas Fault first glimpsed by Mason Hill and Tom Dibblee in 1953. Their view of major motions along the fault, during tens of millions of years, now became an accepted part of the larger plate-tectonic picture.

During these eons, slowly, inexorably, strains had built up as those deep flows of rock pushed at the Pacific Plate. For a century or more the rock along the San Andreas would withstand the gathering strain; then, along some stretch of this fault, there would be a sudden shock. The fault would give way in a great quake, with the coastal lands moving ten or twenty or thirty feet, all within less than a minute. Jagged masses of rock, tens of miles deep and extending along the fault for hundreds of additional miles, would wrench and tear; then they would settle into place during aftershocks, quakes of considerable size in their own right. Then a hundred or so years later the same thing would happen again, along another stretch of the fault some distance away.

There had been at least 200,000 great earthquakes during these geological ages, and maybe as many as half a million. If we could speed up the process 100 billion times over, it could be shown as a movie with a duration of several hours. It would be reminiscent of Andy Warhol's film of the Empire State Building, which shows the movement of the sun as it creates changing lights and shadows over the course of an eight-hour day. If the San Andreas movie were to be made at ground level, it might show landforms in something very much like continuous motion, at a speeded-up rate that would average ninety miles per hour. If the view were from a satellite, we would see the modern shape of the coast emerge. A sliver of northwest Mexico would begin to slide northwestward; it would encounter resistance and fold to form a range of mountains north of present-day Los Angeles. Late in the movie the Gulf of California would begin to open, and Baja California would detach from the mainland, to proceed on its own path.

Such are the conclusions of geologists. We could never hope to see such themes in play during our own lives. We live, as it were, within a single frame of this eons-long movie. Yet we must expect that its theme will affect us, for within the foreseeable future, this film in effect will advance from its current frame to the next one. This shift will take the form of the coming California earthquake.

2

EARTHQUAKES PAST

The first Europeans to explore the land of California were also the first to feel its earthquakes. In 1769, California lay at the far periphery of the Spanish world. The Spanish king, Charles III, set out to solidify his hold on the land by founding missions and colonies. The first step featured a major exploration party under the army captain Gaspar de Portola, which set out from San Diego on a long overland trek for Monterey Bay. On July 28, 1769, this expedition was in camp along the Santa Ana River, close to what is now the town of Orange in the county of that name. Suddenly they felt a succession of violent shocks, four at first, then at least two dozen lesser quakes during the next several days as they continued northward. Portola wrote that although there was strong shaking during the largest of the tremors, it lasted "only about half as long as a Hail Mary"; that is, only a few seconds. At that time he had been in the country barely six weeks.

Six years later it was the turn of the first colonizing party of Spanish settlers, which headed northward from Mexico to Monterey under the leadership of Captain Juan Bautista de Anza. On the day after Christmas in 1775 they were near the present-day town of Anza, west of the Salton Sea. According to Pedro Font, who was in the expedition, "About five in the afternoon we had a temblor with phenomena which lasted a very short time and was accompanied by an instantaneous and loud noise." This quake also was more startling than destructive. Still, like Portola, Anza and his people were simply passing through. What would happen when there were permanent settlements, exposed to earthquake risks year after year?

By the end of that century, the energetic Spaniards had set up nearly two dozen settlements within the coastal areas, and had connected them with a road, the Camino Real. There were pueblos or towns, such as one that had been founded in 1781. The British explorer George Vancouver, sailing nearby a dozen years later, wrote in his log: "A very advantageous settlement is established on a fertile spot somewhere in this neighborhood . . . called Pueblo de Los Angeles, 'the country town of the Angels.' " In addition to the pueblos there also were *presidios* or military posts, and missions. And in this collection of frontier settlements, several of the missions, with their thick adobe walls, would feel the full force of the coming earthquakes.

On October 18, 1800, a Lieutenant Carillo arrived at the Mission San Juan Bautista, which is close to the San Andreas Fault, southeast of Monterey. At supper, he later reported, "a shock was felt that was so powerful, and attended with such a loud noise as to deafen them, when they fled to the court without finishing their supper." A friar at the mission soon reported the damage: "There is not a single habitation, although built with double walls, that has not been injured from roof to foundation, and all are threatened with ruin; and the fathers are compelled to sleep in the wagons to avoid danger, since the houses are not habitable. At the place where the *rancheria* is situated, some small openings have

The San Andreas Fault. (Courtesy Christopher Scholtz)

been observed in the earth, and also in the neighborhood of the river Pajaro there is another deep opening all resulting from the earthquakes." They had reason to sleep in the wagons; during much of October there were continuous tremors, up to six shocks per day.

All this was no more than a prelude to 1812, which was

known thereafter as *el año de los temblores*, the Year of Earthquakes. The worst of it came at San Juan Capistrano, in the south of today's Orange County, where the swallows come back every March. On December 8, 1812, the mission church was crowded with worshipers. It was a Tuesday rather than a Sunday; this was a mass in honor of the Most Pure Conception of the Most Holy Virgin. The church was of heavy stone construction, but the mortar was probably poor in quality. The combination quickly proved fatal.

"A terrible earthquake occurred while the first holy Mass was being celebrated," two of that mission's friars later wrote. "In a moment, it completely destroyed the new church. The tower tottered twice. At the second shock it fell on the portal and bore this down, causing the concrete roof to cave in. Forty Indians, thirty-eight adults and two children, were buried beneath the ruins, only six escaping as by a miracle." One woman and child, buried amid the broken masonry, were dug out the next day and were still alive. But some thirty-six people lay dead within the ruins of the Capistrano church.

This quake caused other damage at the missions of southern California. At San Gabriel, near today's Pasadena, the walls of the mission church were severely cracked, the altar overturned, and statues broken, including one of Jesus. At San Fernando, twenty-three miles to the west, the damage required "thirty beams to support the walls of the church due to the strong and repeated earthquakes." The tremors were felt strongly in San Diego, where a new mission was under construction; but there was little damage. Still, there was to be much more. On December 21 two other quakes, at least as severe, struck in quick succession along the coast northwest of Los Angeles.

This time there was a damaging foreshock, which so frightened people that they ran outdoors. This undoubtedly saved many lives, for only one person died in the main shock, a half hour later. This was a young priest from the mission at Santa Barbara, who was killed by a boulder.

Indeed, Santa Barbara, with its twin bell towers and extensive outbuildings, received the worst of it. A report to the Bishop of Sonora describes a chapel that "fell down completely, and the land was opened up in the vicinity, to such an extent that it causes horror. The Presidio of Santa Barbara is all on the verge of falling down, and there is not one room in it that can be used. People from the Ranchería are living on the plains around the Mission, to where they withdrew since they were very close to the ocean, which threatened to flood them."

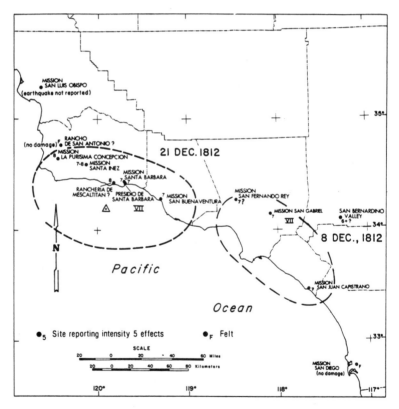

The major California earthquakes of 1812. Numbers represent Modified Mercalli intensities. (After Toppozada et al., 1981)

Other nearby settlements were not spared. At San Buena-ventura, the present-day Ventura, two friars reported "three horrible tremors or earthquakes, during which it seemed to us that the Mission was coming down." At La Purisima Concepcion, in today's Lompoc, "the extraordinary and horrifying earthquake" was reported as having "completely ruined the church. Some of the buildings have been flattened to the ground, and others, after extensive repair, will be usable not as living quarters, but for activities which do not require great safety." There were severe disturbances on the ocean. Near Santa Barbara a ship was carried up a canyon by a wave and then returned to sea. There also were a great many aftershocks. At the Santa Barbara mission, one of the padres set up a pole with a ball tied to it, as a crude seismograph. It shook constantly for eight days, and then continued to move intermittently for the next two weeks, as the aftershocks slowly wound down.

Also winding down, during those years, was the rule of Spain. In 1821 Mexico revolted and won her independence, with California under her flag. Soon afterward, Yankee whalers in the Pacific began to visit the coast in increasing numbers. They needed beef, tallow, and hides, which enterprising missions supplied by running cattle on ranchlands. Among these were the missions of Santa Clara and San Jose, within today's Silicon Valley. Not far away was a settlement at the northern tip of the San Francisco peninsula, which had been neglected and largely abandoned. Richard Henry Dana, author of *Two Years Before the Mast*, visited San Francisco Bay in 1835 and wrote a description:

> Beyond were dreary sandhills, with little grass to be seen, and few trees, and beyond them higher hills, steep and barren, their sides gullied by the rains. [There] was a ruinous presidio, and some three or four miles to the left was the Mission of Dolores, as ruinous as the presidio, almost deserted. There were no other human habitations, except that an enterprising Yankee

had put up a shanty of rough boards. Vast banks of fog, invading us from the North Pacific, drove in through the entrance, and covered the whole bay. The entire region of the great bay was a solitude.

This was the state of affairs in June 1838, when the San Francisco area was rocked by a quake at least as severe as the one in 1906, which left that city abandoned to fire and ruin. At the time of the 1838 quake there was a settler named Charles Brown, who lived in an adobe cabin located almost right on top of the San Andreas fault line. As he later told of it, he went outside immediately after the shock began and saw the earth rising and falling in solid waves. He looked toward the mountains and saw that the redwood trees nearby "rocked like lake-side reeds." Thousands were cracked off and hurled through the air. The ground cracked open and one immense chasm ten to twelve feet wide extended from San Francisco to San Jose.

Brown told this story some forty years later, in an interview with a reporter. Though he may have exaggerated, there are other accounts by which to judge. Adobe walls seven feet thick cracked from top to bottom, and walls were severely damaged at San Francisco, San Jose, and Santa Clara, to as great an extent as in 1906. Moreover, the 1838 tremor was felt far more strongly than the 1906 one at Monterey, a hundred miles distant. An army major stationed there declared that that quake was the severest he had ever experienced; it had seemed to him that the town would be destroyed, and the people of Monterey were frightened out of their wits. By contrast, in 1906 the only damage there was some broken glassware.

Evidently, then, it was only the desolate nature of the San Francisco area that prevented this 1838 quake from being a major tragedy. The land would soon be filling up; the discovery of gold was less than ten years away. But there was still the opportunity for one more quake of exceptional strength, which could strike in full force, yet waste its energies on a nearly uninhabited country. That was the great San Andreas quake of January 9, 1857, which broke along a two-hundred-mile stretch from San Bernardino to central California.

Near San Bernardino, a young woman named Augusta Crocheron was living on a farm. As she later wrote, "I heard a far-off, smothered, rumbling sound that I scarcely noticed, for I thought I was growing dizzy, and not understanding why I should feel so, I started for the house. As I stepped across a narrow stream, the opposite bank seemed at first to recede from me, then instantly to heave upward against my feet." As she fell off balance, the water in the stream emptied out onto the banks, and she saw a man on his knees, crying, the ground rising and falling in billows around him.

"I saw my parents and sisters clinging to large trees," she continues, "whose branches lashed the ground. Birds flew irregularly through the air shrieking, horses screamed, cattle fell bellowing on their knees." The cries of the animals were accompanied by the rattle of household belongings, the sounds of boards cracking and bricks falling, the splashing of water in wells—and the "awful sound of the earth rending open." This rift formed in solid ground some three hundred feet from the house, "a foot wide, a hundred feet long, and so dark and deep we feared even to measure it."

Across the mountains, to the northeast of Los Angeles, a young rancher named John Barker was looking for some missing horses. With him was a neighbor from England. They were close to Tulare Lake, a major body of water some one hundred miles long; but they knew the horses would not drink from the lake water, which was polluted with decaying reeds and other vegetation. Instead, Barker and his neighbor made their search around a group of water holes that fringed the lake, where the water was clear.

They made their way toward a pond surrounded by a fringe of tall willows, hoping to find the hoofprints of their stock. There was a keen frost; a thin film of ice lay across the water. Barker dismounted and led his horse by the bridle as

Portion of the San Andreas that broke in 1857. (After Kerry Sieh, courtesy U.S. Geological Survey)

he walked to the edge of the water. "Just as I reached it," he later wrote, "the ground seemed to be violently swayed from east to west. The water splashed up to my knees; the trees whipped about, and limbs fell on and all around me. I was affected by a fearful nausea. My horse snorted and in terror struggled violently to get away from me, but I hung to him, having as great a fear as he had himself.

"The lake commenced to roar like the ocean in a storm. Staggering and bewildered, I vaulted into the saddle. I found my friend, who had not dismounted, almost in a state of collapse. He eagerly inquired, while our horses were on the run and the lake was roaring behind us, 'What is this?' I replied, 'An earthquake! Put the steel to your horse and let us get out of this!' " They observed a herd of several hundred antelopes running amid wild confusion and terror.

"We returned next day and found that the lake had run up on the land for about three miles. Fish were stranded in every direction and could have been gathered by the wagon-load. The air was alive with buzzards and vultures eager for the feast. We can only imagine what the consequences would have been if a great city had stood on the eastern shore of the lake."

Los Angeles was still far from being a great city, but it was the nearest town of any size. Surprisingly, its buildings were not damaged extensively. Most of them were of only one story, with walls up to three feet thick. Nevertheless, the people were thoroughly frightened. Many of them rushed for the doors. One man mistakenly went out by his window rather than through a door, and was seen running along the roof of an adobe building—"thinking, should it fall, it was better to be on top of it, than it on top of him," according to a newspaper account. Another man fled from his bath completely naked. He rushed to the yard, where a number of women were also seeking refuge. He immediately lay prone and managed to creep under cover, unobserved.

The greatest destruction was near Fort Tejon, in the mountains some seventy-five miles north of Los Angeles. This was an army outpost guarding the main pass that led northward into the Central Valley. Unfortunately, that pass had formed through the motions of the San Andreas Fault. There was a considerable noise from a nearby mountain, and from its peak a mass of rock and earth was forced high into the air.

At the fort, a quartermaster described the quake as "the most terrific shock imaginable, tearing the Officer's quarters to pieces, severely damaging the Hospital, and laying flat with the ground the gable ends of nearly all the buildings. Immense trees have been snapped off close to the ground."

Along the line of the fault, extensive disturbances marked the land. There were sandblows, which blasted through the surface like miniature volcanoes as groundwater was put under pressure from the shock of the quake. These blew sand into the air to a height of six feet, forming damp mounds. One traveler, crossing a stream, wrote that "these appearances were visible as far as I could see up and down the bed of the River. In crossing I tried to avoid those places as much as possible but finally a wheel got into one and down went the wagon to the axletree."

Particularly dramatic were the cracks marking the trace of the fault. One observer described the fracture as "continuing in one uniform direction for a distance of some two hundred miles. The fracture presented an appearance as if the earth had been bisected, and the parts had slipped upon each other. Sometimes the earth on one side would be several feet high, presenting a perpendicular wall of earth or rocks. In some places the sliding movement appears to have been horizontal—one side of the fracture indicating a movement to the northwest, the other to the southeast. The fracture pursued its course over hill and hollow, and sometimes this sliding displacement would give to the points of hills and to gulch channels a disjointed appearance."

This was a fine description of a major fault; but the significance of faults, as the places where earthquakes originate, was not yet understood. That understanding would begin to emerge only following the next great California quake. This was in the Owens Valley of the eastern Sierras, near the Nevada border and almost due north of Los Angeles. The shock struck at 2:30 in the morning of March 26, 1872. Within the town of Lone Pine there were fifty-nine houses, mostly built of adobe. Fifty-two of them were destroyed. Of a population of fewer than three hundred, twenty-seven people were killed and fifty-six were injured as their houses fell upon them. This quake was stronger than that of 1857, and again it was only the sparse population of the country that prevented a far vaster tragedy.

But the fissures and faults in the earth were quite dramatic. In one place an area at least two hundred feet wide sank twenty to thirty feet, leaving vertical walls. Scarps or cliffs up to twenty-three feet tall formed along the eastern base of the mountains. Fences crossing the fault were broken, showing horizontal offsets of up to twenty feet. Such things had happened before, during earlier quakes; for instance, a corral near Fort Tejon in 1857, straddling the fault, had suddenly changed from an enclosure to an open S-shaped structure. For the first time, however, there was a geologist who was ready to take a look.

He was Grove Karl Gilbert, and a century ago he was one of the leaders in American science. He worked closely with John Wesley Powell, who was the first to explore the Grand Canyon. Together they were among the founders of the U.S. Geological Survey, with Gilbert spending several years as its chief geologist. He did a great deal of work in the West, showing, for instance, that in Ice Age times the Great Salt Lake of today had existed as a far larger Lake Bonneville, hundreds of feet deep. He even looked at the moon with a geologist's eye, and argued that its craters had formed from the impact of immense meteors. And when he looked at the Owens Valley earthquake, he saw it in a way that was quite original.

He saw it as a result of the slow upthrusting of the Sierras. The fault, to him, was a crack in the earth's crust along the base of the mountains, which were being uplifted, pushed upward on one side of the fault, while the other side remained level. "It is as though something beneath each mountain was slowly, steadily, and irresistibly rising," he wrote in 1883, "carrying the mountain with it. The upthrust produces a local strain in the crust, involving a certain amount of compression and distortion, and this strain increases until it is sufficient to overcome the starting friction along the fractured surface [of the fault]. . . . Almost instantaneously, there is an amount of motion sufficient to relieve the strain, and this is followed by a long period of quiet during which the strain is gradually reimposed. The motion at the instance of yielding is so swift and so abruptly terminated as to constitute a shock." Eighty years later, it would become apparent that the most important source of strain is the horizontal movement of continent-sized plates of crust, rather than the vertical uplift of mountains. Otherwise, Gilbert had it completely right.

He also noted that houses of wood-frame construction stood up well amid the shaking at Lone Pine, and with that he offered a prediction: "What are the citizens going to do about it? Probably nothing. They are not likely to abandon brick and stone and adobe, and build all new houses of wood. If they did, they would put themselves at the mercy of fire; and fire, in the long run, unquestionably destroys more property than earthquakes." It was the combination of the two that would prove particularly deadly in the great San Francisco quake.

Prior to the 1906 quake, both the fault and the fire danger were known. Andrew Lawson, a geology professor at the University of California, had noted in 1893 that the Santa Clara, San Benito, and San Francisco Bay valleys were remarkably straight and well aligned, forming a major fault. The land there "was marked by tilting and movements that may yet be active." He named the fault after San Andreas Lake, on the peninsula south of San Francisco.

Then in October 1905, six months before the disaster, the National Board of Fire Underwriters issued a report that stated bluntly, "San Francisco has violated all underwriting traditions and precedents by not burning up. That it has not already done so is largely due to the vigilance of the Fire Department, which cannot be relied upon indefinitely to stave off the inevitable." The city's water mains, the report declared, were "inadequate to meet the demands for water flow necessary to fight a conflagration." What was worse, these mains ran through a district in the city's northeast that had been reclaimed from the bay as filled-in land. Here the shaking would be particularly severe, breaking the mains in numerous places and rendering them useless.

The quake struck at 5:13 in the morning of April 18, a violent rip that shook the city for forty-eight seconds. The ground heaved in waves two to three feet high. A roar shattered the morning stillness, as wood frames wrenched and shuddered, while brick, masonry, and glass shattered and fell in heaps. Roofs fell in; walls broke and collapsed; cornices and towers toppled. The bells of the city's churches set up a demented clangor. Then, as the noise reached a peak, the tremor stopped. There was silence. And amid the silence were the groans of the injured, the crackle of sparks from power lines—and the hiss of escaping gas.

Dennis Sullivan, the city's fire chief, woke to the roar of an avalanche of bricks. A tower atop an adjoining hotel had collapsed and punched through his roof, carrying away part of his wife's bedroom. He ran through billowing white dust from the broken mortar, but failed to see that part of the building was gone. He pitched through the gap and fell three stories, breaking his skull, ribs, arms, and legs. He was rushed to a hospital, where he lingered in a coma for three days before dying.

James Hopper, a reporter for the San Francisco *Call,* set out to cover the disaster. He saw a man standing at the window of a broken building, ready to slide down a long piece of cloth in an attempt to reach the sidewalk. Hopper ran in, scrambling over piles of shattered plaster, and found what was left of a room with a bed in it. The bed was covered with debris. A woman's slim hand and wrist reached out from the pile, twisting in agony. Hopper dug into the debris and found her, then carried her to the sidewalk. Then he went back in and rescued a second woman. A third lay dead beneath a mound of bricks.

Then he heard another person wailing in the back of the building. The hallway had collapsed, but a strip of it clung precariously to one wall. Hopper made his way along this ledge and found the hall intact farther on. There, he recalled, "a woman with long dishevelled hair was pacing to and fro, repeating in a long drawn-out wail, over and over again, 'Oh, my husband is dead, and a young man is dead, and a woman is dead.' " Hopper continued farther and found a large pile of bricks. Sticking out from it was a bedpost.

Just then, the fires were beginning.

The combination of broken gas mains and power lines, along with the abundant debris, was an open invitation for fires to spring up in a number of places. With the water mains broken, there was no effective way to fight them. In addition, some people started fires by accident. In one home, which was still standing despite damage, a woman set about the day's activities. Earthquake or not, she still intended to fix breakfast for her family. But the kitchen flue had been damaged, and when she started a fire in her stove, it soon spread to her roof, setting fire to her house. This "Ham and Eggs Fire" quickly spread into the nearby districts.

Along Market Street, the main thoroughfare, firemen from the start had to fall back as building after building ignited. With no hydrants yielding water, the firefighters tried the one expedient that was left: dynamite. By blowing up buildings in the path of the flames, they hoped to clear a fire line, a leveled area that would not easily burn and that approaching flames could not readily leap. It was an old and established technique for use when a city was threatened; as far back as London's Great Fire of 1666, gunpowder had been used for this purpose. But the dynamiters of San Francisco lacked experience, and their efforts sometimes made things worse. In one case, on the edge of Chinatown, their blast blew a flaming mattress across the street, setting fire to a group of houses that until that moment had been spared.

The fire burned for three days, destroying over four square miles of the city—as much as was blasted by the atomic bomb at Hiroshima. At midafternoon on the first day, it formed a dense plume of smoke, hundreds of feet wide, which formed a massive cloud over the city. Buildings were reduced to gaunt façades as their interiors burned brightly, while debris littered the abandoned pavement and smoke rose in columns.

The fires had barely started when the army imposed martial law.

Brigadier General Frederick Funston, the local commander, had taken over the city early on the first morning, in effect deposing the civil government at the point of a bayonet. It was not a very effective government to begin with. Its political boss, Abe Ruef, was a master of the kickback. He and his handpicked mayor, Eugene Schmitz, took frequent payments from the city's brothel-keepers, and were themselves part-owners of one of the larger of these whorehouses. Weak and corrupt, Schmitz yielded readily when Funston sent in the troops. He gave them their orders: Shoot any looters. It did not matter that only the President could suspend civil law by sending in armed troops. Nor did it matter that this law forbade such an order. Funston had in effect torn up the Constitution, at least as far as it applied to San Francisco.

There were instances in which the shootings by Funston's troops at least were in the tradition of vigilante justice. A group of corpses was lying on a pile of rocks. A man approached them and told the soldiers that one of the bodies was that of his mother. Apparently overcome by grief, he threw himself across the dead woman. A moment later, however, one of the troops found that the man was chewing diamond earrings from her ears. "Here is where you get what is coming to you," the soldier declared, and put a bullet through him.

Other cases were far less clear-cut. The fire was a block from one store when a man came out of its door, his arms and pockets full of goods. Three soldiers stood outside, their rifles ready. The man immediately started to run past them, and was still running when one of the soldiers shot him in the back and dropped him. Was he the owner or perhaps an employee who was trying to salvage something? Had he panicked, his nerves on edge from the disaster? No matter. His body lay there in the street for the flames to consume.

There were also instances of mere bullying by armed men. One wagoneer refused to unload a family's belongings. For this, soldiers ran him through with bayonets. A shopkeeper, trying to make a quick profit, demanded seventy-five cents for a loaf of bread. He was marched outside his shop and shot. An Italian man was ordered to help with the firefighting. Perhaps because he knew little English, he failed to respond. A trooper bayoneted him in the back; a civilian who had found himself a uniform then shot and killed him.

What was worse, some of the soldiers themselves turned to looting. One made his way into a woman's parlor; when she told him to get out, he threatened her with his gun. Other army patrols stole cases of beer, wine, and whiskey from boxcars of the Southern Pacific. Arnold Genthe, a news photographer, looked into the rubble of Chinatown and saw men moving through the shells of buildings. From time to time one of them would stoop to pick something up. As they came closer he recognized them as national guardsmen, "carrying off bushels of bronzes, brasses, and partly melted jewelry." Sickened, and fearing for his own safety, he turned and ran. Despite the testimony of Genthe and others, not one of Funston's looting soldiers was ever court-martialed.

And with the fires and the soldiers came the rats. Genthe watched as a pack of them darted toward the fallen dome of a building, which had landed intact on its base. The rats swarmed over it. Beneath it were two crushed Chinese. Some of the rats were gnawing at their limbs. Then other rats approached the burial gangs. These were made up of ordi-

nary citizens. They had been pressed into service at gun-
point to bury corpses that were burned beyond recognition,
missing eyes, lips, and ears. "The bodies had sort of
melted," recalled a twenty-year-old insurance clerk who was
working at the point of a bayonet. "The bits of flesh that
hadn't been scorched looked waxy, the color of dummies in
shop windows. You'd find a lump of fried flesh pitted with
bits of iron, glass and other things. The smell was awful. You
felt sick all the time." Then, with the bodies placed beneath
a thin layer of earth, the rats appeared. This clerk almost
fainted when he saw a rat dragging an arm along the
ground. A soldier stabbed the rat with his bayonet and
threw it into a burning building. In time San Francisco would
undergo an outbreak of bubonic plague.

The fire was eventually contained at Van Ness Avenue, a
wide north-south thoroughfare, nearly two miles west of the
waterfront. General Funston set his artillery to work along its
length, firing at point-blank range into houses on the east
side of the street, knocking them down for a fire line. Other
homes fell to a squad of navy explosives experts, armed with
a ton and a half of guncotton. Some semblance of a water
supply remained there, which gave the firemen something
to work with. The line held; this fire was beaten back. Van
Ness was the final fire line, then, and because of it the city
was saved from even wider destruction. As it was, the death
toll ran to 452, with property losses totaling $350 million in
1906 dollars.

Nor was the destruction limited to San Francisco. In Santa
Rosa, sixty miles to the north, most buildings in the town's
business district were thrown down; fire followed, and fifty-
eight bodies were recovered from the ruins of fallen houses.
At San Jose, with a population of over twenty thousand, not
a single brick or stone building of two stories or more was
left standing. A few miles away a state insane asylum was
entirely destroyed, with more than half the inmates killed or
injured. Stanford University was devastated; only the fact
that spring vacation had emptied the campus kept the death

toll as low as two. All told, the San Andreas Fault broke along a length of 270 miles, from Humboldt County in the north to San Juan Bautista, southeast of San Francisco. The greatest slip along the fault, twenty-one feet, was in Marin County, but offsets of ten to fifteen feet were common. This was the most extensive slip along a fault ever recorded in the United States.

The extent of the damage can be judged by the Mercalli scale, which an Italian priest who was interested in geology had set forth in 1902. In Giuseppi Mercalli's twelve-point scale, as subsequently modified, successive levels numbered I through XII represented escalating benchmarks of terror that described the power of quakes:

I. Not felt except by a very few under especially favorable circumstances.

II. Felt by only a few persons at rest, especially on the upper floors of buildings. Delicately suspended objects may swing.

III. Felt quite noticeably indoors, especially on upper floors of buildings, but many people do not recognize it as an earthquake. Standing motorcars may rock slightly. Vibration is like a passing truck. People estimate the duration of the tremor.

IV. During the day felt indoors by many, outdoors by few. At night some awakened. Dishes, windows, and doors disturbed; walls make creaking sound. Sensation like heavy truck striking building. Standing motorcars rocked noticeably.

V. Felt by nearly everyone; many awakened. Some dishes, windows, etc., broken; a few instances of cracked plaster; unstable objects overturned. Disturbance of trees, poles, and other tall objects sometimes noticed. Pendulum clocks may stop.

VI. Felt by all; many frightened and run outdoors. Some heavy furniture moved; a few instances of fallen plaster or damaged chimneys. Damage slight.

VII. Everybody runs outdoors. Damage *negligible* in buildings of good design and construction; *slight to moderate* in well-built ordinary structures; *considerable* in poorly built or badly designed structures. Some chimneys broken. Noticed by persons driving motorcars.

VIII. Damage *slight* in specially designed brick structures; *considerable* in ordinary substantial buildings, with partial collapse; *great* in poorly built structures. Panel walls thrown out of frame structures. Fall of chimneys, factory stacks, columns, monuments, walls. Heavy furniture overturned. Sand and mud ejected in small amounts. Changes in well water. Persons driving motorcars disturbed.

IX. Damage *considerable* in specially designed brick or masonry structures; well-designed frame structures thrown out of plumb; *great* in substantial masonry buildings, with partial collapse. Buildings shifted off foundations. Ground cracked conspicuously. Underground pipes broken.

X. Some well-built wooden structures destroyed; most masonry and frame structures destroyed with foundations; ground badly cracked. Rails bent. Landslides considerable from riverbanks and steep slopes. Shifted sand and mud. Water splashed or slopped over banks.

XI. Few, if any, masonry structures left standing. Bridges destroyed. Broad fissures in ground. Underground pipelines completely out of service. Earth slumps and land slips in soft ground. Rails bent greatly.

XII. Damage total. Waves seen on ground surfaces. Lines of sight and level distorted. Objects thrown upward into the air.

On this scale the 1906 earthquake, at its most destructive, measured XI.

At that time, the science of seismology was just getting started. An important early group of contributors were the Jesuits, who had a long-standing interest in science. Seismology, they found, was one of the few areas where they could work successfully without running afoul of Church doctrine. Such universities as Fordham, Georgetown, and St. Louis, all strongly influenced by the Jesuits, were among the leaders in this new field. The U.S. Weather Bureau had a modest degree of interest, as did a few astronomical observatories.

However, at the end of the century there still were no good seismic instruments. In 1897, for example, the Lick Observatory, near San Francisco, installed an early seismometer. A San Francisco industrial firm had arranged to set off a chemical explosion, and Edward Holden, the observatory director, decided that his instrument would record it as a test. As Carl Sagan eventually described the incident, "At the appointed moment, no staff member could see any sign of needle deflection except Holden, who promptly dispatched a messenger down the hill to alert the world to the great sensitivity of the Lick seismometer. But soon up the mountain came another messenger with the news that the explosion had been postponed. A much faster messenger was then dispatched to overtake the first and an embarrassment to the Lick Observatory was narrowly averted."

Seismometers were to detect and measure the intensity of earthquake waves; seismographs were to produce permanent records by drawing wavy or rapidly varying lines. But to develop such instruments was not easy. The earth's motions were usually very slight, and an instrument would have to amplify them to make them observable. In an age before electronics, such amplification at first appeared out of reach. Then at the turn of the century the Japanese seismologist Fusakichi Omori solved this problem. He did it by using a lever that would swing with the moving earth, and by arranging for this motion to wiggle a light-spot projected onto a surface. Just as the projected image on a movie screen is much larger than that on the film, so Omori used projection to amplify the oscillation of his light-spot.

His instrument featured a pier or column driven down to bedrock through a hole in the building's foundation. Vibrations in the building thus would not disturb it; only seismic motions would cause this column to move. A long boom was mounted on a hinge at the top of the pier, just above the building's floor. This boom was supported by a cord, leaving it free to swing, oscillating with the pier's vibrations. At the other end of the boom was a plate with a small hole in it. Close behind the plate was a light—a gas flame in the early models—casting its luminance through the hole to produce a bright spot, like that of a movie projector. The "screen," some distance away, was a rotating drum covered with photographic paper and moved by clockwork. The movements of the earth thus caused this light-spot to write amplified records on the film.

This instrument amounted to a specialized darkroom and was unwieldy and expensive. Omori offered to sell such a seismograph to the city of San Francisco in 1904 for two thousand dollars; the offer was refused. But the instrument certainly was sensitive. One was installed at the U.S. Weather Bureau in Washington. The daily visit of a horse-drawn ice wagon that would stop some twenty feet away from the instrument would put enough weight on the earth to warp it downward. This regularly produced a one-millimeter displacement in the seismogram's recorded traces.

With the new century, California began to grow rapidly. Yet in many areas it still was as wild and desolate as when Richard Henry Dana had visited San Francisco in 1835. A naval disaster in 1923 showed that even near Santa Barbara, the coast was still an unsettled frontier.

A squadron of fourteen destroyers, four-pipe veterans of World War I, was steaming southward from San Francisco at twenty knots, bound for San Diego. Naval appropriations were lean in those interwar years, and to bolster public awareness, these ships were to pass close inshore, sailing down the Santa Barbara Channel, where the people could see them. It was early evening and the flotilla was running through fog, with no onshore lights to guide them. But the captain in the lead ship was prepared to rely on his dead reckoning, based on his speed and compass course. He heeled that destroyer to port, making a left turn that he believed would take the squadron into the channel. But his calculations were off; the destroyers were ten miles too far to the north.

That lead ship, the USS *Delphy,* ran straight onto the rocks near Point Arguello, west of Santa Barbara. The others were close behind, and one by one, a total of eight other destroyers crashed upon the coast in turn. Of course, as these ships' officers recognized that they had run aground, they began blowing loud blasts as warnings, using steam-driven horns. But the momentum of the ships was such that only five managed to stay offshore altogether, within this group of fourteen. Two more, having run aground, later worked themselves free. But seven naval vessels lay trapped and listing, with a total of sixty seamen dead in the disaster. The coast was so dark, so uninhabited and lacking in lights, that the ships had had no warning.

During the next four years, two major quakes struck close by. On June 29, 1925, it was Santa Barbara's turn. Again, nearly all the brick, concrete, and stone buildings were demolished or seriously damaged, and thirteen people lost their lives. A four-story office building, only two years old, was reduced to a pile of rubble. Inside, rescuers found the mangled and still-warm body of a dentist. The walls of a four-story hotel crumbled into heaps. In another large hotel, a five-story concrete tower crumbled with the shock, plunging through three floors of rooms and down into the lobby. Another building collapsed, leaving only the front wall, on which the owner had hung a long banner reading, I FACE RUIN. The owner had been conducting a fire sale.

Twenty-eight months later, a much heavier shock struck along the coast to the northwest of Santa Barbara, near Point Arguello. There were heavy rockslides on steep slopes, while tidal gauges recorded a seismic sea wave that ran six feet high. Chimneys were wrecked in the town of Lompoc; the quake was felt from San Jose to Pasadena, a distance of some three hundred miles. It was also felt at sea, where two captains reported by wireless that their ships experienced heavy shocks twenty-five or more miles from the shore. But this part of the California coast was nearly as wild and desolate as in the days of the Spaniards. The tracks of the Southern Pacific ran close to the sea, and were disrupted; trains were held up for several hours. Otherwise, though, it was mainly a country of sheepherders and ranchland, and no lives were lost.

During the mid-1920s, the man whose name would become synonymous with earthquakes was starting his career. He was Charles F. Richter. Richter grew up in the Wilshire district of Los Angeles, went to Stanford, and tried chemistry as an undergraduate. Unfortunately, as he later recalled, "I was quite nervous and tended not to be neat, particularly with my hands, and this is fatal in a chemistry laboratory. So after some unfortunate experiences, I felt that this wasn't for me." He switched to physics, graduated with his degree at age twenty in 1920, and promptly experienced a nervous breakdown. His mother steered him to a psychiatrist, who helped him get his bearings, and with this he proceeded to work.

His first job was as a messenger boy at the Los Angeles County Museum. Then he worked in a warehouse for a hardware company. But in 1923, his prospects changed dramatically. The California Institute of Technology was growing in nearby Pasadena, under the leadership of George Ellery Hale, one of the famous astronomers of the day, and of Robert Millikan, who that year won the Nobel Prize in physics. Richter wasn't about to miss the opportunity to attend Millikan's lectures, and he soon left the hardware warehouse to enter Caltech as a graduate student in physics. Soon he was deeply involved in studies of atoms and electrons.

Hardly a dozen years had passed since the men of Cambridge University's Cavendish Laboratory, Britain's leading physics lab, had gathered at a dinner and had raised their glasses in a toast: "To the electron! May it never be of any use to anybody." J. Robert Oppenheimer, who in two decades would be directing the Manhattan Project, was a student at Caltech and an acquaintance of Richter's. At a discussion, the question came up of the usefulness of physics. Oppenheimer said, "As far as I'm concerned that's of no importance. I do this kind of work because it interests me, and it is there." To work as a physicist was to live in an ivory tower, studying a field that was almost considered a branch of philosophy.

But the field was yeasty with new ideas about atoms, and Caltech attracted a number of the world's leaders. They were mostly from Germany, and in those days of slow travel by rail and ship, they would come for extended visits. Richter met Hendrik Lorentz, whose work had helped lead to Einstein's, and got his autograph. Max Born came to lecture; he was a leader in the study of atoms, nuclei, and electrons. Another such leader, Erwin Schrodinger, also came to speak. Richter remembered him as "a decidedly good lecturer, and he was speaking of a very fresh and new subject which was not completely worked out, as he pointed out himself." At one point, Schrodinger was discussing how to extend a certain treatment to take account of Einstein's work. He said, "Now, of course the generalization is not unique." He stopped for a moment and then said, "Of course not, otherwise it would not be a generalization." Richter regarded this as a very profound observation.

His office-mate for a time was Boris Podolsky, a graduate student who later worked with Einstein. Podolsky's family lived nearby, and working for them as live-in help was a young woman named Lillian Brand. "She was born in Los Angeles," Richter recalled. "She always considered herself very exceptional, being the native daughter of a native daughter. There aren't many of those." They soon were seeing each other frequently.

He wrote his Ph.D. dissertation on the study of the hydrogen atom, basing his work on the new concepts of quantum mechanics, a branch of physics that had come into existence during his years as a grad student. Earlier studies of the atom had applied the idea that an electron followed a well-defined orbit within the atom, like a planet. Quantum mechanics brushed this aside on the grounds that such an orbit could not be observed. Indeed, Werner Heisenberg, who, along with Born and Schrodinger, had founded this field, had written of the importance of "attempting to secure foundations for a quantum theoretical mechanics which is exclusively based on relations between quantities which in principle are observable." This attitude, that of basing his scientific work exclusively on what was observable, stuck with Richter. It later led to an important feature of his earthquake scale: that the magnitude of an earthquake would be defined exclusively in terms of what could be measured on a seismogram.

In addition to showing that he had talent in atomic physics, his dissertation research also showed that he had the versatility and inventiveness that would allow him to enter a field where little was known, where creativity was at a premium, and where even the basic concepts were often matters of controversy. That was what quantum mechanics was like during his graduate years. It also was a good description of the state of seismology, the science of earthquakes.

He got his degree in 1927, and soon found a job. The Carnegie Institute of Washington was putting money into a Pasadena research center, the Seismological Laboratory. They needed a research assistant, and Robert Millikan, president of Caltech, recommended Richter for the position. Richter had absolutely no background in geology, but Millikan had been impressed with Richter's ability to enter a new field that lay on the frontiers of science, and proceed to solve a problem. That was what would count in studying earthquakes, which were as poorly understood as atoms, and as open to new insight and ingenuity.

The Seismo Lab was out to describe what was happening seismically in southern California, starting at the most basic level: mapping faults, recording quakes, and determining their locations. This meant devising better seismographs. It meant spending long and tedious hours making measurements and calculations from the seismograms to try to determine the locations of the weak tremors these instruments were picking up. Richter's boss told him he didn't have to concern himself with these routine tasks. He could rely on another staff member to take care of all that. But Richter soon found that he could accomplish little without doing a goodly amount of this work himself.

The following year, he married Lillian Brand. She taught creative writing at a local college, and did some herself. Over the years, they did a variety of things that raised eyebrows among their friends. To begin with, they both were nudists, and this sometimes made Caltech officials nervous. What was more, they always spent Christmas apart. She would travel to some distant place—one year it was Timbuktu in west Africa, simply because she was intrigued with its name—while he would take long hikes alone in the mountains, an activity that particularly pleased him. Yet their marriage was satisfying to both of them. A woman who knew both Richters stated that "they each got what they wanted from the marriage. Lillian got a feeling of security, of belonging, of having someone to look up to, and Charlie got someone who worshiped him. He was very proud of her and her writing."

Richter had not been long at the Seismo Lab when he was joined by one of his most valued colleagues, Beno Gutenberg. Gutenberg had come over from Germany, where he had held a low-ranking academic position in Frankfurt. Richter, himself of German descent, described the position as Professor Extraordinarius. One of the extraordinary things about it was its low salary, and Gutenberg had been supporting himself largely through income from his family's soap business.

He was a pioneer in using earthquake waves to map the earth's interior. In particular he relied on the fact that "shear waves"—those that oscillate from side to side—do not travel through a liquid, but only through a solid. The earth's core was known to be a liquid because shear waves did not pass through it, and Gutenberg set out to find its size. He had determined that he needed to study certain specific types of recorded shear waves, had searched seismograms to find them, and had measured the depth of the earth's core— 2,900 kilometers—with an accuracy that still stands. Gutenberg stood five feet one inch and was nearly bald. Once, being photographed alongside a colleague who stood at six feet, he remarked that this was the long and short of geophysics.

Despite the Depression, by the early 1930s the Seismo Lab had installed a network of seven seismographs throughout southern California, and was preparing to issue regular bulletins describing the observed quakes. That meant they would need a convenient way to refer to them by magnitude. The Mercalli scale was still an important method for describing a quake's felt effects; in fact, Harry Wood, Richter's boss and the head of the Seismo Lab, was busy revising it to fit the types of buildings common to the United States. But to use that scale, it would be necessary to send interviewers to every location that recorded a tremor, asking people what they had noticed and whether there was any damage. And with several hundred quakes expected every year and detectable with their instruments, this was out of the question. What was needed was a way to describe the size of a quake using data that could be measured on the seismograms.

Richter was working with Wood, trying out various ways of comparing their local tremors, and they weren't getting anywhere. Then Richter read a paper by the Japanese seismologist Kiyoo Wadati, which gave a rule describing how the strength of a seismic wave diminishes with increasing distance from the source of the tremor. This was important; knowing this, it would be possible to adjust the instrument readings to take account of this distance. Then Gutenberg suggested that they should plot the data on a logarithmic scale. On such a graph, successive steps upward would represent a sequence of numbers such as 1, 10, 100, 1,000, and so forth. By contrast, on an ordinary graph, successive steps would give a sequence such as 1, 2, 3, 4. A logarithmic scale thus was a convenient way of presenting the data when its values ranged over an inconveniently large extent, as was the case when comparing large and nearby quakes with small and distant ones.

Another part of their approach would be understood by anyone who has ever been in a moderate quake. First there is a sudden shake that continues steadily; then, a moment later, comes a more intense shock, which rattles more strongly but which quickly dies out. The initial shake comes from the quake's pressure wave or *P wave,* a wave of compression radiating from the epicenter. The quake also sets up a shearing wave or *S wave,* whose sideways motion also passes through the earth, but more slowly. The S wave is more intense than the P wave, but it arrives later. A seismogram shows both the P and S, and also has precise time information, so that the interval between these waves' arrival is easy to measure. That interval, in turn, tells the distance to the epicenter: the longer it is, the greater is the distance.

Gutenberg and Richter knew that their seismograms would have accurate timing information. They expected to use a new type of seismograph, coinvented by Harry Wood, with a timing system devised by their colleague at the Seismo Lab, Hugo Benioff. Benioff's timers allowed a single drum to record a full day's worth of seismogram tracings, accurate to better than a tenth of a second. Thus, from any single seismogram they could read off the interval between the P and S, and determine the distance. Using Wadati's rule, they could adjust the measured quake intensity and determine its strength at a standard distance of one hundred kilometers. Then, taking the logarithm of the adjusted measurement, they would have a number like 2.6 or 4.2. This would be the magnitude of the quake on their scale. While Richter was concerned mainly with the earthquakes of southern California, Gutenberg, who had a wide knowledge of seismograms from other areas, pointed out that this scale could be used for quakes all over the world. This would become known as the Richter scale. Richter called it simply the magnitude scale; he did not attach his name to it for many years. It was Perry Byerly, a seismologist at the University of California at Berkeley, who introduced the term "Richter scale." Nevertheless, Richter wound up with more credit than he deserved. "There is simply no question that it should be known as the Gutenberg-Richter scale," one longtime colleague of both said later. "But for many, many years, Charlie did very little to emphasize Beno's role. If you wanted to think it had all been Richter's doing, that was okay with Charlie."

By whatever name, the scale measured the quakes they were recording. It also was possible to dig out the old seismograms from previous decades and determine the magnitudes of the quakes they had recorded. The 1906 San Francisco quake measured 8.3. The 1925 Santa Barbara shaker got a 6.3, while the stronger Point Arguello tremor was put at 7.3. As a logarithmic scale, each one-unit increase meant a tenfold jump in the size. The San Francisco quake thus was ten times greater than the Point Arguello tremor, and a hundred times greater than the one at Santa Barbara.

Meanwhile, Caltech was continuing to attract famous visitors from overseas. One of them was Einstein. He frequently was the subject of notices in the weekly calendar, which would read, "Physics seminar, subject and speaker to be announced." That was nearly always Einstein; Caltech preferred not to put his name on the calendar because it tended to attract cranks and curiosity-seekers. After one such seminar, Gutenberg and Einstein fell in together and began walking across the campus, talking about Gutenberg's studies of seismology. They both were so engrossed in the conversation that they failed to notice anything unusual around them. Then a colleague came up to them and asked, "Well, what did you think of the earthquake?'' Their response was, "What earthquake?"

It was the Long Beach tremor of March 10, 1933, magnitude 6.3 on the Richter scale. It broke the southern part of the Newport-Inglewood fault, which runs south of Long Beach between the towns of those names. The epicenter was in Huntington Beach, close to its pier, but Long Beach was badly hit and gave its name to the quake. Some 115 people were killed and $40 million worth of damage was done—in the depths of the Depression, with all the nation's banks closed by presidential order.

"When the earthquake struck," reported the *Los Angeles Times*, "it came with a roar and a crash that sounded like an explosion." Hospitals were pushed beyond their capacity, as ambulances brought in the injured. A pretty blond girl, about four years old, was carried in unconscious. Her arm was crushed at the elbow, which meant she would need an amputation. She lay pale, awaiting her turn on the operating table. Not far away was a woman of about sixty. Her hair was gray, her face was the same color, and as the *Times* remarked, "earthquakes seem to do that to people." In the next room was a man identified as John Doe. He lay dead, his head caved in by a falling brick. Another unidentified man was seen in the debris of a collapsed building. Its destruction was followed by a fire, and the body could not be recovered.

As the years went by, and the earthquakes kept coming, Richter remained actively involved in his seismology research. In 1957 the Seismo Lab moved into an elegant mansion in Pasadena. There were marble floors, paneled work areas, individual fireplaces, and private bathrooms for each professor. There also were gardens and a private tennis court. When an earthquake occurred, though, Richter would grab the item that mattered most—the lab's telephone. He would sit with it in his lap and ask the anxious callers, "Where are you calling from?" He marked their positions on a map of southern California. As the calls from different places came in, Richter could estimate the quake's location as well as its magnitude.

The Seismo Lab continued to grow. Large closets in the mansion became students' offices; the billiard room was converted into a place for reading seismograms, and the kitchen became a drafting room. An inner patio became a computer room, and a walk-in safe was made into a storage vault for technical papers. Even the garage became a high-pressure laboratory. Then the hallways began to overflow with seismic records and publications, and it was clear that the Seismo Lab was running out of space. By the early 1970s it was preparing to move to new and much larger quarters, on the Caltech campus.

Richter, meanwhile, had caught the attention of the university's satirists, the English professor J. Kent Clark and his close friend and tunewriter Elliot Davis. They wrote a number of songs, in the tradition of Tom Lehrer, concerning Caltech and its people; an outfit calling itself the Caltech Stock Company performed them in campus revues, and some of these songs were recorded in an album, *Let's Advance on Science*. Their song, "The Richter Scale," had the following lyrics:

Charley Richter made a scale for calibrating
  earthquakes
Gives a true and lucid reading every time the earth
  shakes
Increments are exponential, numbers *0* to nine
When the first shock hit the seismo everything went
  fine,
It measured
One two on the Richter scale, a shabby little shiver
One two on the Richter scale, a queasy little quiver
Waves brushed the seismograph as if a fly had flicked
  her
One two on the Richter scale, it hardly woke up
  Richter. . . .

Some day pretty soon we fear our many faults will
   fail us
Slide and slip and rip and dip and all at once assail us
Seismic jolts like lightning bolts will flatten us that day
When the concrete settles down geologists will say, it
   measured
Eight nine on the Richter scale, it rocked 'em in Samoa
Eight nine on the Richter scale, it cracked like Krakatoa
Waves crunched the seismograph, just like a boa
   constrictor
Eight nine on the Richter scale, it really racked up
   Richter.

Richter did not like this song at all. Weeks after its performance, he told a friend why he had been so offended: "My science is *not* a joke."

Yet in the early 1970s, there was simply no basis for saying that the Big One might strike "pretty soon," or at any foreseeable time in the future. There had been major quakes in 1812 and 1857; the ones since then had been moderate, compared with the destructive San Francisco tremor. So far as anyone could tell, this state of affairs might continue for another century or longer. The historical records showed less than two hundred years of earthquake activity, and this was simply not enough to give a valid reading of the risk. To learn more, it would be necessary to uncover the earth's geological history; and the man who began that task was Kerry Sieh.

At the time Sieh began his work, in the early 1970s, there was only one way to learn about California's earthquakes: by studying the written records, both descriptive and seismographic, from the tremors of the last two centuries. Sieh went deeper. He showed that by careful study of the disturbances that prehistoric quakes had produced in the soils, it was possible to learn of the occurrence of great quakes as long ago as two thousand years. With this, it was possible to answer a number of important questions: At a given site, had the fault been inactive, or had major tremors occurred? How often did they take place, and how long had it been since the last one? If that last one was several hundred years old, should the next big quake be expected soon, or not for additional centuries? And how big would it be? All these issues now could be addressed using his methods. What was more, he was actively continuing with this research, and had invited me to come out and see what he was up to.

3

DIGGINGS

On a bright but smoggy day in late October, I went out to visit the San Jacinto Fault near San Bernardino. There is a good deal of mystery about it. It is a major and damaging offshoot of the San Andreas; its central part, which broke in 1918, produced a quake of magnitude 6.8 that devastated the small towns of San Jacinto and Hemet. This had followed an even stronger shaking on Christmas Day, 1899, centered thirty miles away, that killed six people. And in 1890— before anyone had proper seismographs—there had been another very strong tremor east of Los Angeles, in country that was then almost uninhabited. Did it or didn't it break the northern San Jacinto Fault? The answer is not known. If it did, it relieved the strain and probably left that stretch of fault safe for our time. If it didn't, however, and if that quake broke a different fault, then the northern San Jacinto has probably had no major quake while Europeans and Americans have lived in southern California. This would mean that this stretch is strained severely, and such cities as Riverside and San Bernardino are in danger of a shock of about magnitude 7. This would be enough to kill hundreds of people.

I drove on the freeway beneath a three-level interchange. I could picture it toppling from a height of fifty feet, crowded with cars, in the shock of a quake that might strike at five in the evening. Nearby was a tall grain elevator; I wondered about its solidity. Power lines, probably carrying 138,000 volts, maybe 245,000, were strung between steel towers. I exited onto local streets and crossed a set of three railroad tracks on the main line running east from Los Angeles. I recalled how such tracks had twisted in a major 1952 quake in Kern County, north of Los Angeles.

Near this tract was a cleared field, and in the middle was a yellow backhoe, piling up earth alongside a trench. Somewhere along its length was the trace of the San Jacinto Fault itself, carrying its record of past earthquakes, and its possible clues concerning the next one. On a side street adjoining the field, a white station wagon stood parked. Its doors were marked with large logos showing a map of the world with the continents in orange and a seismographic squiggle crossing the Pacific, along with the words SEISMOLOGICAL LABORATORY. A tall, tousle-haired man in work clothes came over, a shovel in his hands. This was Steve Wesnousky, who was working closely with Kerry Sieh. I asked him about the overpasses and chimneys.

"Your concern is well taken," he replied. "This is a major crossroads: the railroad, the freeway interchange linking the main highways in and out of California. In fact, the major problem might not be the shaking right away, but the problems in bringing in supplies."

He looked around at the nearby homes. "It's true that the laws in California do not let you build directly over a known fault trace. You see the San Jacinto running over there; it's a greenbelt." That is, the builders had left grass in place along the fault, rather than straddle it with buildings. That would keep houses from being physically torn apart by offsets along the San Jacinto. But what about chimneys coming down? "I would suggest yes. You can expect some large damage. The fault does go through the overpass; it goes through San Bernardino Valley College. There's a motel over there that is known to lie directly atop the fault. And you can trace the fault on through that department store." Early in the 1970s, the state legislature passed a law stating that when a developer started to build, he had to bring in geologists to locate any fault. But a great many structures had been built before that law was passed, and will be with us for a long time.

He pointed me in a different direction and returned to his trench. I walked along a narrow strip of land overgrown with tall grass—the "greenbelt"—and soon came to another field with more dirt piles. Next to one of them was a narrow pit fifteen feet deep, the backhoe's limit. A thin steel tape measure hung the length of one trench wall to measure the depth of the different layers within the soil. The backhoe had left a small, benchlike shelf along the narrow, sloping pit wall that gave access to this hole. On this shelf of earth was a large soft-drink container from Del Taco, and a few small packages of aluminum foil. At the bottom of the hole was Kerry Sieh. He had a small trowel in his hand, as he carefully scraped away at the compacted sand of the pit wall. He wore a yellow hardhat, a T-shirt, and "gray, ugly, holey" pants. "I'm finding black gold," he grinned. "This soil is an old lakebed. There were fires in the brush up on the hills, chaparral that burned from lightning strikes. Then in winter the rain would wash the burned leaves and twigs down to this pond. This is old peat."

He was searching for bits of carbon that could be dated. When he found them, he wrapped his samples in the aluminum-foil pouches. Even small bits of carbon, fragments of ancient leaves a few milligrams in weight, would serve. A new technique, employing a particle accelerator, could study the carbon-14 atoms in such a sample, and determine its age. But this method was somewhat inaccurate. The older and more conventional technique required more carbon but it could give a date accurate to thirty years, which is excellent precision when you are thinking in thousands. The two dating techniques would each give independent ages, serving to check the other. "I'm getting enough carbon for a conventional date," he added, "as well as by the accelerator method."

The point of his work was that, unlike many geological formations whose ages were in the millions of years, the soil layers had been laid down within the past few hundred years, more or less concurrently with the earthquakes. The field was part of an ancient "sag pond," a low spot along a fault where water would collect during the rainy winters, depositing silt. Sometimes there had been dry years; then the deposits would show windblown dust. At other times heavy rains had led to floods, which had covered the pond bottom with coarse material that included small stones and gravel. And amid all these deposits were bits of carbon, washed down or blown in as leaves or twigs, which had grown and died at the same time that the sediment deposits were forming. Dating the carbon thus would give these sediments' ages.

By careful study of the soil layers that lay exposed within the walls of a trench, Sieh and his colleagues could list them in a sequence. Like a layer cake, these deposits lay in beds with recognizable colors, textures, and depths. Those that contained useful amounts of carbon could be noted. Within this sedimentary layer cake, the earthquakes had left their marks. Any individual quake ruptured the sediments and shifted them to form offsets, all the way to what had then been the surface. But subsequent deposits, laid down after that quake, would build up undisturbed. The key then was to look for soil disturbances that were clearly the work of such quakes. These would run only partway up the trench walls, stopping at some well-defined soil layer that represented the next bed to be deposited after that particular tremor.

Two types of disturbances were particularly useful. The first was the sandblow, a miniature, volcano-like eruption of sand or mud. The sag pond's bottom had usually been waterlogged but firm; individual grains of sediment had water between them, but touched each other and formed a cohesive mass. But in an earthquake the seismic waves would push the water between the grains' contact points, separating them and turning the wet pond bottom to quicksand. These earthquake waves then put pressure on this muck, causing it to blow through the surface.

The sandblows left easily recognizable traces amid the sediments within the trench walls. New sediments covered them cleanly, giving sharp separations between the pre- and postquake layers. Different quakes tended to produce sandblows at different locations, so their traces would not lie on top of one another in a confusing way. And because larger quakes produced larger sandblows, their sizes, which could easily be measured, gave valuable clues as to the intensities of the ancient quakes.

A second disturbance came from slippage along the fault itself. There was usually some vertical movement, with the soil on one side of the fault being pushed somewhat higher than that on the other side. In the trench walls, this meant the soil layers could be seen to have broken along the line of the fault, forming vertical offsets. These too ran only part way up the trench walls, and gave independent determination of which layers had or had not been disturbed in any particular quake. The combination of sandblows and vertical offsets, along with the ages of the layers as determined by carbon 14, then gave the age of the youngest layer of sediment to form after a given quake. This could be taken as the age of the quake itself, since such layers had been forming continually and without interruption.

There was more. With additional work, Sieh could develop a three-dimensional view of the buried sediments. Any one trench gave a two-dimensional view, a cross-section. But Sieh was prepared to dig several such trenches, one next to the other, each of them crossing the fault like crossbars on a telephone pole. This would give a number of cross-sections, allowing individual features within the soil to be traced from one trench to the next. This collection of sections thus amounted to the three-dimensional view.

It was particularly useful when Sieh could find a buried streambed, the remnant of a creek or channel that had crossed the fault. It was in the nature of such streams to flow in reasonably straight courses; they did not make jogs or zigzags, at least not within a length of a few meters. But the three-dimensional view of the ancient stream would often show just this type of zigzag, at the fault. The clear conclusion was that the fault's motions had broken and offset this channel. Hence, by measuring the offset, Sieh could determine the shifts in the land produced by the quakes. This gave an entirely separate determination, independent of that from studies of the sandblows, to show the size of the ancient quake.

"We're interested in identifying prehistoric earthquakes," he went on, "since we don't know when the last one took place. There are at least three earthquakes recorded here in these sediments, so it's important to know the date of the oldest one." Sieh's earlier work had uncovered soil disturbances that showed the three former earthquakes. But he had not succeeded in dating them, and this was the goal of his present effort. Within his pit, he was searching for carbon with which to date the soil layers. And within the field a short distance away, Steve Wesnousky, with his trench, was looking for the trace of a buried streambed that might show an offset. The size of this offset, then, would show how dangerous was the local fault.

Sieh had tried to determine the quakes' ages fifteen years earlier, but without success. "Back in 1972 the National Science Foundation was trying to seduce students into research," he recalled. "We decided to work here in our own backyard. We applied and got the money, to our amazement and astonishment. In '72 we did a lot of excavation.

We could see the fault trace; we could see the record of prehistoric earthquakes, and we collected a lot of charcoal. But when we sent it off to a lab to be dated, the radiocarbon dates were bogus. We got nice big samples of carbon, but we got screwed." The lab had made a mistake, and the dates it reported were worthless.

"We came back in '79 and tried again, but that was a very wet year. We had a trench dug across the fault only a few yards from here, and when we got back the next day it was a puddle. Wooden planking had floated out; the trench was completely full of water." (The land had once been a low-lying pond, after all.) "We couldn't get back for more than a year. By the time we did, the developers had eviscerated the fault, dug it out to build a drainage ditch. This is really our last chance here, with this property under development. Here we have a great example of how builders destroy the very data that could help us understand the seismic hazards they face." Still, he now was finding what he needed. In one of his most important pouches he had about two grams of carbonaceous material. "That's enough for a conventional date, with high precision."

I walked back to Steve Wesnousky's long trench. With him was Carol Prentice, a graduate student working on her Ph.D. She had been at Caltech since 1982, and was studying ancient earthquakes along the San Andreas north of San Francisco to learn when a great quake like the one of 1906 might recur. Right now she was helping Steve shore up the sides of their ditch so there would be no danger of a cave-in. The shorings were made from long aluminum plates resembling planks, connected by cross-braces with built-in pistons. With a hook and chain, Steve lowered each shoring into the trench. Then, using a pump, Carol forced fluid into the cross-braces and pushed the plates tightly against the walls of the excavation.

By the end of the afternoon the backhoe operator was nearly at the end of the long red line that had been painted on the ground to outline where he should dig. Carol was with Kerry in his trench, taking down notes in a logbook as he dictated. They needed a "trench log"—a description of the various soil layers with their measured depths. A little later the backhoe operator drove over with his rig, a versatile, tractorlike vehicle that could dig with its long boom and shovel, or bulldoze with a wide blade across the other end. He was to begin filling in Kerry's pit—that was the agreement with the landowner—but he was leaking hydraulic fluid, which lay in long dark lines across the bare soil. He would have to work quickly, while he still could. As he shoveled the dirt pile directly into the deepest part of the hole, a plume of brown dust billowed upward in the light of the setting sun.

I went back two weeks later. They had installed more shoring along the main trench, and had cut a short trench to form a cross with the first. The walls of these excavations then showed the cross-sections of soil they needed for a three-dimensional view. And they had found what they were hoping for. Carol led me down into the trench to show me. We scrambled down a steep, sandy incline, ducking under one of the shorings, then making our way past the trench walls. These walls had been rough at first, crudely dug, scarred with the marks of the backhoe, but Carol and Steve had smoothed their surfaces so that their detail could be seen. They then had found the fault. "We missed it at first," she remarked. "It was hidden behind one of the shorings." Sitting in the dirt, she pointed it out. It was a thin crack in the packed earth—and that was all.

I recalled a cartoon from *The New Yorker,* tacked outside Kerry's office. Two archaeologists, shovels in hand, had just uncovered a small, pyramid-shaped form protruding from the desert sand. One of them was saying, "This could be the discovery of the century. Of course, it all depends on how far down it goes." This unprepossessing crack ran down for tens of miles, north and south for about a hundred. Yet because the weight of the soil had packed and pressed its sides together, it was thoroughly unobtrusive, and would remain so—until the next quake.

But this wasn't what had the geologists excited. Nearby,

Carol pointed out another part of the trench wall, slightly coarser than the fine sand of its surroundings, a bit lighter in color. These differences would easily escape the notice of you or me, but to the experienced eyes of Carol and Steve, they stood out. They marked an ancient, buried streambed, a narrow channel that had flowed toward the fault. At least one ancient quake had broken this bed and shifted its offset parts; within a few days they expected to trace its course. This old and long-forgotten stream was their discovery.

A few days later, Kerry told me the news. They had indeed measured the offset: ten meters. The streambed showed a zigzag of this length, where it crossed the fault. This meant the local fault not only was actively straining; it was dangerous, capable of causing major quakes. Here was proof of the danger to San Bernardino and Riverside. And with their charcoal samples, it soon would be possible to say just how long ago the quake had occurred that broke that stream. One step ahead of the developers, in the last opportunity before that land would be covered with a growing town, Kerry and his colleagues had seized the necessary data. In a year or two they would write a paper describing their evidence for prehistoric quakes. It would stand as part of the groundwork for all subsequent studies of seismic hazards along the northern San Jacinto fault. And it would be one more successful use of the trenching techniques Kerry had introduced during the 1970s.

Kerry Sieh spent his first twelve years in Cedar Rapids, Iowa, spending many summers on his grandparents' farms. "I don't think I knew what science was when I was a boy," he recalls, "but I had a strong interest in nature." There were creeks to dam, woods and fields to wander through. In later years, when he was working in the outdoors as a geologist, it would be like coming home.

Then, in 1962, his family moved to Costa Mesa, near

beaches southeast of Los Angeles. He was a student in one of California's better high schools, Corona del Mar High, in the wealthy town of Newport Beach. His sophomore biology teacher got him interested in butterflies. "I had no idea there was such a range of animal life," he declares. He chased them through fields with a butterfly net—"it's much easier than fingers"—and mounted them in a collection, with mothballs for preservation. He fell in love with the ancient world through a Latin class, taught by an ex-seminarian. In his senior year, a friend led him to an a cappella chorus of eight men and eight women that sang madrigals from the seventeenth and eighteenth centuries. The teacher in charge wanted A students who knew how to sing, and this group often gave performances in the area. Kerry recalls the "electric atmosphere of exhilaration" of performing. They'd give a concert, then go down to the beach in their tuxedoes and run around, or go out for hamburgers.

Within the next two years, some of Kerry's friends were applying to Ivy League schools and getting in. His grades were as good as theirs, and he applied to Stanford, Princeton, and Cornell. All three schools turned him down. He was thoroughly devastated.

He thought of enlisting in the Navy, but decided to try for one of the branches of the University of California. That spring, UCLA was wait-listing applicants. Every other university in the system was entirely full—with one exception. The branch at Riverside was taking anyone they could get. Riverside was less appealing than the other campuses—it was smoggy, it was far from the beach—and it gave Kerry a chance.

"The first year was a horrible experience," he states. "I was away from my madrigal friends and an hour away from my family. I didn't know what I wanted to do, but found I couldn't do music; I wasn't talented enough." He was taking several science courses, going to classes and doing homework, and he was feeling, "What am I doing here?" He was doing well in his work, but he felt his life lacked purpose, and he was filled with self-doubt.

Kerry fell in with a senior named Dave Gerry, a geology major. He also was a fundamentalist Christian. Kerry argued with him about the latter, but he was very interested in the former: "On weekends I'd be studying math and chemistry in my cubicle, losing more and more of my Newport Beach tan. And this guy would come back from his field trips, intellectually and physically just beat. And I thought, 'Now that's the life!'" Dave was spending weekends in the field, hiking over hills, minutely examining rocks and other features, struggling to make sense of what he was seeing. Very soon, Kerry declared a geology major. "Geology wasn't like doing problem sets for homework," he remembers. "There was more reality to it. The problems were untidy. They were tactile; you could touch the rocks."

The combination of using his brain and his body, out in the field, appealed to him immensely. "When you walk on the ground, you walk on something that has a wonderful story to tell, almost anywhere on earth. There were these fabulous stories—the evolution of the earth, the evolution of life." What was more, he had entered the field just as plate tectonics was sweeping all before it, for the first time giving a unified system for understanding the workings of the earth. "It was exciting to be learning the basics at a time of revolution," is how he describes it. "It was a time of tremendous ferment." One of his professors, Will Elders, spotted his talent and enthusiasm, and invited Kerry to be his student assistant. This gave Kerry a chance to read the recently published papers that were laying the groundwork for plate tectonics. He helped prepare maps for one of Elders's papers, which dealt with the opening up of the Gulf of California, a topic that was very much in the mainstream of this subject. Elders had other lessons for Kerry as well. "He was excited about it," Kerry remembers. "His attitude was, 'Be critical of new ideas, but don't be afraid of them.'"

The summer of 1971, following his junior year, saw him

join a field camp in Nevada, organized by Elders. He and some other students would spend six weeks making geological maps in the rocky terrain. The students slept on a ranch in an old bunkhouse, got up in the cool morning, then hiked out with a detailed topographic map, a contour chart showing mountains, forests, and canyons. On such maps he and his fellow students would note the various beds of rock, as well as their orientations and relations to one another. The country featured tall, hilly ranges rising from a valley floor, with mountains approaching eight thousand feet, covered with pine trees.

Back at school that fall, a classmate handed Kerry a brochure for a program called Student-Originated Studies, saying, "Dr. Elders just handed me this; it's from the National Science Foundation. You can write a proposal; they're encouraging topics that are environmentally related. Dr. Elders suggested we work on the San Jacinto Fault. It's close by; nobody knows much about it. Let's see what we can do!"

Kerry had heard a talk a few months earlier, given by a geologist who'd been digging trenches in the Bay Area to locate faults. He now recalled that seminar and thought, "Surely they can do something more sophisticated! With these sediments exposed, they should be able to tell when earthquakes happened, what the offsets are—not just where the fault is." In his senior courses, Kerry was learning how lakes and rivers deposited sediment, how to interpret what different sand-grain sizes meant. "Really, I was in the right place at the right time," he explains. "I'd taken that classwork just as the idea of trenching was coming along, making artificial excavations. Geologists are not accustomed to making such excavations; usually they look for outcrops of rock to study."

Those geologists in the Bay Area had had courses like Kerry's in their own undergraduate days, learning about sediments and their deposition. But that had been long ago; to these experienced people that material was old-hat. They had dug their trenches for the simple purpose of locating faults; it hadn't occurred to them how they might go further and study the quakes that had occurred on those faults. But to Kerry the study of sediments was fresh and new, as was the idea of trenching as a part of geological fieldwork. In his mind these two concepts fitted neatly together: trenching would uncover the sediments, while studying them in detail would give information on ancient quakes.

Working with Elders and other students, he spent two weeks preparing the grant proposal. He was proposing to study the San Jacinto Fault with an eye to determining whether it posed a significant earthquake hazard. To do this, he and his colleagues would dig a trench across the fault, laying bare the sediment layers, and determine the sequence in which these layers had been laid down. He would then look for breaks in the sediment, where quakes had pushed the beds upward on one side of the fault, with these beds then buried by younger deposits that had formed after a quake. He also would collect carbon samples that would likely be mixed in with the sediments, and send them off to a lab to be dated. That would determine the quakes' ages.

All this was far more than most other student projects would attempt. It would be an entirely new way of examining earthquakes; it would amount to inventing a technique for studying prehistoric tremors, which no one had even tried to study before. Again, this was a tribute to the originality of Kerry's thinking. The grant thus was quickly approved. Kerry now found himself the principal investigator on a research project funded by a grant from the National Science Foundation—a position that many of his professors would have been glad to be in. To Kerry, it was quite heady. "There was the thrill of learning—and also the more mundane fact that I'd probably be employable with this." This grant award would look quite good on his resume.

His first task was to locate the fault with precision. He studied aerial photos, and found eroded scarps or cliffs that marked the path of the fault. They also showed that the fault crossed the floodplain of the Santa Ana River, where he hoped to find deep sediment deposits. He bored with an auger into the soil to check it out, then got a backhoe to dig a trench fifteen feet deep. "We put a tape across the top, measured distances to features in the trench wall, and made a map." Among those features were the signs left by prehistoric earthquakes. "We could see places where the layers of sediment were broken, so we knew they had been laid down before the quake occurred." They had been broken by motions of the fault. "Then we saw rubble that had collapsed from a scarp face very soon after the quake." The shifting masses of rock and soil, on either side of the fault, had upthrust low, steep cliffs, which fell to produce layers of rubble. By finding charcoal within these layers, both before and immediately after each large quake, he could determine the dates of those ancient tremors using carbon 14.

There were at least fifty carbon-14 labs to choose from, and Kerry knew almost nothing about carbon dating. He picked his lab on the recommendation of somebody he knew, sent off the charcoal samples, then waited. Every week he phoned the lab, only to be told, "We don't have your dates yet." Finally, months later, the dates were in. He carefully compared them to the information in his trench logs, the records that showed what he had seen within his excavation.

These logs showed the sequence of the sediment beds, bottom to top, which lay exposed within the trench. Those at the bottom were the oldest and had formed first; they had then been overlain by successively younger deposits. Thus, Kerry expected that charcoal from deep layers would yield measured ages far older than carbon from layers higher up in the trench. But that was not what the data from the lab showed.

The dates from that lab were entirely wrong. The carbon from the deepest layers, which should have been oldest, instead had been dated as the youngest. For charcoal from the topmost and hence most recent sediments, the carbon-14 date was the oldest. The sequence of carbon dates thus was entirely upside down, and hence valueless. He knew right away that the whole summer's work on the San Jacinto was largely for naught.

"My first reaction was supreme disappointment," he relates. He called the lab back and said that the dates were obviously wrong. The man there replied, "Maybe the section of land is overturned." Kerry knew that idea was ridiculous. When he told Will Elders about it, the professor was furious. He got in touch with the lab himself, saying, "What is going on here? These dates are blatantly incorrect!" To prove his point, Elders showed them Kerry's trench logs, which proved that the sediments had been deposited in a regular sequence; in no way had the strata been overturned. The man at the lab agreed to rerun the dates—and strangely enough, now that he knew the proper order of the layers of sediment, this time all his dates were consistent. Kerry remained unconvinced: "At that point, would you trust someone, once he has the beds in front of him and knows which one is younger and which is older? The dates may have been right the second time, but I didn't believe him." The completion of the work on the San Jacinto would await his return to the area fourteen years later, in 1986.

In 1972 he entered graduate school. Because of his National Science Foundation project, plus his straight A's in geology, a number of universities had been courting him—Harvard, Stanford, MIT. He picked Stanford for a good reason: he wanted to study earthquake faults. "The faults were all on the West Coast, and I wasn't impressed with the notion that you could study them at MIT," in earthquake-free Boston. He took his B.S. with considerable confidence: "I felt pretty good about my background at the end of my senior year. I thought I knew most of what there was to know in geology."

He didn't know what he didn't know. He soon discovered there were gaps in his background wide enough to make him feel like a freshman all over again. He had no concept that you could use math and physics to understand geological processes. He didn't understand as much as he thought he did about igneous rocks, about groundwater. He hadn't learned much about stress and strain, which was essential in understanding earthquakes. There were significant topics that he didn't even know existed, such as the study of fossilized shells of microscopic plankton in the ocean. Because different species had flourished at different times and depths, such shells could not only serve for determining ages, they could show the depth of water at the time their rocks had formed.

That first year at Stanford, he chugged away, taking lots of courses. He had stayed in touch with his old friend Dave Gerry, who helped him locate a four-bedroom apartment in the nearby town of Mountain View, which he shared with three roommates. His summer of work on the San Jacinto had earned him a total of $950, out of which he bought a ten-speed bike for commuting. He had a fellowship, and was given an office on the third floor of the geology department. It was on Stanford's sprawling campus of low, Spanish-style sandstone buildings, roofed with red tiles and linked by arched walkways. And he started looking for ways to pursue his interest in faults.

He found a key opportunity in 1973, during his first year at Stanford. He'd met a group of engineering geologists who were working to locate active faults. One of them later phoned him and invited him to come to Alaska for the summer. Thus he went to work on the Alaskan pipeline, mapping such faults along the length of its route, from Prudhoe Bay to Valdez. He flew first to Fairbanks. It was quite exhilarating; he'd never been anywhere but Iowa and California, and now felt as if he were on his way to the Gold Rush.

There were no roads where he was going. He flew in to a work camp that featured a large number of mobile homes, all brought in by helicopter, along with immense fuel tanks. Enclosed corridors ran for hundreds of feet, with trailers branching off to the sides. This camp at Deadhorse, on the North Slope, appeared to house some five thousand men.

"They had wonderful food," Kerry recalls. "They'd have fifteen kinds of baked goods: cookies, pastries, tarts. Steaks, too. Some of the guys were fishermen; they'd catch trout or salmon on their lunch breaks." A helicopter would set a man down on the banks of a promising stream, then return in an hour or so to pick him up.

The work week ran to eighty hours. Kerry spent much of that time in helicopters, looking for the traces of faults. His camp was north of the Arctic Circle, so the sun never set. Forests of birch, aspen, and spruce grew all around. In late June, however, a storm blew in; they were snowed in for three days. Then the clouds broke and he flew down to do some work in the Brooks Range, the tall, mountainous spine that crosses the northern part of Alaska. At midnight they knocked off, and flew back to camp by flying directly into the sun, which was due north.

One of his friends was a young geologist with a Ph.D., Gary Carver. "He was such a powerful, intelligent guy," says Kerry. "He knew what to look for, what questions to ask. I didn't." For instance, they were flying amid volcanoes and glaciers. The glaciers in places had bulldozed long lines of rubble ahead of them, then melted and retreated, leaving the rubble long as moraines. They could be mistaken for the lines produced by scarps along a fault, but Gary could tell the difference.

Kerry returned to Stanford that fall. It was time to start thinking about the research that he would do for his Ph.D., and he knew that he wanted to study the San Andreas Fault. Seismology had been an active field of research for the whole of the twentieth century, but in 1973 that major fault was still largely a zone of ignorance. It was known to have broken in great quakes in 1838, 1857, and 1906, and it was known to exist in segments, each with a different history and behavior. The southernmost part, running from the Mexican border past Indio to the San Bernardino area, had not broken in historic times. Then there was a two-hundred-mile stretch from San Bernardino to Paso Robles in central California that had broken in the great 1857 tremor. To its north, running to San Juan Bautista, was a "creeping" segment. Recent work, around 1960, had demonstrated that the fault in this section was yielding, the two sides slipping past each other at about three centimeters per year. And from San Juan northward to the coast at Mendocino was a fourth segment of the fault, which had broken in the great quake of 1906.

To Kerry, all this raised more questions than it answered. Was the southern segment dormant, or had it accumulated stress that could lead to a major quake? What exactly had happened along the length of the 1857 break? What previous earthquakes had occurred along the fault, and when? At what rate was the fault accumulating strain? At what average rate was it slipping, releasing this strain? How did these rates change along the fault's length? If there were large changes, would that mean that great quakes were more frequent along some stretches than along others? And what about the next one?

In 1973 there simply was no basis for answering these questions. An essential piece of data, associated with the concepts of plate tectonics, still lay undiscovered. These concepts described the San Andreas as a boundary between two major plates of the earth's crust, the Pacific Plate and the North American Plate, which were sliding past each other. At what rate were they sliding? This essential datum, the "plate rate," would soon be sought by two geophysicists from Caltech, Jean-Bernard Minster and Tom Jordan. Their finding, an average of 5.6 centimeters per year for the past 3 million years, would be essential in any estimate of earthquake hazard. For example, suppose you believed the San Andreas Fault was slipping at full plate rate. Then, knowing that the 1906 quake had produced offsets of five meters, you could divide five meters by 5.6 centimeters per year and estimate that such a quake would happen again after ninety years—in 1996, give or take a few decades.

And if the San Andreas was not being stressed at the

whole of the plate rate, then some of this motion between the plates would be straining other faults, which would be dangerous in their own right. The San Jacinto was one such fault. Others were known to exist on the east side of San Francisco Bay: the Hayward fault, and the Calaveras. The Hayward, for one, had broken in 1868, wrecking and damaging buildings, killing some thirty people. When might it happen again? Measuring the average San Andreas slip rate would give a clue.

Nor could anyone declare that all the active faults were known. There was also the question of faults running out to sea, being strained by the motion of the plates, yet not easily studied because they were underwater. One such fault had turned up early in the 1970s, to the intense embarrassment of Pacific Gas and Electric, the major utility firm. PG&E was proceeding with plans to build two nuclear plants at Diablo Canyon, a remote coastal spot eighty miles north of Santa Barbara. The builders had selected Diablo in part for its remoteness from faults on land, but had neglected to look under the sea. Then in 1971 two geologists from Shell Oil, E. G. Hoskins and J. R. Griffiths, published their discovery of a major fault running less than three miles from the plant site. It came to be known as the Hosgri fault, a name derived from its discoverers. The U.S. Geological Survey concluded in 1975 that this fault might well have broken in the major Point Arguello quake of 1927, magnitude 7.3. By that time the nuclear plants were more than 75 percent complete. PG&E eventually succeeded in adding enough structural bracing to win an operating license and allow these plants to open, but the cost of this extra work ran into the billions.

Kerry, as a doctoral student, aimed to do more toward understanding the San Andreas than had been done in the eighty years since Andrew Lawson at Berkeley had discovered it. To the faculty at Stanford, this quest seemed entirely quixotic. Kerry wanted to look for surface offsets, features visible at ground level that would show the fault's shifts in the 1857 quake. Why should he believe they were there to be seen, after more than a century of weathering and erosion? He wanted to dig trenches and look for evidence of ancient quakes. That too was new and unfamiliar to his professors; they had no experience with such an effort, and the debacle of Kerry's carbon dates from his San Jacinto work hardly increased the faculty's confidence. Kerry also hoped to find carbon for dating, in soil layers along the San Andreas. But much of the country was a near-desert; why should anyone believe that carbon was there to be found? It could only come from dead plants, after all, of which there had been very few.

The usual procedure was for a grad student to tag onto a professor's grant, sharing in a part of his research. The professor would assign tasks and give the student responsibility for this part; with several years of effort, the student would carry it through and qualify for the Ph.D. Sometimes students undertook original research, but the Stanford faculty was accustomed to seeing their students propose projects that were far less sweeping than Kerry's. He thus faced a problem: he would need a faculty adviser to act as his sponsor before he could proceed. He talked with some of the professors he knew, but couldn't find one who would believe in him.

During Christmas of 1973, he visited his family in southern California. While there, he took a day to visit Caltech, where he made an appointment with one of the nation's leading seismologists, Clarence Allen, who had come up as a student of Richter. Allen suggested that Kerry try to win the support of Richard Jahns, the dean of Stanford's school of earth sciences. To Kerry, Jahns was a remote and almost inaccessible figure who virtually walked on water. Still, early in the new year, he arranged a meeting. "I walked out feeling six inches off the ground," Kerry remembers. "He had confidence in me."

For Kerry to gain formal approval for this research, it had to be voted on by a panel of three professors, including Jahns. Kerry made his presentation—and was turned down, with only Jahns voting for his plan. The others felt he would fail to find traces of the 1857 quake after nearly 120 years, or that he would be unable to find charcoal where the San Andreas ran through desert land. Kerry was devastated. Jahns told him, "We could agree on one thing: you're bull-headed." They wanted him to rethink his proposal, and gave him some suggestions. He beefed up some of his ideas and wrote a new proposal—not to professors within his department, but to the U.S. Geological Survey. Then a curious thing happened. The paperwork at Stanford got lost, and there was no official record of the panel's rejection of his first plan. By slipping through the bureaucratic cracks in this fashion, he gained what amounted to approval to proceed. The USGS soon assented as well and provided $25,000.

Part of his work involved old Spanish newspapers with articles from 1857, describing *el temblor grande.* Those became important in one phase of his USGS-sponsored research: to describe, from contemporary sources, the 1857 quake. Harry Wood, Richter's old boss, had written a paper, but Kerry felt that Wood's search for sources had been rather hit-or-miss; it would take a professional historian to do the job properly. Kerry knew such a historian, Dan Burd, a former roommate. Using funds from his USGS grant, he hired Dan to search through the archives at the Bancroft Library in Berkeley, the leading repository of Californiana. Among the nineteenth-century letters, diaries, and newspapers there, Kerry expected there would be much more material than Wood had been able to locate. "Dan came up with a lot of great stuff," Kerry summarizes. "Accounts that no one had ever seen before, describing what happened during the earthquake."

From those old accounts, he sought much more than descriptions of panicky horses and falling walls. He was after a scientifically accurate account of the 1857 quake. Such an account would be based on the Mercalli scale, which, as noted in chapter 2, featured twelve successively higher intensities, each with greater levels of damage. This scale differed from the Richter scale in that it described the felt effects of a quake rather than its actual magnitude. To appreciate this difference, suppose that a quake takes place that measures magnitude 7 on the Richter scale. Anywhere in the world, seismologists will measure its waves and come up with a consistent conclusion: The quake was indeed of magnitude 7. The waves weaken with distance, but the calculation of Richter magnitude allows for this, so that seismic stations at different distances can come up with the same measurement.

But what is it like in the quake's immediate vicinity? Close to the epicenter, there might be a region of Mercalli intensity VII: "Everybody runs outdoors. Damage . . . considerable in . . . badly designed structures." Surrounding this region, in the fashion of a bull's-eye, are zones at increasing distance with steadily diminishing intensities. The first such zone is of Mercalli intensity VI: "Felt by all; many frightened and run outdoors. . . . Damage slight." The second one, as we move outward from the epicenter, is of intensity V: "Felt by nearly everyone; many awakened." The Mercalli scale, unlike that of Richter, explicitly describes how a quake's intensity falls off with distance, as determined by the quake's felt effects.

A map of the region around the quake's location, showing concentric curves with intensities that fall off from the center in this fashion, is called an *isoseismal* map. It stands as a scientifically useful description of a quake's effects. Furthermore, each Mercalli category, or degree of intensity, contains points that would be observed in the country as well as in the city, and in the last century as well as this one. That was the point of Kerry's historical research. For instance, if newspaper accounts from some town described such effects as "everybody runs outdoors; some chimneys broken," then the 1857 quake in that town had been of Mercalli intensity VII. The collection of all such accounts then would give the descriptions that he could match up with the proper Mercalli intensities, to construct the isoseismal map.

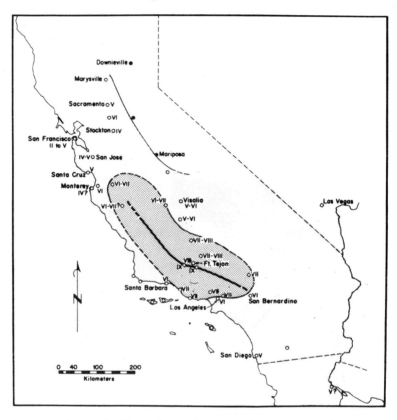

Isoseismal map by Kerry Sieh, showing felt intensities of the great earthquake of 1857. Roman numerals indicate intensities on the Modified Mercalli scale. The shaded region represents the zone of intensity VII or higher, where major damage occured. (After Agnew and Sieh, courtesy Kerry Sieh)

Why was this important? By constructing such a map, he was in a position to state with some confidence what would happen at any location in southern California, in the event of a repetition of the 1857 quake. That would stand as a welcome contrast to such sensational popular books as *The Last Days of the Late Great State of California*, which had predicted that a coming great quake would cause Los Angeles to split off from the mainland and fall into the sea. Such a fate would hardly be worse than that of experiencing the highest Mercalli intensity, XII: "Damage total. Waves seen on ground surfaces. Lines of sight and level distorted. Objects thrown upward into the air."

But Sieh concluded that even at the epicenter, which was near Fort Tejon, north of Los Angeles, the 1857 tremor had been no higher than intensity IX: "Damage considerable. . . . Ground cracked conspicuously." And from Los Angeles to San Bernardino, the intensity was even less, amounting to a VI: "Some heavy furniture moved; a few instances of fallen plaster or damaged chimneys. Damage slight." The interiors of homes might be wrecked, in other words, but the houses themselves would not fall down. A repetition of the 1857 quake thus would strike Los Angeles far less severely than would a repetition of the 1906 tremor in San Francisco, where the peak Mercalli intensity was XI, approaching the worst.

Digging in libraries was only the beginning. As a central aspect of his research, Kerry planned to walk along much of the San Andreas, studying the ground like an old-time prospector. But his commitments at Stanford during the school year meant he could do this only in the summer, when temperatures would reach over one hundred degrees in the shade. And where he was going, there wouldn't be any shade, for he was bound for the Carrizo Plain.

The Carrizo lies due west of Bakersfield, between the Temblor and Caliente ranges. In aerial photos, the San Andreas stands out as a great gash, a straight line running like a seam, as if the land had been stitched together. Hills drop toward it, then yield to flat desert on its other side. Gullies shift their course when they cross the fault; long, linear valleys appear where it traverses hilly uplands. A sickly yellow grass covers the ground, with occasional green and leafy mountain oaks standing starkly as single trees or as small copses. Ranchers run cattle over the land's emptiness, where each cow requires tens of acres if it is to survive. Yet to Kerry the land was bountiful. Here he hoped to find small streambeds, offset in the 1857 quake, which would tell him how the fault had broken and slipped.

He started working his way along the fault with a backpack. He would drive across the fields, chaining his bike to a suitable tree or fencepost, then drive on for several more miles and park his car. By hiking toward his bike, he then would have transportation on his return leg. He carried a notebook, and made sketches of small features that looked like offsets, but which were not likely to show up in aerial photos. "The first day was really depressing," he recalls. "I could hardly find anything." He took a break at midday, then he trekked on. People had been using insecticides nearby; he saw dead foxes, coyotes, rabbits, and birds. But by the end of that day he had seen something new. In three places, small gullies or streams crossed the fault, and had deposited silt on its other side. The gullies and their deposits had been offset by six meters. Evidently the fault had slipped this distance in 1857. "I was ecstatic; I was just thrilled," he declares. "It looked like there was data to be had."

That night he decided to camp out. He drove into the nearby mountains, near the treeline, where the piñon pines gave way to scrub. He found a flat area off the road where he could park. It was a little-used campground; there even was a spigot for water, which meant he could wash off. Soon he settled into a routine. It was a half-hour drive down to the Carrizo, and he could buy crackers, peanut butter, and fruit in small nearby towns such as Taft and Maricopa. "There's no 7-Eleven on the Carrizo Plain," he warns. He found it "hot, dry, lifeless, almost barren of people."

Some lived there, nevertheless. The land was harsh on the impatient. In winter the roads washed out in downpours; there was nothing to do but hole up with the provisions on hand, then ride horses to check the fences. One ranch manager told Kerry, "Well, it's gettin' time to be movin' on. The place is gettin' too populated." His nearest neighbor was five miles away.

As he worked his way north, he soon found himself in the country of the Grants and the Twisselmans. The central-California counterparts of the Hatfields and McCoys, they had settled the land a hundred years earlier. One day Kerry was noting some three-and-a-half-meter offsets near Cholame when he went up to a ranch house. A young man of his age greeted him, and invited Kerry to join them for dinner. He was raising a bald eagle in the house. He had stolen it from its eyrie as a chick, and the eagle now stood two feet tall. This was blatantly illegal, but the young man's attitude was, "It's fun." Kerry felt that this was just one more unusual thing that a man of the Carrizo might do.

Later that summer, Kerry doubled back nearly two hundred miles to explore the fault in the San Gabriel Mountains, near the town of Wrightwood. The Angeles National Forest lay around him, thick with pines. When he looked down, he found offsets of around four and a half meters—only half the length in the Carrizo. But he could also look up, and he saw something new. From time to time he would see an oddly shaped tree that had broken near the top many years earlier and subsequently regrown. He realized he was seeing trees that had been heavily damaged by motions along the San Andreas, and that this might offer him a new set of data with which to learn about the fault.

These explorations filled the summer of 1975. Back at Stanford, Kerry arranged a meeting with Richard Jahns to show him the data. He had some 150 offsets recorded in his notebook. Jahns wasn't impressed. The sketches weren't to scale, and Kerry had exaggerated some features for clarity. Jahns then accompanied Kerry for a five-day trip to the Carrizo, helping him make proper observations. "He taught me how to do it, and allowed me to see a great scientist observing," Kerry remembers. He had a lot more experience than Kerry in interpreting features, for instance, and his perceptions were well honed. He could look at the marks of a flow and tell just what had happened.

They documented what had happened along the fault in 1857. The offsets in the Carrizo ranged up to ten meters—

and there were fainter and older offsets, twenty and thirty meters in length. They began to develop the idea that previous great quakes had been about the same size, that the fault had repeatedly broken with slips of ten meters or so. But near Wrightwood, to the southeast, the offsets were only four to five meters. What did this mean? Did both stretches of fault have quakes equally often, but with differing amounts of slip? Or did the Wrightwood area have great quakes twice as often, to keep pace with the larger offsets in the Carrizo Plain?

To answer this question, Kerry needed to determine the slip rate, the average rate of movement along the fault. The way to do this was to find a place where the fault had offset some stream or creek by a hundred meters or more. That would show the cumulative effect of a dozen great quakes, maybe of several dozen, shaking the land across thousands of years. He would use carbon 14 to determine the age of the stream's formation. Then, by measuring the length of the offset, he would have the desired slip rate.

He studied aerial photos and found what he was looking for. In the southern Mojave, east of Palmdale and near the desert town of Pearblossom, a tiny stream known as Pallett Creek made its way down from the mountains and out onto the plain. As it crossed the San Andreas, it jogged to the southeast for 130 meters, then resumed its course. It looked to him like an old glacial stream that had formed during the last Ice Age, and had probably been accumulating its offset for the past ten thousand years. He found a map by a geologist who had lived in the area, which stated that there was peat below. And as he sat in his Stanford apartment, he realized that if he could date the peat, he could date the stream.

The area around Pallett Creek had often been marshland, with tall grasses and reeds. As the stream wandered back and forth, its waters made the ground lush with rank growth. In the summer the grasses would dry, and would burn from lightning. At times, storms would sweep down the mountains, burying the land in gravel and sand. Then the dead reeds and grasses turned to layers of peat. In time the stream had ceased its meanderings and cut a permanent channel. Its waters no longer made frequent course changes; the land had dried up, and little grew beyond the banks. That meant the peat had stopped forming at the time the stream had cut its channel. The channel then had been offset in the earthquakes. Better still, the stream had cut its way through six meters of soil, like a miniature Grand Canyon. The entire layer cake—the peats, the sands and gravels, as well as windblown dust—thus could easily be seen. Here no dun-colored earth revealed its secrets in the most subtle differences of texture and hue. The contrasts between the various layers would be dramatic enough to stand out in news photographs.

Kerry collected peat samples from the top and bottom of the channel. He expected the top sample, reflecting the age of the offset, to be about ten thousand years old. The bottom one, whose age would equal the time required to accumulate such deposits, might be around twenty thousand. He sent the peat off to a lab—one he knew he could trust—and waited. In November 1975 the dates were in. He phoned the lab from Stanford—and his jaw fell like a brick. The top peat was only two hundred years old. The bottom peat was not twenty thousand, but only two thousand years old. His immediate reaction: "I was horrified. There just couldn't be a 130-meter offset forming in just two hundred years. Something was terribly wrong."

Then, almost immediately, he realized that he was looking at Pallett Creek from the wrong perspective. "This is a two-thousand-year record in a six-meter-high cliff. The rate of sedimentation would be about a foot per century. And if earthquakes break the sediment every hundred years or so, there should be good separation between successive quakes." Now he saw that Pallett Creek could serve to show the great quakes of the past two thousand years. "I became extremely excited. There was a chill up my spine. I realized

I had a potential treasure trove there, and I was very eager to get back."

However, he had commitments at Stanford and had to leave his treasure buried for a while. There were a few things he could learn, even so. For instance, if that offset was only two hundred years old, then how had it formed? The answer was that it wasn't an offset after all. By chance, there was a slight rise in the land at that point, which had caused the stream to make a detour. He had been fooled: "Sometimes my intuition isn't all that hot." This meant he could not easily determine the slip rate along the fault, which he still wanted to measure. However, he had the opportunity to study ancient earthquakes directly from the records they had written in the earth.

Finally, during spring break in 1976, he got back to Pallett Creek. He found the fault covered with broken rock. Using a shovel and pick, he started to dig. There was a small break in the strata that ran upward into a deposit of gravel. That might be the mark of an earthquake. He went ahead by hand, continuing to dig. The slope-wash, the eroded material that had covered the fault, kept getting thicker, but Kerry kept shoveling. Finally he saw "this monstrous offset, half a meter high or more." He was so excited that he kept on shoveling until he had exposed the entire trace of the San Andreas. He then had to go back to Stanford, but he knew he had it.

Kerry found the land-ownership records at the county seat, then arranged permission to bring in a backhoe and a bulldozer, with the money coming from his USGS grant. He also hired his brother Rodger to help with the digging.

There was a great deal to learn. Some eighty distinguishable soil layers had been laid down in the past two thousand years, to a depth of six feet, and all had to be examined in detail. The backhoe dug two long trenches, with the bulldozer cutting a third. These exposed hundreds of square meters of area in their walls. Kerry's wife, Laurie, marked them off in one-meter squares, using string secured with nails, forming a thin white grid that stood out against the earthen colors.

It was very hot there in the Mojave; flies swarmed nearby. Kerry proceeded to make meticulous diagrams of the sediment layers, mapping about three square meters of trench wall per day. Evidence for past quakes lay amid these layers, in breaks in the beds, vertically shifted strata, and sandblows. These had disrupted the even accumulations of the beds, and these disruptions had to be disentangled and sorted out with care. Eventually he deciphered the puzzle. The evidence showed twelve great quakes along that part of the San Andreas, dating back to the time of the Roman Empire. With a possible error of no more than a few decades, their dates were as follows:

260 A.D.	845	1350
350	935	1550
590	1015	1720
735	1080	1857

Their average interval had been 145 years.

"Here geology was running concurrently with European history," he would remark. The geological events—the quakes—had occurred during mere hundreds of past years, in contrast to the millions of years for many other geological processes. "This fascinated me; I love working with geology that I can put in a human context. It's tough having a sense of time when you're talking of billions of years. But here you can see evidence of a quake that was in the time of Charlemagne, big kettle-drum-shaped features that formed when he was unifying western Europe. Or you can see a quake before that one, from the time of Muhammad. Then there was one near the Battle of Hastings, in 1066. We thought for a while we had one around 1215, which would have coincided with the Magna Carta. Then the more recent ones, around the time of the Black Death, 1350, and of Michelan-

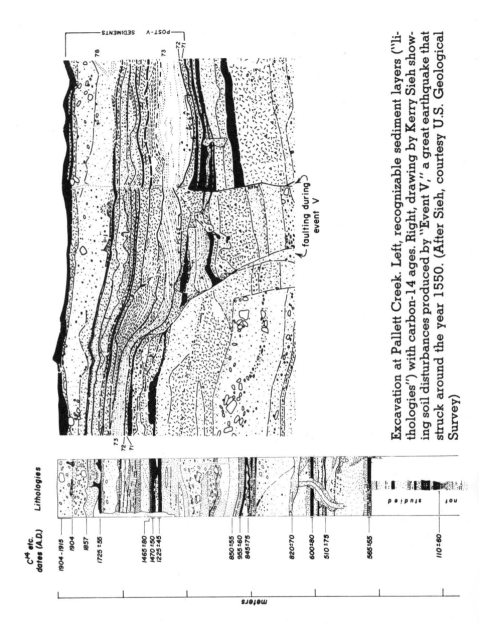

Excavation at Pallett Creek. Left, recognizable sediment layers ("lithologies") with carbon-14 ages. Right, drawing by Kerry Sieh showing soil disturbances produced by "Event V," a great earthquake that struck around the year 1550. (After Sieh, courtesy U.S. Geological Survey)

gelo in 1550." Nevertheless, these insights had not come easily: "All this work was wearying and exhilarating."

One major piece of the puzzle still was missing, however: a determination of the slip rate along the fault. Kerry went back to the Carrizo Plain, guided by aerial photos he had borrowed from a friend at the USGS, Robert Wallace. These photos showed that a stream had flowed out of the Temblor Range and onto the plain, being repeatedly offset where it crossed the San Andreas. The present channel showed an offset of 128 meters. With the 1857 quake having produced about nine meters of slip in that area, this offset could be expected to represent about fourteen great quakes. To the northwest lay an old and well-eroded dry channel, offset by 380 meters. That stream course thus had probably accumulated the slip of some forty-two such earthquakes. And there was an even older creekbed, offset by 475 meters.

The stream had no name, and Kerry christened it Wallace Creek, after his friend. Unlike Pallett Creek, it had no meanders or jogs to fool an unwary geologist. Instead, it had repeatedly flowed directly onto the plain, providing an initial straight line that had then deformed. Indeed, a rancher who lived nearby told Kerry that during a recent rainy winter, water in the creek had spilled over the edge of the bend that had formed where it crossed the fault. It was easy to imagine that the stream would soon cut through its bank and form a new channel, once again running straight across the fault, ready to be offset anew by the quakes of future centuries.

At Pallett Creek, Sieh had had to distinguish twelve different earthquakes from one another, determining the date for each one. At Wallace Creek, there was a single geological event that most concerned him: that of the stream having changed course some fourteen quakes ago. It had abandoned its former channel and flowed onto the plain in a new course, which would be offset by 128 meters prior to the present day. There also was a single date that mattered most: that of this abandonment. Yet the Wallace Creek problem proved much harder to solve than those at Pallett.

At Pallett the sediments had been laid down smoothly in a sequence, one atop the other, from oldest to youngest. There were no breaks in this sequence, no events amounting to erasures where strata had eroded away and been lost, leaving a gap in the record of time until newer beds could form and accumulate. This unbroken sequence thus served as a reference for comparison. Broken or shifted beds, disturbed by old quakes, could be sorted out and the quakes identified through comparisons with this reference.

At Wallace, by contrast, no such regular sequence of sediments existed. In principle it might have been there, layered within the streambed; but that was not the nature of such streams. Rather than accumulating deposits evenly and in an unbroken sequence, they were prone to floods that would destroy the geological evidence. Such floods, on occasion, would scour out previous deposits, eroding the stream's channel to some depth. At other times they would transport new supplies of sand or earth, laying them down within the channel as a new deposit. Such deposits could be dated by carbon 14 in the usual way, if they contained charcoal from range fires amid the dry grass of the area. But these carbon dates would tend to tell the date of past floods in the creek, which had no relevance to seismology. Sieh's problem was to find dates that would tell him about earthquakes.

He proceeded to map the soils along the creek with great care. Along the upper channel, in the hills adjoining the San Andreas Fault, the stream's banks showed numerous thick and jumbled deposits of sand and gravel. These appeared to be debris flows, resembling mudslides, which took place only rarely. The abandoned channel, the former stream course that showed a 250-meter-long offset, was filled with such deposits, which Sieh called "high-channel alluvium." But there was no such material in the modern channel, with its 128-meter offset. Evidently, any high-channel alluvium in

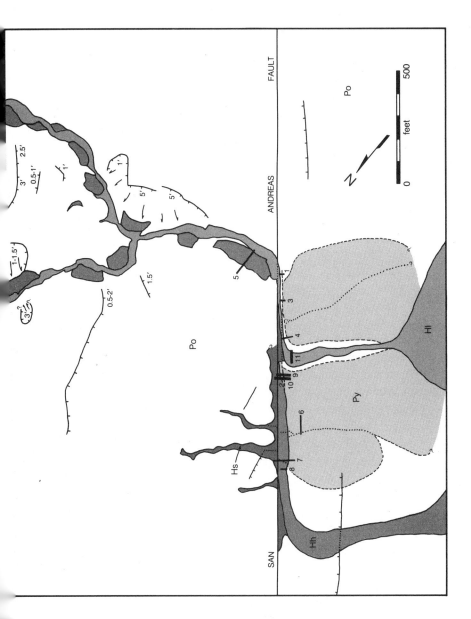

geological map of Wallace Creek. The Y-shaped feature is the upstream portion of the creek. Blocky formations along its banks are deposits of high-channel alluvium. The San Andreas Fault runs as a straight line below the middle of the map. The L-shaped feature marked Hh is the ancient abandoned channel. The similar feature Hl is the modern channel, which flows out onto the plain. (After Sieh and Jahns, courtesy Kerry Sieh) this present-day channel had been scoured away by floods, and had been lost.

There was carbon in the deposits of high-channel alluvium, giving the times of deposition. Along the banks of the upper channel, the youngest such alluvium had a measured age of 3,680 years. In the abandoned channel, the youngest age was 3,780 years. Within the errors of measurement, which were accurate to no better than a century or so, these dates were identical. A single flow of high-channel alluvium must have come down in a major mudslide, forming deposits along the hillside banks, filling the downstream channel that now lay abandoned.

It took about five years and the careful study of eleven trenches cut across the creek—compared with three trenches at Pallett—before Sieh could learn what he wanted. This deposit of high-channel alluvium had been the last such flow, and had choked the existing stream course when it came down, some 3,700 years ago. The stream, blocked from its prevailing course, then had very quickly broken out of the old channel to flow directly onto the plain and across the fault, in a new channel that had since accumulated its offset of 128 meters. Dividing this offset by the age, 3,700 years, gave the slip rate along the fault: 3.4 centimeters per year. Sieh thus solved the problem of using data concerning ancient floods to learn about earthquakes. More specifically, he showed that an ancient mudslide with a determinable date could force the stream to change course, cutting a new channel whose offset would record the motion along the fault from such quakes.

Wallace Creek also featured a much older offset, 475 meters in length, which proved to have an age of 13,250 years. This gave a slip rate of 3.6 centimeters per year. Within the limits of accuracy in the dating techniques, the two rates agreed. The resulting measured rate was also very close to the slip rate along the creeping section of the San Andreas, southeast of Monterey, where the fault was yielding. And Sieh later determined similar values for the slip rate at Pallett Creek, and near Indio.

Except in the creeping section, however, the fault was not sliding freely at this rate. This was the long-term average, over thousands of years. During any one year the fault would not slip but would build up strain, which would be released every century or so in a great quake. Evidently, along much if not all of the San Andreas, such strain was accumulating at a rate of about 3.5 centimeters per year.

This simple fact told a lot. For one thing, the plate rate, or speed at which the Pacific and North American plates were moving past one another, was 5.6 centimeters per year. Bernard Minster and Tom Jordan had published that figure in 1978. This meant that in no way could the San Andreas be slipping at the whole of the plate rate. As Sieh put it, "You could not stand astride the fault and say that each foot was on a separate plate." The rest of the slip, over two centimeters per year, had to be going into other faults: the San Jacinto, the Hosgri, the Hayward and Calaveras near San Francisco.

Here was a clear measure, then, of the long-term motion along these other faults: they had to be accumulating strain at this rate, two centimeters per year, with this strain also being released from time to time in major quakes. If the San Andreas had proved to be slipping at or close to the plate rate, then these nearby faults would have been taking up little strain; their major quakes would therefore be few and far between. But at two centimeters per year, each such fault could readily produce a damaging quake nearly as often as the San Andreas itself. And while the Hosgri was out at sea, the Hayward and Calaveras ran through the populous East Bay region, with the San Jacinto traversing areas close to the cities of Riverside and San Bernardino. Sieh's work thus had shed a good deal of light on the long-term earthquake hazards to these cities, from faults other than the San Andreas.

Additionally, the measured offsets along the San Andreas now could serve to estimate intervals between great quakes. In the Carrizo Plain, with its nine-and-a-half-meter offsets, the interval would be around three hundred years. This interval could be calculated as the offset divided by the slip rate:

nine and one-half meters divided by 3.4 centimeters per year equals 280 years. With the last big quake having taken place in 1857, the next one would not be expected till the middle of the twenty-second century. In Sieh's words, "It's a pretty safe bet we won't see a big earthquake there in our lifetime."

That was the good news. The bad news came from Pallett Creek, only forty miles from downtown Los Angeles. Here the offsets were only four and a half meters. With the slip rate also being around 3.5 centimeters per year, the interval between quakes proved to be about 145 years. Such quakes had produced only half as much offset as in the Carrizo, but had occurred twice as often. And with 130 years already having elapsed since the last major one in 1857, another such major quake appeared dangerously near. That finding proved to be the basis for Sieh's conclusion: A great quake is to be expected along the San Andreas near Los Angeles, within the next few decades. The techniques used at Wallace and Pallett could not give forecasts to better accuracy than this. But they were sufficient to show that such a quake was due, and must be expected relatively soon.

Moreover, Sieh later went on to explore the San Andreas to the southeast of Los Angeles, digging trenches north of Indio. The fault's slip rate there was the same as elsewhere, 3.4 centimeters per year, as revealed by the dates of offsets formed within the beds of sediment. The time between successive great quakes was around 250 years. The last one had occurred around the year 1680. Thus, as at Pallett Creek, there was good reason to believe that the fault was strained sufficiently to produce a major quake, and that such a tremor could take place soon. Indeed, it might well already be overdue. Moreover, such a tremor taking place along the section of fault that includes Pallett Creek, north of the city, could well rip the fault to the southeast and trigger a further continuation of the quake along the sector that includes the excavations near Indio.

What all this means is that within the next fifty years, the chances range from 50 percent to 90 percent—virtually certain—that a quake of magnitude 8 or higher, an earthquake fully as severe as those of 1857 and 1906, will strike along the San Andreas from the Tejon Pass, due north of Los Angeles, to the Salton Sea. It will strike through Los Angeles, Riverside, and San Bernardino counties, where more than 11 million people live today. It will not waste its force on the Carrizo, where few people live, but will break where it can do the most damage. If there is any solace, it lies in the creeping section. Geodetic measurements show that the fault there is creeping or yielding rather than accumulating strain. This section thus effectively separates the San Andreas into northern and southern parts. At least it does not appear possible for a single superquake to rip along the entire length of the fault, from Cape Mendocino to the Mexican border. Such a supertremor would devastate Los Angeles and San Francisco simultaneously. As it is, these cities will most likely undergo their shakings at different times.

Still, there remains much to learn, even concerning the ancient quakes whose repetitions form the basis for such a forecast. Most recently, Kerry has been working with an entirely new technique for dating such quakes: tree rings. Trees growing astride the fault have at times been shaken so severely that they have lost their branches, or had their roots partly destroyed. The resulting damage shows in the rings, which record patterns of growth.

A tree grows a new ring every year. Thus, the age of any ring may be found merely by counting them backward from the outermost one, just below the bark, which formed in the year the tree died. But the rings are not of the same width. In dry years, when the tree is under stress, its rings are thin. Trees have thus served for the study of prehistoric climates, since their rings can tell when there have been rainy years and when the rains have failed to come. Sieh's hope was that earthquakes would affect the subsequent growth of tree rings in similar fashion.

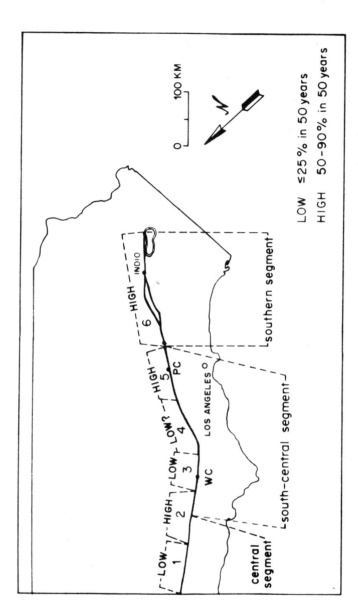

Map by Kerry Sieh showing earthquake potentials along the San Andreas over the next fifty years. (Courtesy Kerry Sieh)

The sequence of all tree rings then would resemble the sequence of soil layers he had studied at Pallett Creek. In both trees and soil, a continuous progression of layers, growing one after the other, would serve as a recording medium on which the quakes' effects would have written their marks. The soil layers went back two thousand years but gave few clues to their age; that had to be found by carbon dating, which was somewhat tricky. The record of the trees went back perhaps five hundred years, in the oldest cases. But their rings could be dated simply by counting. They thus offered a new route to the study of at least the more recent of the prehistoric quakes—and with not only much greater convenience than at Pallett Creek, but with far better accuracy. A quake that left its mark in the soil might be dated to an accuracy of a century, but if it affected the growth of a tree, its date could be found to an accuracy of a few months—the time for the ring's growth.

What was needed would be to find several such trees along the San Andreas, in the forests north and northeast of Los Angeles. Their rings would then be compared with those from trees that lay off the fault, to distinguish evidence for quakes from that of other natural events such as lightning strikes and droughts. Lightning might damage a tree and produce slow growth of a ring during the following year. But that would not be expected to happen to more than one tree in a group. Drought, by contrast, would narrow the rings of all the trees, both on and off the fault. The best evidence for quakes would come if there was a pattern of narrow rings in more than one old tree that straddled the fault, all with the same age, and with this pattern not showing in trees that grew away from the fault.

Kerry had pursued this method of dating quakes since his days as a grad student. He read a 1972 paper by the seismologist Robert Wallace, who had set forth this idea while working with the tree-ring expert Val LaMarche. "Bob precedes me everywhere I go," Kerry remarks. "He always comes up with the idea first; then I come by as his lackey and develop the details." (Wallace had discovered and mapped the creek in the Carrizo that bears his name, and had appreciated its significance in determining the slip rate. But he had not determined the ages of its features; that had been left for Kerry.) In his early work on tree rings, he did not believe that his idea would bear fruit.

To test this approach, Sieh wanted to look for evidence in tree rings of the known quake of 1857. He began by using Wallace's corer, to examine the tree's patterns of growth. The corer was a wood auger that could cut a slim cylinder from the trunk of a tree, showing its rings, but would not harm it, any more than we are harmed if a doctor cuts away a small tissue sample from an organ. Kerry's first tree was smack on the fault and quite large. He drove his corer right through the tree's center—and found that it had started growing in 1858, one year after the big quake.

He proceeded to work in the pines of the Angeles National Forest near Wrightwood, a short drive from Los Angeles. The trees were magnificent. Many soon proved too thick for his borrowed corer, so he bought a bigger one, powered by a gasoline motor. One ponderosa pine was 390 years old. It had been topped in the 1857 quake; that is, its top had broken off, giving it an unusual shape within the forest. This had brought a slowdown in its growth that could easily be seen in the rings. Another tree showed a similar slowdown, and by counting the rings inward from the bark, Kerry dated the retarded growth to 1834. There had been no important quake that year in southern California, so he wrote it off to damage from lightning. By examining a number of trees in this fashion, he showed that the great quake of January 9, 1857, showed in the tree rings as having occurred between September 1856 and March 1857. This fact was important. It showed that the technique worked, when tested against the date of a known quake. As Kerry put it, "It sure beats carbon dating, because you can date it to the nearest season."

During the mid-1980s, he began to work with a tree-ring

expert from Columbia University, Gordon Jacoby. In April 1985, Jacoby came out to California, and they sampled a number of trees near Wrightwood. He took the cores back to New York to study; one pine went back to 1382. Then after a couple of months he told Kerry, "It looks like we have something in 1711 or 1713." That was close to the carbon date of 1720 for one of the quakes at Pallett Creek; it looked promising. There appeared to be other possible events as well, in 1455 and around 1570.

In October 1986, Gordon returned. He arrived at the Siehs' one Sunday evening and during dinner later that night, he said, "I've got bad news: 1711–1713 just aren't there." A more careful study had shown that there was no tree-ring record of a great quake at that time. Further, the 1455 and 1570 events also were spurious. Kerry was crestfallen. He had been preparing a proposal for further research, based on the idea that those events had been major quakes. Over the artichokes, pork chops, and cherries jubilee, here was one more research idea that looked as if it were shot full of holes.

"Well, Gordon," Kerry asked, "that tree you cored near Wrightwood—when was it topped?" It was the same tree whose abrupt shutdown in growth Kerry had attributed to lightning. Gordon replied, "Well, it's not 1700, I'm afraid; it's historical." That meant it was within the last two centuries, and Kerry thought, Oh great, another lightning strike. "We couldn't even count past 1812," Gordon continued. "The rings were so narrow; there were missing rings."

At this, Kerry suddenly became excited: "Eighteen-twelve! Was it during the growth season or at the end of the growth season?" Gordon replied, "We don't know, but we counted the 1812 ring and that was the last we'd counted." Now Kerry's excitement intensified.

"Do you realize there were three great earthquakes in 1812? They're usually placed offshore—San Juan Capistrano and Santa Barbara."

"No! I didn't know about that," Gordon answered.

Those quakes occurred on December 8 and 21 of that year, after the growth season. Because the Spanish reports came from the missions along the coast, the quakes were believed to result from offshore faults. But now Gordon's tree-ring data was suggesting that at least one of them had been a great quake on the San Andreas, a possibility never before considered.

Kerry pulled out the data on a tree he had cored several years earlier, which he thought had been struck by lightning in 1834. He hadn't known that he shouldn't have naïvely counted the rings backward from the bark. He had thought that a ring would form each year, even though it might be quite narrow. He hadn't appreciated that when a tree was severely stressed it could fail to form growth rings, sometimes for an extended period. This effect is easily overlooked, but Gordon had found the missing rings by careful comparison with healthy trees nearby, undamaged by any earthquake.

These trees showed continuous and unbroken ring sequences, to the present day. They also showed the narrow rings of ancient drought years, which thus could indeed be dated by counting backward from the bark. With no rings missing, this count would give accurate dates for those drought years. Moreover, Jacoby had recognized those same drought years in cores taken from trees along the fault, which thus gave benchmarks for dates prior to the shutdown in their growth. Counting forward in continuous sequence from such benchmarks, Jacoby then had found that this shutdown had occurred in 1812.

The fact that the trees straddled the fault, and that major quakes were known to have occurred in that year, told Kerry that the shutdown in growth must have been due to a previously unknown great quake on the San Andreas. He said, "Gordon, you've got to go out to Wrightwood tomorrow and re-core that tree, because I'll bet it has twenty-two missing rings. I bet it was topped in 1812, at the end of the growth season." He became increasingly excited as he continued, "Gordon, the only places that reported earthquakes were on the coast, where the missions were. We don't even know what the intensities were out toward the San Andreas. They could have been much higher."

That was on a Sunday night. Gordon went out to Wright-wood and called on Tuesday with the news: "Kerry, you were right. The 1834 tree was topped in 1812, at the end of the growth season." Moreover, he had found several other trees that also showed the effects of an 1812 quake. Now Kerry looked at the historical accounts. He decided the December 21 events could be ruled out; their intensity at Santa Barbara had been even higher than the one in 1857, too high to fit. That had to be due to a local fault. But for the December 8 quake, he asserts, "if you explain away the high intensity in San Juan Capistrano as due to a structural defect in the tower, causing it to fall—then you've got it. There's no reason why it's not perfectly consistent with a great quake on the San Andreas."

What does it mean if the San Andreas near Los Angeles broke on December 8, 1812? Did two major tremors occur only forty-four years apart, alleviating the strain for our time? Will a century or more pass before the Big One, making its timing consistent with the data from Pallett Creek that shows intervals often approaching three centuries? Do the quakes of 1812 and 1857 form a pattern echoed in the great quakes near San Francisco, in 1838 and 1906? Or must we fear that the next great quake will strike on schedule, within the next few decades—and then be followed by one of equal size some years later, within the lifetimes of many of the people who will survive the first one? And what was the extent of that 1812 event? "It could have ruptured all the way to the Salton Sea," Kerry adds, "and it would have been consistent with the reports at San Diego."*

Thus research on past quakes continues to raise new

*A forthcoming paper, "A Very Precise Chronology of Earthquakes Produced by the San Andreas Fault in Southern California" (K. Sieh, M. Stuiver, and D. Brillinger, authors) is to appear in the *Journal of Geophysical Research* late in 1988, and addresses these issues.

questions. For Kerry, the approach to finding the answers is clear. "One underlying sentiment I have is that the Holocene record is highly underrated," he says of the geologic record of the time since the last Ice Age. This record exists within the top few meters of soil and sediment, literally under our feet. "An enormous amount of data can be drawn from the sediments of the last ten thousand years. And it's just barely been explored."

If earthquakes were regular and periodic, as predictable as the return of Halley's Comet, then this data would be very useful for prediction. We could look toward a day when the quakes of recent centuries would be mapped and dated, accurate to within a few months, using tree-ring data. For instance, we might find that major quakes could be dated in this fashion as having occurred in the years 1723, 1589, and 1455. Earlier than that, there might be no surviving trees, but still one might find older quakes through their disturbances in the soil, as at Pallet Creek. Carbon-14 dating, which is accurate only to about a century or so, then might give those previous earthquake dates: 1340, 1150, 1070, 950, give or take a few decades. We then could say that all these data fit a consistent pattern: that magnitude-8 quakes strike along the San Andreas every 134 years, on the dot. That means the next one would come in 1991.

But quakes are not so neatly predictable. The record at Wallace Creek, for instance, shows a thirteen-thousand-year-old offset produced by more than forty great earthquakes. Even if we could somehow know the exact dates of each, accurate to the correct day, that would give no clear prediction of the next one. The reason is that these dates would show no regular or periodic pattern. They would amount to a mere recording of historical moments, akin to a list of the days when the forty kings of France, from Clovis to Louis XVI, had their coronations. Those kings had reigns of highly varying length, and the time between quakes has been similarly variable.

Sieh's approach thus amounts to an extrapolation from

past records, in asserting that a particular quake is likely to strike. This approach, then, is similar to predicting the length of a particular reign on the day of coronation: one knows that the king will die and that the quake will eventually take place, but the most that can be said is that these events will happen sometime within the next few decades. That is all the accuracy that can be expected from such extrapolations, because of the inherent irregularity of the occurrences.

But if we observe the king closely and monitor his health, we will have a far better chance of knowing how long he will reign. In particular, doctors are capable of detecting warning signs indicating that his life is likely to end in a few years, or even in the coming months. Similarly, by close examination of faults, seismologists have often succeeded in finding physical phenomena suggesting that a quake is likely to take place reasonably soon. These phenomena are known as *precursors,* and it is possible to say a good deal about them. If Sieh's approach amounts to studying the ancestry of the coming California earthquake, the study of precursors could be compared to examining the patient directly.

4

PRECURSORS

It was an unprepossessing three-page article in the April 16, 1976, issue of *Science*. The title, "Aseismic Uplift in Southern California," was the sort of deadpan statement that scientists love. On its face, it asserted nothing more than that the land had pushed its way upward aseismically or without producing an earthquake. But the map on the article's first page was dramatic indeed. It stated that between 1959 and 1974, a stretch of land along the San Andreas had been uplifted by at least ten inches. What did it mean? Was this a warning, an indication that this part of the fault might soon break? George Alexander, the science writer at the *Los Angeles Times,* soon christened it the Palmdale Bulge, after the town that lay at the center of the rise. The people of Palmdale understandably preferred to call this feature the Southern California Uplift. By whatever name, it was bound to stir controversy. And at the center of the controversy were the geodetic measurements that had led to this discovery.

These measurements featured a simple surveying technique known as *leveling*. It was carried out by a surveyor using an instrument called a level, along with two "rodmen," each wielding a three-meter-long rod that is marked with a precisely ruled scale. To begin, the first rod is set vertically on a benchmark, a permanent elevation marker. The surveyor walks a hundred feet ahead, while the second rodman goes a hundred feet farther still. The surveyor's level is a telescope with a bubble like that in a carpenter's level, guaranteeing an accurate setting on the horizontal. Its viewer peers at the first rod, swivels to look at the second, and notes the elevation difference which is easily seen by using crosshairs. Then, while the second rodman stands in place, the first man moves two hundred feet farther on, while the surveyor takes up a position midway between them to make a new pair of sightings. This measures the next change in elevation along the survey line. The three workers will repeat this procedure several hundred times over a route of thirty miles or so, to determine the elevation of a second benchmark, which is located at the end of that route.

However simple, this procedure can measure astonishingly small elevation changes on lines that cross rugged terrain and even mountains. The accumulated error can be less than a centimeter, along a thirty-mile distance. Civil engineers use such leveling surveys to develop a network of benchmarks with precisely determined elevations. These serve as reference points in building railroads, pipelines, aqueducts, and highways. Moreover, these surveys have been repeated along a number of routes in southern California every few years; there has been a great deal of data. And the Palmdale Bulge elevation change amounted to twenty-five centimeters, according to the 1976 paper. Thus, even though Palmdale lay on the other side of a three-thousand-foot mountain range from the reference benchmark, which was at sea level, these measurements had to be taken seriously.

Robert Castle of the U.S. Geological Survey, author of the paper in *Science,* was at the center of all this. His tall, lean, and rugged appearance showed him to be a man of long experience in the field. His office door carried a sign, in old English script: "Ye Olde Throne Room." Also, there was another posted item: "No, the Wizard will not see you." His taste ran to sweatshirts, comfortable corduroys, and casual shoes. He had been with the Survey since 1950.

Early on, he had found an opportunity to join a small USGS office at UCLA, doing fieldwork in the Baldwin Hills near Los Angeles Airport. Close by was the Baldwin Hills Reservoir, whose dam collapsed late in 1963. Because Castle knew the area, the director of the USGS thus asked him to make a report on why the dam had broken. From an initial review of the available data, Castle concluded that it was the result of operations in a nearby oil field, which had produced earth movements that had led to strains along a fault. The fault then had slipped, causing the dam to break. This conclusion stirred arguments. Senior people at the USGS decided that Castle's viewpoint was not adequately supported by his data, and edited his report heavily. Castle regarded this as censorship, and took his name off the report. He then redid his study in far more detail, confirmed his earlier conclusions, put out a formal report—and convinced his superiors that he was right.

This work at Baldwin Hills introduced him to geodetic measurements. They had been important in observing the deformation of the land in the area, which had ultimately led to the failure of the dam. As he recalls, "I was impressed with the inherent accuracy of geodetic leveling. I was also impressed with the enormous volume of data." The data was in city and county records spanning some seventy-five years, and contained the results of the large number of surveys that had been made since late in the nineteenth century. He began to work with this information, hoping it would prove useful for some problem in geology.

His work received a considerable boost in 1971. On February 9, a small fault north of Los Angeles gave way in the San Fernando quake, magnitude 6.4. It was the worst one to strike the city since the 1933 Long Beach tremor, killing fifty-eight people, destroying some eight hundred homes and buildings, and causing half a billion dollars in damage. This quake took place amid a dense geodetic net, an array of lines that had been repeatedly resurveyed and leveled. Moreover, in the wake of the tremor, all the local benchmarks had to have their elevations redetermined. This meant that Castle would learn not only what had happened as a result of the quake, but also what had occurred before. "There were several items of interest," he remembers. One survey line, during 1968 and 1969, had shown an uplift of seven centimeters—and its location was nearly the bull's-eye of the eventual 1971 epicenter. Evidently, this motion of the land had been a precursor, signaling that the quake would occur there a couple of years later. This could be understood by thinking of the fault as a fracture sloping or dipping sharply into the earth, like a steep ramp. At a depth of several miles, the fault had slipped under its stress without producing a quake, as if a vast block of rock resting on the ramp had slid upward because of a push from below. This slippage then had pushed other rock formations upward along the dip of this ramp, straining the upper fault and producing the uplift. The motion of that subsurface mass of rock had pushed the ground upward; it also had loaded new strain onto the upper fault, hastening the quake.

To seismologists, this was highly reminiscent of events in Japan only a few years earlier. Surveyors there had made repeated levelings, beginning in 1898. In central Japan, near the city of Niigata, these surveys showed a steady uplift throughout the first half of the century, reaching a peak of sixteen centimeters by 1955. Then the deformations subsided rapidly during the next several years. In 1964 the fault broke in a quake of magnitude 7.5. With this and the new results from the San Fernando quake, there was the clear suggestion that changes in geodetic leveling patterns—a subsidence in Japan and perhaps now an uplift in California—could signal a forthcoming earthquake.

In searching through the data, Castle and his colleagues found other odd things. Along another line, between the towns of Saugus and Palmdale, there apparently had been an uplift of eighteen centimeters between 1961 and 1964. That was an enormous change. Jim Savage, one of Castle's friends at the USGS, suggested that they check it by looking at the previous leveling, in 1955. "The effect of that was actually to *increase* the signal," Castle asserts. Since 1961 the measured uplift had been eighteen centimeters; but since 1955 it appeared to have gone up a total of twenty-five centimeters.

"There's a certain tendency to guess that if we see a deformation along that line, it's tied up with the San Andreas," he declares. "We viscerally jumped to the conclusion that there may be a relation." The Saugus-Palmdale line of leveling measurements had stopped just short of the San Andreas; now they began examining data from lines that actually crossed the fault. They found that the uplift extended well into the Mojave; on the view that it had to stop somewhere, they decided it was likely to peter out somewhere west of Barstow, a town that was nearly halfway to Las Vegas. From examining what Castle describes as "all the geodetic data we could lay our ruddy hands on," they eventually concluded that a broad band of territory, covering 32,000 square miles—an area as large as South Carolina—had uplifted by as much as forty-five centimeters.

What did it mean? There were plenty of people willing to speculate that it was a precursor, an indication of a major quake in the offing. One of these was Frank Press, who had headed Caltech's Seismo Lab and who would soon join the White House staff as President Carter's science adviser. At a meeting in December 1975, Castle gave a presentation to Press and told what he had learned: the bulge was large, additional measurements had shown its extent, and it had gone up quite rapidly. Castle even said that most of its swelling had occurred during a few months in 1961, based on data from surveys made just before and after that year.

Press went to the blackboard and plotted how a point in the region would have gone along at a steady elevation—and then zip, it was up. He then said, "Someplace in here we're going to have a big one, aren't we, Bob?" Castle replied, "If you'd like to say that, that's fine." Castle wasn't a seismologist by trade and didn't feel qualified to propose that a big quake was in the offing. But Press was one of the nation's leaders in the field, and felt that Castle was quite entitled to draw such a conclusion.

Press also had very good connections in Washington. At a meeting of a presidential science committee, attended by Vice-President Nelson Rockefeller, he explained the situation. In January he wrote a letter to Rockefeller, which soon reached the desk of President Gerald Ford:

> The discovery, which will soon be released publicly, is most disturbing because such uplifts in the past have preceded earthquakes of great destructive power. . . . The effect on Los Angeles of an earthquake in the region of the uplift would be disastrous. A structural engineer at UCLA, Professor Martin Duke, has estimated that as many as 40,000 buildings would suffer collapse or serious damage.
>
> There is no question that the uplift must be taken very seriously, even though geophysicists have, as yet, no clear understanding of its origin or significance. . . . The region of the uplift should now be subjected to a most intense scrutiny. . . . In Japan, a geophysical anomaly of this magnitude would trigger an intensive study or a public alert.

Ford responded by asking for more information, which Rockefeller provided in three memos. Ford then arranged for an extra $2.1 million to go to the USGS, to monitor the fault. In the low-budget world of seismology, this was an enormous windfall.

In mid-April a seismologist from Caltech, James Whitcomb, predicted an earthquake would occur. He declared that it might strike within a year, and could be as strong as the San Fernando quake. He hastened to say that there was no way to determine the chance that such a forecast would prove correct, but that did not soothe the Los Angeles city council. There was talk of suing Whitcomb, and anyone else who made such predictions, if real-estate values should drop.

As the excitement over the bulge continued to rise, several scientists launched a strong effort aimed at making it go away. Their hope was to explain away the measurements as the results of systematic errors. The key to this lay in the likelihood that heated air, rising from close to the ground, would have distorted the images of the rods as seen through the surveyors' telescopes. At each step in the leveling this would have introduced a small misreading, and these errors then might have accumulated over the hundreds of steps in each survey. It was a commonplace view that such distortions would be insignificant, but the experiments that had led to this conclusion had been carried out in Finland, where the air was always cool. Charles Whalen and William Strange, of the National Geodetic Survey in Rockville, Maryland, then made measurements aimed at determining the distortions that might be seen in sunny California. They found that the resulting errors could amount to ten centimeters or more. Strange then found that around 1960, just when the Palmdale Bulge had supposedly arisen, surveyors had changed their procedures in ways that would have helped the bulge appear to pop up.

But while such findings could deflate the bulge, they couldn't make it disappear. Errors in measurement might account for half of the forty-five-centimeter rise that Castle was claiming existed, but there still was that other half. The bulge thus was as enigmatic as ever, and as a possible precursor it was just as problematic. This enigma continued for several years without resolution. Then Castle dropped the other shoe. In 1986 he announced that further studies of the geodetic data, going back to the late nineteenth century, had cast the problem of the bulge in an entirely different light. It was not just a recent feature that had emerged in our time and that could thus well be an earthquake precursor. There had been an era of uplift just after the turn of the century, and no major quake had followed that earlier bulge. It thus had definitely not been a precursor.

The data he was relying on consisted of the penciled notes of the survey crews. These surveys had not been carried out according to the strict standards of present-day work. For instance, nowadays it is common to check a set of leveling results by running the survey in both directions along a line; at the turn of the century this was less frequently done. But in working with that old data, Castle had two things going for him. The first was that in those days, surveyors had been educated men who usually worked with integrity. Their profession carried prestige; they remembered that George Washington had started his career as a surveyor and they regarded themselves as gentlemen. The second was what Castle calls "the absolute, nearly ordained-by-God requirement that no one may erase anything. Cross it out, but do not erase." This meant he could reconstruct how the leveling crews had worked, and where some of them had blundered.

"Surveyors have been known to fudge," he remarked. "We practically got to know the personalities of some of these people, based on their data." One crew had approached a benchmark whose elevation had recently been determined in earlier surveys—and found that they were off by a foot. Evidently the levelman had misread a rod, in sighting through his telescope. He didn't want to go back and redo the work, so he crossed out his final measurement and wrote in a number one foot different. On another occasion, a rodman had his rod upside down, and the surveyor fudged a whole series of numbers to try to cover his mistake. "We discovered compelling evidence of twelve major blunders, all identified with the work of a single levelman," he added, "seventy-five years after he did the work. It's too late to fire him, may he rest in peace."

Still, there was no reason to question the work of the other crews. And from these data, Castle concluded that California had not just bulged, it had jiggled. An enormous uplift, extending from the Pacific eastward, perhaps as far as the Colorado River, had risen to heights of up to fifty centimeters, between 1902 and 1928. It then had subsided and sunk back. Then, between 1959 and 1974, the modern uplift had formed across the entire southern part of California. In more recent years it too appeared to have subsided, at least in part. And with this, it appeared that this recent bulge, like the earlier one, also was no precursor of a major quake on the San Andreas. Instead, it was part of a process of regional uplift that had been thrusting mountains into the sky. "We're looking at a deformation that has been proceeding through recent geologic time," was Castle's conclusion. "Half a million years is probably a reasonable figure."

The Palmdale Bulge thus was a seismic will-o'-the-wisp, having no direct connection to the San Andreas. Yet in those same years when Castle was wrestling with his geodetic data, an entirely different approach to identifying precursors of major quakes was coming to the fore. This might be called the dog-that-didn't-bark approach; the following exchange appears in Sir Arthur Conan Doyle's short story "Silver Blaze":

> "Is there any other point to which you would wish to draw my attention?"
> "To the curious incident of the dog in the night-time."
> "The dog did nothing in the night-time."
> "That was the curious incident," remarked Sherlock Holmes.

The dog that did not bark finds its counterpart in earthquakes that do not happen. Such quakes, which are expected and even overdue, nowadays are serving to indicate that a big one is near.

This approach got its start in Japan, in the decades following the 1906 San Francisco quake. Akitsune Imamura, a young seismologist in Tokyo, knew that a large tremor had destroyed that city in 1703, killing 32,000 people. It bothered him that no similar quake had taken place since. He argued that a repeat of the 1703 catastrophe was likely to occur, and that Tokyo was no better prepared than San Francisco had been. As a result, this quake would likely claim as many as 100,000 lives.

His views drew strong opposition from a more senior seismologist, Fusakichi Omori, the man who had invented a seismograph and then tried unsuccessfully to sell one to San Francisco. Omori saw no reason to think that earthquakes would strike twice in the same place, and he denounced his younger colleague for sowing social unrest. For well over a decade Imamura was often dismissed as a mere crackpot and his life was miserable.

During the summer of 1923, Omori sailed off to Australia to attend a conference. While there, he arranged to visit an astronomical observatory in Sydney, where a seismograph had been installed. He was at the observatory on September 1 when the instrument began to trace out the record of a large and distant earthquake. It was the great Tokyo quake, magnitude 8.2 on the Richter scale, which Imamura had foreseen and which, true to his prediction, razed the city and killed 140,000 people. For Omori, the shock of being wrong was more severe than that of the quake itself. During his voyage home, his health declined sharply, and he died shortly thereafter.

Imamura, for his part, was free to forecast more earthquakes. His technique was similar to Kerry Sieh's: to examine old records and look for patterns, and to note where major quakes seemed to be overdue. But he did not have to dig trenches or take cores from trees. He had something better: the centralized records of Japanese tremors, which had been accumulating in Tokyo ever since the establishment of a unified government in 1588.

Those records were the counterpart of the contemporary

accounts of the 1857 quake that Kerry Sieh's historical research had turned up in the Berkeley library. Those Japanese archives had reported the dates as well as the towns where there had been damage or death, permitting Imamura to estimate the quakes' locations and magnitudes. Moreover, the data went back far enough, and the major tremors of his country had been frequent enough, that he could begin to see patterns of recurrence.

A stretch of the Pacific coastline in southeastern Japan drew his attention. Very large quakes had occurred there, in 1707 and again in 1854. The interval had thus been 147 years, and on that basis the next one in the series might not be expected till 2001. But Imamura, made cautious by his Tokyo experience, stated that this interval might well be shorter, with the next major quake coming much sooner. He did not try to estimate when, but it was not long, as these things go. In 1944, on the third anniversary of Pearl Harbor, part of that fault broke in a shock of magnitude 8.0. Two years later the other part broke, magnitude 8.2. Imamura's contribution had been to show that this historical data could forecast that a quake of a certain magnitude would strike again in a certain place. This idea appears obvious today, but it had never been previously put into practice.

A Soviet seismologist, S. A. Fedotov, was the next to make a contribution. In 1957 he was a young physicist who had just received his Ph.D., and the International Geophysical Year—a coordinated program of research in the earth sciences—was about to get under way. Fedotov was soon sent off to serve the motherland without having very much to say about his assignment. It proved to be the Kuril Islands, rocky, desolate, storm-swept, racked by earthquakes. The Kurils lie across the mouth of the Sea of Okhotsk, between the northern tip of Japan and the south point of the Kamchatka Peninsula. A ship left him on the beach with supplies and equipment and his assistants, a long way from home.

It was a more remote place than Siberia. At least Siberia had a railroad, but the uninhabited Kurils could be reached only by the ships of the Soviet Navy. Sometimes, when the storms were particularly fierce and prolonged, even they couldn't get through. Fedotov proceeded to set up a seismic network, an array of instruments that would observe the islands' frequent tremors. On November 6, 1958, the area was jolted by one of the greatest shakings ever measured, magnitude 8.7. The authorities in Moscow were very pleased with Fedotov's detailed recordings. They were so pleased, in fact, that they ordered him to keep at it. He thus was on the scene when an even larger quake struck, five years later. These hard-won seismograms would be hailed as perhaps the best data ever obtained for truly great quakes, those of magnitude 8 or more.

Soon after, he was released from his exile and permitted to return to Moscow. There he proceeded to write up a theory he had developed. (Small, rocky islands sometimes bring them out in people; think of Darwin in the Galápagos.) He argued that the main fault along the Kurils existed in segments, each of which would break more or less regularly, in quakes of characteristic sizes. He set forth a list of segments where the big earthquakes appeared to be overdue. These lengths of fault came to be known as *seismic gaps*. If you looked at a map that showed where major tremors had taken place in recent years, such gaps stood out like missing teeth. During the years of 1965 to 1973, five of Fedotov's gaps were filled by large quakes.

All this amounted to addressing in a systematic way the warning of the seismologist Perry Byerly of Berkeley: "The further you are from the last big earthquake, the nearer you are to the next." It meant forecasting earthquakes on the basis of recent seismic records, rather than of old government reports or other historical papers; but it still meant using such information to estimate the frequency of quakes and then extrapolating to the next one. And such extrapolation still was likely to be rather imprecise, because of the irregular occurrences of the quakes. It was Kiyoo Mogi, in Tokyo, who found something more. He had squeezed rocks under high pressures in his lab to learn how they might behave in fault zones. During the mid-1960s, student riots at Tokyo University closed down the school and shut Mogi out of his laboratory for several years. Fortunately, he had a lengthy catalog of Japanese earthquakes at home, recorded during the previous century.

He proceeded to plot up the data, looking for patterns. That was an old practice in science; it was how Kepler had found the laws of planetary motion, decades before Isaac Newton had shown where these laws came from. Mogi found that a number of large quakes had been preceded by seismic gaps. He created the concept of the "Mogi doughnut": that prior to such a quake, around its eventual epicenter, small tremors would stop occurring or would fall off sharply, while in the surrounding area such small earthquakes would continue as before, or even increase their rate. On a map these quakes then would form a ring around the eventual epicenter, but close to that center there would be seismic silence. Such rings or doughnuts might not show up convincingly; they might be identified after the fact. But the quiescence, the lack of normally expected small shocks near the epicenter, proved to be a particularly important concept.

It meant that there was a useful way to tell if a particular seismic gap was likely to rupture soon in a large quake. The thing to do was to monitor the small quakes of the region. If they stopped, that would be ominous; it would amount to the calm before the storm. All this could be understood by thinking of a fault as locked in place by some large protrusion. The surrounding rocks would not be solid, but would have numerous fractures. As the stress increased along the fault, it would strain these cracks, which would pop in frequent small tremors. As the stress continued to build, it would force these cracks shut while concentrating its force onto the protrusion. In its vicinity, then, the fractures would be pushed so tight they could not give. That would produce the seismic quiescence, even while the surrounding area, less severely strained, would continue to experience small quakes as before. Finally, amid the calm, the large tremor would break, at the moment the stress became too great for the protrusion or locked portion to withstand.

This meant there were two kinds of seismic dogs that didn't bark, offering a two-step procedure toward earthquake prediction. The first step would use historical records to find that there was a missing large quake, along a stretch of fault where it was expected or overdue. This constituted a seismic gap. Such a quake would be of magnitude 7 or larger. Observations with seismographs might then show that small quakes—magnitude 4 or less—were missing or absent within that gap, when compared to the rate at which they were expected to pop. That would be seismic quiescence, and finding it would be the second step. It could serve as a signal that the overdue big quake would take place fairly soon—say, within the next few years, or even the next few months. This would not permit a true prediction, accurate to within a day. But by narrowing the uncertainties to perhaps a hundred miles, and a year or more in time, these techniques would stand as important steps toward prediction.

A capable and lucky seismologist then might beat a quake to the punch, arriving on the scene in time to look for the detailed patterns of activity that might permit yet more accurate forecasts. The person who has done this most successfully is Karen McNally, a professor at the University of California at Santa Cruz.

She was born Karen Cook, early in 1940, and grew up on a farm in the small town of Clovis, near Fresno. By the time she was five years old, her dad had taught her to drive a tractor. Even then, her father encouraged her to look beyond Clovis and to think of becoming a doctor. In 1966 she went off to the University of California at Berkeley, to major in geophysics. After taking courses for several years, she got a part-time job filing seismograms. That work was quite boring, but it helped introduce her to seismology.

She got her B.S. in 1971, then went on to graduate

school, with the help of a research assistantship. "That drew me toward earthquakes," she says, "even though I hated filing seismograms." Her assistantship required her to study earthquakes occurring along the San Andreas, in a special project funded by the Pentagon. The air force wanted to learn more about quakes, because they might be confused with underground nuclear explosions, which the Defense Department was very interested in detecting. She started by soldering circuit boards for instruments, working with engineers who were building equipment for use in the field. "I felt very comfortable in that environment," she notes. "It was like being back on the farm with practical-minded people."

They were working along a stretch of the San Andreas east of Monterey, at the south end of the length that had broken in 1906. This part of the fault had had moderate-sized quakes, magnitude 5 or so, as well as large numbers of smaller tremors. She began to see a pattern to this activity. It appeared that a cluster of small quakes would occur in the area during the years immediately preceding a magnitude-5 event; these would serve as precursors. Though early in her graduate studies, this idea of hers proved to be significant. It formed the basis for her dissertation, and she continued to pursue this research after she got her Ph.D.

There was no useful understanding of what would trigger an earthquake, what would cause it to happen. Lacking such understanding, she had fallen back on the age-old recourse of the scientist: collect data and look for patterns. The patterns she sought were arrangements of small quakes by time, location, and magnitude, which had sometimes been followed by the larger tremors that she was hoping to predict. Her method was to set forth mathematical descriptions of such a pattern, and to use statistical techniques to show that if its appearance was soon followed by the occurrence of a magnitude-5 earthquake, this was very unlikely to be due to chance.

It was very much like the work of economists seeking to predict a business downturn or recession. Such economists also must proceed in the absence of a clear understanding of how the economy works. They too have emphasized gathering data, manipulating it through statistical techniques, and trying to show that there are patterns that precede such downturns, in a way that also is not due to chance.

Seismologists and economists have been working in this manner for a simple reason: they cannot carry out controlled experiments. There is no way to put earthquake faults or national economies on a lab bench, or even to observe them with the sort of clarity that led astronomers to formulate the laws of celestial motion. In the nineteenth century, for example, detailed lab experiments led to mathematical laws governing electricity and magnetism, laws that still stand. They could never have been found by standing at a distance and watching how lightning flashes. But seismology was still in the lightning-flash era, when basic relationships of cause and effect lay undiscovered. McNally's work amounted to a search for such relationships, if they were there to be found.

She proceeded to work with two professors in the department, Tom McEvilly and Lane Johnson, who had done a good deal of work on San Andreas earthquakes. She had filed all those seismograms while working as a clerk; now she had the pleasure of taking them down from the shelves and working with them. Their squiggly lines included time signals; she had to check and remeasure them, reading off data that could be fed into a computer. "The wave patterns became interesting," she states. "It was as if the traces from different stations, from different quakes, had different personalities." The data from these seismograms eventually filled boxes of computer cards, at two thousand cards to the box. She also developed statistical techniques for analyzing the data, mathematical methods that would allow her to find patterns and give descriptions of her earthquake swarms. The resulting program filled additional boxes. Finally, she took all these keypunched cards to the computer center, where she'd work all night. Her discoveries did not come by brilliant flashes of insight, but by slaving away in a lab in the basement.

After several years, Tom McEvilly told her she had done

enough and could graduate. She felt there was a lot more to do, but it was the custom for grad students to take their degrees after a few years, then continue with their research in postdoctoral positions. Her other professor, Lane Johnson, suggested she apply to Caltech for a postdoc; he knew the people there, and had reason to believe they'd be interested in her work on earthquake precursors. She had made no breakthroughs, but her colleagues wanted to hear what she had been doing. She went down and gave a seminar in the Seismo Lab, describing her findings. Soon she was off to Caltech, with an office in the Seismo Lab, just down the hall from the seismographs. And very soon she was working closely with a new professor, Hiroo Kanamori.

He was only four years older than she, but while she was a research fellow, the lowest faculty position available, he had been a full professor for some time. His father had been a minister in the Japanese government. During World War II, he and his family had survived the air raids by hiding in shelters. After the war his father rejoined the cabinet, helping to write Japan's new constitution. As the educational system revived, young Hiroo made his way through to Tokyo University, emerging in 1964 with a Ph.D. in geophysics.

In 1976 he was refining the Richter scale. Based on measurements of the peak of a seismogram trace, the scale usually gave a consistent reading of the size of quakes up to about magnitude 7. Such quakes broke only short lengths of fault; they were like explosions that occurred in a single place, and the resulting seismograms were like recordings of the blast and shock from such detonations. But in measuring greater quakes, the Richter scale often gave inconsistent results. Such tremors often ruptured considerable lengths of fault; rather than resembling explosions, they were like lightning bolts, which flash suddenly over extended distances. Their seismograms were like records of thunder, which could spread over a considerable length of time. For such quakes, the single measurement of peak intensity on the seismogram could easily be misleading.

Kanamori's solution lay in a concept called *seismic moment,* which is a measure of the energy released in a quake. The seismic moment could be measured by determining the volume of rock within the earth's crust along the fault, which had released its strain in the quake. That volume, in turn, could be found by measuring the slip or offset produced by the quake, along with the length and depth of fault that had broken. The length and depth, for their part, could be determined from observations of the aftershocks, the small tremors that would continue to pop for some time along the newly broken fault. All this meant that seismic moments were rather cumbersome to determine, but in sum, they offered an accurate measure of the strength of great quakes.

When Richter was developing his scale, he had made good use of work by the seismologist Kiyoo Wadati, who had shown how seismic waves would die out with distance. Now, more than forty years later, Kanamori found what he needed in the work of another Japanese seismologist, Keiiti Aki. From studies of waves produced by the 1964 quake at Niigata, magnitude 7.5, Aki had shown that seismic moments could be determined directly from the seismograms. The key point was that modern instruments could record seismic waves of low frequency, and that the amplitude of these waves, measured by the instruments, was directly proportional to the seismic moment. A measurement of this amplitude thus could serve to define a new earthquake scale.

Kanamori's new scale resolved the old discrepancies. For instance, there had been damaging quakes at San Francisco in 1906 and in Chile in 1960. Both had been assigned the same Richter magnitude, 8.3. Yet the Chile earthquake had ruptured a much longer stretch of fault and had caused damage over a wider area. Its seismic moment had been forty times greater. Its seismograms, moreover, had clearly shown the low-frequency waves, which had produced slow, stately oscillations of the instrument needles two and even three days after the main shock. Now, on his seismic-moment scale, Kanamori gave the San Francisco shaker a magnitude of 7.9. The Chile cataclysm, by contrast, went up to a magnitude of 9.5—the largest earthquake ever recorded.

Karen's own research had featured years of studying seismograms, but she had never come close to discovering anything so significant as a refined Richter scale. She was quite prepared to regard Kanamori as Mr. Seismology, as a new Richter. They proceeded to study tremors along the San Andreas, exploring with a mobile array of trailer-mounted seismographs. "Hiroo was a very polite person, and a penetrating scientist," she says. "He was very inspiring, because he is very generous in sharing his thoughts and observations. He finds all earthquakes interesting." All this was part of the spirit of the Seismo Lab, which was a much more genial place than Berkeley. There her companions had mostly been fellow students, with an occasional discussion with McEvilly and Johnson. She rarely met with the rest of the faculty.

At Caltech, the atmosphere was far more open. For grad students and faculty members alike, there was coffee in midmorning and midafternoon. At lunchtime, several people would gather for a long stroll down the Olive Walk, crossing the campus to the Athenaeum, the faculty club. There, on an open and columned terrace, they'd talk of items they'd just read or noticed. Hiroo might say, "I looked at this seismogram this morning. It has very peculiar long waves in it; it's a different waveform." He would describe it, then add, "I wonder if this might be similar to some other earthquake." They would then fall to discussing other quakes, comparing them in accordance with seismological relations. Then Don Anderson, director of the lab, might bring up questions dealing with the relations themselves, and the talk would shift to understanding what they could mean in the light of plate tectonics. These noontime discussions thus covered a rich variety of topics in geophysics.

It was in the course of one such discussion that McNally learned about a forecast that a major quake would occur soon in Mexico.

Mexico, along with Japan, Alaska, Chile, and other Pacific regions, shares the dubious distinction of being among the world's most earthquake-prone areas. Around much of the Pacific rim, immense plates of the earth's crust—the seafloor of that ocean—force and thrust their way beneath the surrounding continents. The resulting quakes have often been awesome; most of the largest ones have occurred in these zones. Along the south coast of Mexico, between 1898 and 1978, over forty quakes of magnitude 7 or larger took place. Along the California coast, in that same period, there were only six such tremors. Mexico was experiencing six times as many severe temblors, and might therefore teach six times as much.

In 1973, a group of American geophysicists—Lynn Sykes of Lamont-Doherty Geological Observatory, John Kelleher of the Nuclear Regulatory Commission, and Jack Oliver of Cornell—had written an important paper on the earthquakes of Mexico. They showed that in any given area, the *recurrence interval* or expected time of repetition between such major quakes was only thirty years. This contrasted with intervals of 150 to 300 years for the great quakes of California. However, along a number of stretches of Mexican fault, no such tremor had occurred for up to fifty years. For instance, near Oaxaca, southeast of Mexico City, there had been no quake of magnitude 7 since 1928. The Oaxaca area thus constituted a seismic gap, and there were a total of nine such gaps along that coast. In that same year, as if to underscore the importance of the paper's finding, the gap around Colima, due west of Mexico City, was suddenly struck by a quake of magnitude 7.6.

Further study was done in 1977, when three other seismologists—Masakazu Ohtake in Tokyo, along with Tosimatu Matsumoto and Gary Latham at the University of Texas in Galveston—announced that the seismic gap at Oaxaca was also a zone of seismic quiescence. During the previous decade, two large quakes had marked the ends of this gap: one of magnitude 7.6 in 1965, and the second of magnitude 7.1

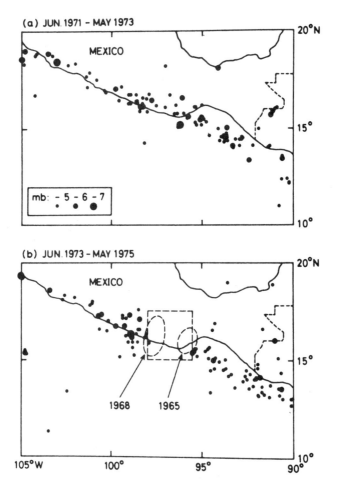

(a) JUN. 1971 – MAY 1973

MEXICO

20°N

15°

mb: – 5 – 6 – 7

10°

(b) JUN. 1973 – MAY 1975

MEXICO

20°N

15°

1968   1965

10°
105°W   100°   95°   90°

Mexican seismic gaps. Top, normal seismicity seen during 1971–73 along Mexico's south coast. Bottom, seismic quiescence or an absence of quakes during 1973–75 within the Oaxaca gap, a region bounded by the sites of major quakes in 1965 and 1968. Closed curves indicate fault areas that have broken in major quakes within recent decades. The Michoacan gap, marked with a dashed curve, was filled after 74 years by the great earthquake of 1985, magnitude 8.1. The Guerrero gap, which is immediately adjacent, is currently over 76 years old and remains unbroken. Opposite page, the situation today. (Courtesy *Engineering and Science* magazine, California Institute of Technology)

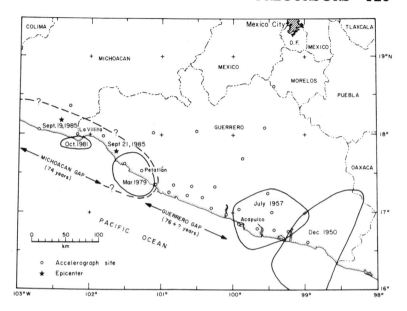

in 1968. Prior to each of these tremors, the continual popping of small quakes had stopped for a time, then resumed
shortly before the main shock. Now, in 1977, these seismologists found a similar cessation of such quakes within the
Oaxaca gap. This halting of seismic activity had taken place
in 1973, according to the available records.

The Pentagon had set up a worldwide network of seismographs during the 1960s to monitor underground nuclear
explosions. This network could detect earthquakes as low as
magnitude 4, the equivalent of fifteen tons of TNT. At that
level, the limit at which earthquakes could be detected,
there had been no quakes within the Oaxaca gap during
the previous four years. This was ominous. It was all too
reminiscent of the seismic quiescence that had preceded
the large quakes of 1965 and 1968. And on this basis, the
three seismologists asserted that the pattern would repeat.
There would be a resumption of minor earthquake activity
within the gap, to be followed by a temblor of magnitude
7.5 or greater. They did not predict when this would hap-

pen, but they stated that the location would be midway between the city of Oaxaca and the coast.

McNally, along with Hiroo Kanamori, soon learned of the paper that set forth this prediction, and both were concerned. "We thought that looked significant, that there was something real there," she recalled. It was not long before she became involved at first hand.

As an undergraduate at Berkeley, she had taken her daughters and some windfall money she had saved and spent six months in Santiago, Chile, at the Universidad Nacional. She was far from fluent in Spanish, but she gamely attended university courses.

Then in 1973, while Karen was at Berkeley, the Chilean army seized power in a coup and overthrew the established government. The new dictator, General Pinochet, proceeded to fill the jails with political prisoners. One of them was a seismologist, Lautaro Ponce. Karen had never met him, but her colleagues remembered she'd been to Chile. Her department organized a letter-writing campaign, seeking to put pressure on the Chilean junta to release Ponce and other prisoners, and Karen took an active part. After several years they were successful. Ponce was given his freedom, and soon made his way to Mexico City, where he joined the faculty at the university.

Early in 1978, Karen attended a conference of seismologists and saw his name tag. She exclaimed, "You are Ponce!" He replied, slowly, "Yesss." He was of medium height, with black hair streaked with gray that turned into a nearly bald spot above a cranial treeline, and was several years older than she was. She told him how she'd helped win his freedom. He invited her to give a seminar in Mexico City. Since she was expecting to attend another conference that summer in Caracas, Venezuela, she could easily stop in Mexico on the way back.

At this point her invitation was a matter of academic courtesy. It soon became more significant. In August, Ponce phoned her and told her that a quake had occurred within the Oaxaca gap. It was no more than a modest tremor, but it might mean that seismic activity was resuming. If so, it would be in line with the prediction by Ohtake, Matsumoto, and Latham that this resumption would take place and would precede the main shock. Karen had built her professional reputation with her work on such precursory swarms of small tremors; she was likely to know if such a swarm meant that a big quake was coming. Her experience and interests would be of particular value in Mexico City.

While she was there, another quake took place that seemed to come from the Oaxaca area. They went to a seismological station, looked at the seismograms, and convinced themselves that it was indeed near Oaxaca. Moreover, Ponce and his colleagues were keenly interested in the paper by Ohtake and the others. With this, he and Karen agreed to work together, putting in a network of portable seismographs near the Oaxaca gap.

These instruments had a fair degree of similarity to cassette recorders and were no larger than carry-on luggage. There was a sensitive pickup, resembling a microphone, to detect vibrations in the earth. Electronic circuitry then amplified these vibrations, and the instrument could be switched to high gain or sensitivity, to record particularly faint tremors. But the recording medium was not a reel of magnetic tape. Instead, it was a sheet of paper mounted on a slowly rotating drum, turned by a motor like that in an electric clock. To prepare the paper for use, a technician would hold it over a kerosene lamp, blackening it with soot. The amplified seismic vibrations then made a sharp stylus wiggle back and forth, scratching off the carbon in fine lines somewhat like the grooves of a phonograph record. A finished seismogram, recording two days' worth of such oscillations, then would be preserved against smearing by being sprayed with lacquer.

The clocklike drum drive included a circuit that would put a recognizable jog in the stylus trace every minute, as a time signal. Several such instruments, placed at different locations, thus would record the same small tremor at recognizably different times. These tremors were never hard to see in the seismograms; they stood out as flurries of sudden oscillation that soon died out. The oscillations came in two parts: an initial P wave, followed a few seconds later by a rather stronger S wave. With the locations of the instruments being known, and with measurements from the seismograms giving the different times of arrival of both these types of waves, there was enough data to calculate with accuracy both the location and the Richter magnitude of any particular quake.

A network of such instruments would then allow Karen and Ponce to monitor the area's small earthquakes, yielding data that might show a precursory swarm. They hoped this might help develop a view of a major quake in the making. However, no one was counting on anything so dramatic as an earthquake right under their noses. That would have amounted to predicting the quake's time of occurrence— and everyone knew there was no way to do that.

Karen returned to Caltech, and she and Ponce inventoried their equipment. How inexpensively could they possibly set up the network of seismographs? And how quickly? She was working with a grant from the USGS, and she called Jack Evernden, who was managing its earthquake prediction effort. He agreed that she could redirect $3,500 of what she had, and go do it. They had battery-powered seismographs, radiotelephones for communications, and field equipment such as shovels. Putting it all together, there was enough money for a month in Oaxaca.

The state of Oaxaca was mountainous and thickly forested, but it was not exactly trackless. There were maps of the area, though they generally left much to be desired. Still, Ponce and his colleagues were geologists, and were quite accustomed to preparing charts in the field. They started by flying over the area, plotting paths that ran through the jungle. There was a maze of back roads cut by the passage of horses and, infrequently, motor vehicles. Mapping them was a matter of noting such things as, "Here's a hut with a red roof; if we turn left there, we can get to the ocean."

They set up a base in the coastal town of Puerto Escondido. It had a single paved street, and water ran through the town in an open gutter. Some of the houses were adobe; others were *palapas,* grass-covered huts. Their roofs were of corrugated metal, dull gray where they were galvanized, rusty red or brown where the zinc coating had worn through. Chickens scratched around in the yards. Near the beach was an attractive and inexpensive hotel, not frequented by the American tourists. It had no hot water, but there was a choice of accommodations. For the students and technicians in the project, there were grass-covered cubicles with hammocks in the middle, open on one side to the sea. The faculty, by contrast, had the best rooms in the hotel, with real beds, adobe walls, and heavy tiled roofs. Ponce didn't have the heart to tell the hotel people that he was expecting an earthquake.

Karen flew down to Mexico City with her seismographs and other equipment checked as overweight baggage. Ponce met her at the airport, and she flew on to Acapulco. From there she was driven to Puerto Escondido. The party had a Land-Rover, along with some old rented trucks and carryalls. She saw how the jungle came up to the edge of town and soon discovered the local peddlers, who carried coconuts on their backs. "You would cut a coconut open," she smiles in remembering. "Sometimes you'd have a little rum with coconut milk, sip it in the afternoon when it was very hot. That was nice." The country had tarantulas, too, enormous black spiders that would lumber across a road. Children would play with them while standing by the roadside, holding them in their hands, trying to impress the visitors so they might receive a coin.

The visitors strung their instruments in a loop that ran for thirty miles up into the mountains and then back to the coast at Puerto Angel, thirty miles to the east. These seismographs were placed in the shade, under temporary shelters built with poles and with grass or palm fronds across the top. Their locations were clearly marked on maps. The paper seismograms had to be changed every day or two, but commuting from Puerto Escondido was out of the question. It still rained frequently, and a sudden storm could block the view only ten yards ahead and make the roads impassable. Rivers lacked bridges. Tracks ran through dense jungle to elevations of more than a mile. Under the best of conditions, a driver might make twelve miles an hour, along twisting, bone-jarring, wearying paths.

Several of the technicians, then, lived out in the field, in remote villages. Amid these country people, largely of Indian descent, the Mexicans from Mexico City were almost as foreign as the Americans. In some of those places, little Spanish was spoken. A technician's quarters might be two hours from a seismograph. Accommodations were either a grassy *palapa* or a small and weatherbeaten hut built of boards with a corrugated-iron roof, but either one was better than a sleeping bag in a tent. Between visits to the instruments, they kept in touch by radiotelephone.

The effort proceeded in this fashion for the entire month of November. Ponce, along with the students and engineers, was at Puerto Escondido. Karen took the long and rutted route to visit the technicians in the field, like a general rallying her troops. Mostly, though, she made trips back and forth to Mexico City as well as to Caltech, bringing additional equipment and supplies. And as the days passed, the data began to come in. They had come to study quakes of magnitude less than 4, which could only be monitored locally. Such quakes were soon seen on the seismograms.

For some time, even the small tremors were absent. Evidently the seismic quiescence was still continuing, with just a few microquakes at the edges of the Oaxaca seismic gap, a zone sixty miles across. Then a cluster of tiny tremors broke this silence in a quiet region east of Puerto Escondido. The quiescence returned, but a drum-patter of other small quakes appeared again around the edges of the gap. Then, on November 27, and continuing for about a day, a few quakes of magnitude 2.5 or so occurred close to the center of the gap, with slightly stronger ones appearing at the edge of the region and migrating toward the center. Then even these stopped. During the next seventeen hours there were only three small tremors, which now moved outward from that center. It was November 29, and the expedition had money for only two more days.

Then the silence was shattered by a quake striking with a magnitude of 7.8, making it nearly as great as the San Francisco quake of 1906. It was right in the center of the gap, close to the coast, and its epicenter was only thirty miles from the location predicted more than a year earlier by Ohtake and his colleagues.

Karen was back at Caltech on a supply run. She was driving to the lab when she heard a radio news report: a big quake in Mexico. She thought, That's it, and I'm here! She flew back as quickly as she could. Fortunately, the damage from the tremor was not large. Familiar with earthquakes, the local people had succeeded in building sturdy structures. Still, as Karen slept in her adobe-and-tile room at the hotel in Puerto Escondido, there were some large aftershocks. "There were a few times when I jumped out of bed and ran out the door," she declares.

They had not predicted the exact time of this quake, but they had been on the scene to trap its precursors in their seismic net. The two-step forecasting procedure, that of the seismic gap followed by a finding of seismic quiescence, had worked to perfection. At first there had been the examination of the historical record by Lynn Sykes and his colleagues, in their 1973 paper. That record had not been one of quakes inferred from soil disturbances, as at Pallett Creek, or of government archives, as in Imamura's studies in Japan. Instead, much as with Fedotov's work in the Kuril Islands, it had consisted of an earthquake catalog: a list of the location, date, and Richter magnitude of each major quake observed using seismographs within this century. But in all these cases the historical record served the same purpose: that of showing the approximate frequency of large tremors in any location, so that if the next one was due or even overdue, that fact could be noted. That was what had led to the finding that Oaxaca was a seismic gap, a place where a quake was expected.

The second step had been the identification of seismic quiescence in this gap, in the 1977 paper of Gary Latham and his associates. This had come from the study of quakes of magnitude 4 and above, recorded at large distances from Oaxaca, using the worldwide seismic net. The existence of this quiescence, along with the fact that there had been major quakes in recent years at both ends of the Oaxaca gap, meant that this gap was showing the same behavior as a similar and nearby one, called the Colima gap. That one had experienced a large quake in 1973. The reasoning was this: The Colima and Oaxaca gaps both had had earthquakes at their ends, followed by seismic quiescence within their interiors. The Colima gap, a few years afterward, had had a large quake; and the Oaxaca gap was not far away and should behave similarly. Therefore, a major quake was due on the Oaxaca gap, and seismologists should be on the lookout for any further Oaxaca activity that appeared to echo the earlier events along the Colima.

Ponce had seen such activity in the summer of 1978: a small quake within the Oaxaca, followed by another one while McNally was visiting. This suggested that the Oaxaca gap was about to rouse from its seismic slumber, for just such stirrings in the Colima gap had preceded its own major quake. That was what led them to mount their exploration. Their goal was to observe the Oaxaca area at close range, in hope of seeing more clearly how a fault zone might behave in the months or years before a great quake. They were indeed expecting such a quake, but only within that level of predictive accuracy: months, maybe years. Instead, they struck it lucky and saw the quake take place right under their noses.

The important new thing they had seen was the foreshocks, in the days and hours prior to that quake. That such foreshocks might exist was well known; but to McNally, steeped in the idea that they would form patterns, they proved to be particularly revealing. The key point was that these foreshocks had migrated, in ways that gave valuable insight into the way the fault had worked.

The way to think of this fault was that it was under great strain but was pinned in place by a number of protrusions, each holding a fair share of the stress. The early foreshocks, seen that summer, suggested that one and then another of these protrusions had been stressed too strongly and had let go, popping in small quakes and releasing some strain. That meant they were no longer carrying their fair share; this released strain passed quickly to the other protrusions, loading them more heavily. Soon they too began to pop, in the initial foreshocks of the major quake. When these foreshocks migrated in location, that could mean that several such protrusions existed in a line and failed in quick sequence, like falling dominoes. All the while, the strain on the fault was being held back by fewer and fewer protrusions. Finally there was one too few, and then the whole fault went at once in the great earthquake.

But if protrusions were giving way and passing on their strain to others in this fashion, why had there been no chain reaction in which the first such pops would quickly bring a failure of all? The answer was well known to specialists in the behavior of rocks. They had long since shown that brittle materials, such as glass or stone, show what is called "static fatigue." If you suspend a heavy weight from a rod of glass, the rod will carry the load for a while, but will eventually break. When a protrusion gives way within a fault, passing on its load of stress, the other protrusions will also bear it for a while, but through static fatigue they too will give way in time.

This explanation of the foreshocks might not be the correct one, but it represented a set of ideas that might be tested and studied further, in future quakes. That was what science was all about, after all: developing concepts or theories and then testing them. In the meantime, for the practical problem of earthquake prediction, those foreshocks in themselves might have proved to be valuable. As McNally later stated, "We were able to see clearly that in this last thirty-two-hour period before the main shock, there was a distinct clustering of earthquake activity that was quite different from any previous activity." That would not have led to the sort of disaster alert we receive when there is a known and imminent danger, but it might well have led to a warning, something like, "There is a 50-percent chance of a major quake within the next twenty-four hours."

Karen was already well known in the world of seismology; now she became famous in the scientific community at large. Caltech asked her to give one of its most prestigious lectures. And other universities soon were asking her to consider joining their faculties. "I was deeply engrossed in my research," she says. "I wasn't looking for a job. But I decided this must be the time in my career when universities might make such approaches, and I should think seriously about this." Some of the offers were generous, and one invitation, from the University of California at Santa Cruz, was particularly appealing. The department's interests closely matched her own. In 1982 she joined the Santa Cruz faculty on the university's beautiful campus, featuring redwood forests and a sweeping view of Monterey Bay.

She maintained an active interest in the earthquakes of Central America by working to set up a permanent network of seismographs in Costa Rica. She also kept a wary eye on Mexico. There still were a number of seismic gaps along its west coast. Two near Acapulco, in Guerrero and Michoacan states, looked particularly worrisome. The last major tremors in those gaps had taken place no later than 1911. In the summer of 1984 she told me of a theory explaining how such large quakes might develop. It was based on the idea that the quakes were resulting from a massive slab of Pacific seafloor slowly sinking into the earth under its weight, producing a steady "downdip tugging" on the upper parts of this slab, where the quakes would occur. Then she said, "If the model is correct, there should soon be an earthquake of magnitude 7.5 or more in the Acapulco region." And just to its west was the gap in Michoacan. A tremor of magnitude 7.3 had broken right in its middle, late in 1981. But she judged that a still larger tremor was to be expected, for that gap had not seen a major quake for at least seventy years, and still held considerable strain.

In the spring of 1985, working again with colleagues in Mexico, she led another expedition to the Guerrero region, placing seismographs in a temporary network as in 1978. They had seen quiescence at one edge of the Guerrero gap in 1982, followed a few months later by a temblor of magnitude 6.7 on the edge of that quiescent zone. That was enough to launch this new expedition.

Their base was in a small, bright blue hotel in the town of San Marcos, just down the road from Acapulco. The hotel lacked a terrace and hot water, but at least there was electricity. The upper floors housed roosters, which were being raised for cockfights that were held twice a year. Across the road was a grass-topped restaurant with a floor of carefully swept packed earth. A pig tied by its door served as the automatic garbage disposal. Its owner and his family lived there, weaving hammocks when they weren't serving food. Karen and her party often ate there, for the food was hard to beat. There was beef, pork, seafood, plenty of tortillas, lots of melons, and papayas.

In the tight collegial world of seismology, this Guerrero seismic gap was notorious as the most likely place for a major quake. This notoriety spread to the East Coast. On September 19, 1985, seismologist Chris Scholtz was in his office at Lamont-Doherty Geological Observatory, near New York City. It was early in the morning, and he heard the clatter of feet in the corridor as colleagues ran down the hall toward the seismographs. Scholtz went down to join them, and saw a large quake coming in on the instruments. He asked a student, "Where's it coming from?" "From the southwest," was the reply. Scholtz then said, "It must be

Acapulco." The students later were very impressed, for the tremor indeed was on Mexico's west coast—but it wasn't in the Guerrero gap. It was in the nearby Michoacan gap, farther west. That long-overdue disaster measured 8.1 on the Richter scale.

Its energy traveled inland to Mexico City, shaking it with enormous force. Some 250 buildings collapsed; many more were badly damaged. Nine thousand people lost their lives. Many were trapped in the ruins of buildings, and on the world's TV sets, the destruction left lasting impressions of what an earthquake can do. With these appalling losses, Karen and her colleagues had to face a fact that was more appalling yet: this was not the quake they had anticipated. The Guerrero gap was still there, and more ominous than ever. The 1985 quake had marked its western end, as the 1983 tremor of magnitude 6.7 had done for its eastern end. That could only mean that another major shaking lay ahead, probably within the next few years.

All this has a good deal of relevance for southern California. From the work of Kerry Sieh, we know that the most likely location for the coming California earthquake is along the lengths of the San Andreas between the Tejon Pass, due north of Los Angeles, running southeast nearly to the Mexican border. Our best estimate is that the probability of the Big One is 25 to 40 percent during the next thirty years, or 50 to 90 percent during the coming fifty years.

Karen McNally's work offers the prospect of a more closely focused prediction. The key will be seismic quiescence: a stopping or near-cessation of small and moderate-sized quakes, magnitude 4 or less, along some length of the fault. That will be the ominous calm before the storm. It will provide a warning time not of decades but of years; the next great quake then will be that close. It will be possible to examine the region minutely, seeking signs and changes that may help make better predictions. Rather than a foreboding presence looming in the uncertain future, the coming California earthquake will be imminent. People and governments can begin to take precautions that may save many lives. The question then will be whether the quake can be predicted with better accuracy, or whether it will strike as a surprise.

5

SURPRISES

For a while, back in the mid-1970s, it looked as if the problem of predicting earthquakes was about to be solved. The key was a concept that comes into play whenever you walk barefoot on the beach in damp sand.

Think about the last time you were walking at the shoreline. When you put your foot down on the sand, a dry spot appeared around each footprint. Had your weight pushed the water from the sand, as if from a sponge being squeezed? The explanation is a bit more subtle. When you make a footprint, you are squeezing the sand from a single direction; that is, from the top. The sand then responds by expanding in the other directions, off to the sides—and by a greater amount than it compresses in response to your weight. Your foot's pressure, then, actually causes the volume of the sand to increase, with the spaces between sand grains becoming larger. This appears paradoxical, for the volume would certainly diminish if the sand were loaded or compressed from all directions. The increase arises because the sand is loaded from only one direction. With this expansion, the sand with its enlarging interstices acts like a sponge and draws its water downward from the surface. This is what makes the dry spot appear around your footprint.

This effect, the net expansion or enlarging of a porous material in response to compression in one direction, is called *dilatancy*. Osborne Reynolds, a British physicist, discovered this phenomenon in the late nineteenth century. Then, in the early 1980s at MIT, the geophysicist William Brace discovered that dilatancy could be seen in solid rock, too. He and his grad students placed cylinders of rock in a press that would squeeze them from top to bottom. As the pressure built toward the breaking point, tiny cracks began to develop within the rock, increasing in number and size as the compression progressed. These cracks made the rock expand; the developing breaks played the same role in the rock as the spaces between the grains of sand at the beach.

Chris Scholtz, who in 1985 looked at a seismograph and decided immediately that its quake had to be coming from Acapulco, was then a grad student in that MIT lab. "Up to that time," he asserts, "it had not been realized that there was such pervasive fracturing inside a rock before it would fail and break under the stress." In his Ph.D. research he used instruments to observe the formation of the cracks. He used what amounted to a microphone to record the clicking noises within the rock: "It was somewhat like using a seismometer to record small foreshocks before an earthquake." Indeed, the snapping and popping of these fissures formed patterns resembling those of swarms of small tremors. Then, as the hydraulic press loaded its rock sample more severely, he recalls that "there would be a chain reaction of cracking in a narrow zone. Finally the rock would fracture very suddenly, with a loud report." These experiments were producing what amounted to small earthquakes, complete with precursors, right there in the lab.

However, these tests differed from earthquakes in an important way. Earthquakes rarely involve the breaking of solid masses of unfractured rock. Instead, they take place amid rock masses that have already broken. Such masses press together along the fault, just as the weight of a block of stone presses it heavily against a pavement. The seismic stresses, then, are like horses pulling on the stone, trying to drag it sideways. Friction locks that block in position, just as it locks the rocks at the fault, preventing them from shifting in a quake. But if the horses are strong enough, the block moves. The important point is that the stress required to overcome friction and cause rock masses to shift or move, causing an earthquake, is much less than the stress needed to break a virgin extent of rock. To Brace and his grad students, then, there was no obvious connection between their work and the behavior of rocks in fault zones. Still, dilatancy was well worth studying in its own right. These researchers proceeded to measure the properties of rocks as they swelled under pressure: their porosity or diminishing resistance to the flow of water, their electrical properties, even the speed of pressure and shear waves—such as might come from a quake—as they passed through the dilated samples.

Amos Nur was the grad student working on these waves. He was from Israel and wanted to study geophysics, but Israel had no university programs in the field, so he came to the United States in 1963. After a year at Southern Methodist University he transferred to MIT, where he soon joined Brace's group.

For his Ph.D., he conducted experiments on two varieties of waves with characteristically different speeds. There were pressure waves, resembling sound as it passes through air or water. Nur found that as the rock became dilatant—began to swell under pressure—these waves slowed down. Also there were shear waves, which do not pass through air or water but which do travel through rock, shaking it from side to side. These shear waves characteristically had lower velocities than the pressure waves, but Nur found that dilatancy had little effect on their speeds. Thus, if you looked at the ratio of these velocities—pressure speed divided by shear speed—this ratio would drop in the presence of dilatancy.

In 1971, while he was at a conference in Colorado, a set of seismic results elicited great excitement. In the province of Tadzhikistan in the Soviet Union, a remote and mountainous district where China's Tien Shan range extends westward toward Afghanistan, a group of seismologists had monitored the local earthquakes. They had found changes in the speeds of the pressure and shear waves. Specifically, the ratios of these velocities had dropped off noticeably in the years prior to significant quakes, then returned to normal. Very soon afterward, the tremors had struck.

With this, says Nur, "I put two and two together." The changes in velocity reported by the Russians were just the sort of thing he'd seen in his lab at MIT. He argued with Brace that the two sets of data fitted together; the Soviet data could be understood using the idea of dilatancy. Back at MIT, he wrote up a paper about this idea over a weekend. For a while it looked like it might launch a revolution in geophysics.

At that time, data was coming in from upstate New York. The region had been rattled by moderate quakes from time to time, cracking plaster and throwing down chimneys. One such tremor hit New York City in 1884; others had struck to the north in 1914, 1925, 1929, and 1944. In an effort to learn more, several East Coast universities set up networks of seismographs. Early in the summer of 1971, the network run by the Lamont-Doherty Geological Observatory picked up a number of small quakes near Blue Mountain Lake in the Adirondacks. A group from Lamont set up a temporary network of portable seismographs in the area, like Karen McNally's arrays in Mexico. During the next two months the instruments recorded a swarm of such quakes, the largest being of magnitude 3.6.

At the end of the summer the data was in. The tedious job of analysis fell to a graduate student, Yash P. Aggarwal, from

Pakistan. He soon realized the seismograms showed something unexpected: the velocities of the pressure and shear waves were behaving much as they had in the Soviet Union. The pressure-wave velocities were diminishing, then returning nearly to normal; within as little as a day or two, there would be a moderate-sized quake.

By then Scholtz was at Lamont. He had not worked closely with Amos Nur while they were both at MIT; he was only vaguely aware of Nur's work on the speeds of earthquake waves. But Nur sent a draft of his paper to his colleagues at Lamont. Suddenly, Scholtz realized that he was within reach of striking scientific gold, for he had his own lab results from dilatancy experiments: "We immediately realized that the idea of dilatancy could be used not only to explain the velocity changes, but that it implied changes in electrical conductivity of the rock, permeability, pore pressure, seismicity, and lots of other things." Scholtz, after all, had been studying these very matters while working on dilatancy at MIT. "And we realized there had been a lot of observations of changes in these phenomena, made haphazardly over the previous twenty years. But they had never been studied systematically. Not knowing how to predict earthquakes, you couldn't very well pose the problem."

In 1972, Aggarwal went to another conference and gave a paper on his work with the quakes near Blue Mountain Lake. In the audience was another seismologist, James Whitcomb of Caltech. Whitcomb realized that he could test the idea of dilatancy by searching for velocity changes in waves from earthquakes that had preceded the recent San Fernando tremor, magnitude 6.4. He had the necessary seismograms from the Seismo Lab; better still, he had the ear of Don Anderson, the lab's director. Whitcomb proceeded to look for the changes—and soon he was asserting that he had found them. He began working on a paper with Anderson. And with Anderson on board the dilatancy bandwagon, the new theory was likely to sweep the field, because of his strong reputation.

"Our groups were working on these two papers almost simultaneously," Scholtz remembers. "It was a sort of *samizdat,* papers going back and forth between the coasts. It was an exciting time. We pulled all these observations together. People had made them without knowing what they meant. But they could all be explained on the basis of dilatancy."

The following spring, the American Geophysical Union hosted its annual meeting at the Sheraton-Park Hotel in Washington, D.C. The conference sessions had been scheduled months earlier, based on short descriptions or abstracts of the scientists' papers. Scholtz had been too late for the abstract deadline, so he couldn't expect to get on the schedule. Nevertheless, one of the session chairmen agreed to put Scholtz in at lunchtime, following the morning presentations. His paper created a sensation.

"It was in a ballroom at the Sheraton," he recalls. "The room was just packed. It hadn't been formally scheduled, but the word had gotten around; the whole meeting was buzzing. There were maybe five hundred people, some of them standing. I talked for forty-five minutes; then there were forty-five minutes of questions afterward, so everybody missed lunch. It was very new; people were quite excited about these ideas. But they were also skeptical, so it was scary. They wanted to shoot the ideas down; they would be asking the nastiest questions they could think of. After all, this was a paradigm in the making."

What Scholtz was proposing was nothing less than the first fundamental advance in the physical understanding of earthquakes in ninety years. In 1883, Grove Gilbert had proposed that earthquakes arose from slippage along a fault. Everything since then had been built on this essential idea. Now Scholtz explained the behavior of the rocks within a fault zone prior to a quake, basing it on the concept of dilatancy and of phenomena that he and his colleagues had actually studied in their labs.

Events leading up to the quake would begin with a slow buildup of strain along a fault, stressing the rocks with steadily increasing force. Eventually the increasing stress would begin to produce dilatancy. Cracks would begin to form and grow; the rock would swell. Moreover, groundwater would be present naturally amid the rock. As with the sand on the beach, as the rock swelled, it would become drier. It would increase its volume more rapidly than the rate at which groundwater could flow into the newly formed cracks. These cracks, being dry, would tend to hold firmly rather than slip in minor earthquakes.

But this volume increase would actually strengthen the rock against an increase in the cracking rate, an effect called *dilatancy hardening.* This hardening of the rock under strain would resemble the "stress hardening" of steel and other metals, which stiffen as they deform or yield under an increasingly heavy load. Stress hardening occurs when a metal is forced through a die, for example; it prevents metals from being pulled apart like taffy. Dilatancy hardening would slow down the cracking rate, allowing the groundwater to catch up with the increasing volume of the rock's cracks, percolating into its fissures. Eventually the rock's pores and cracks would be fully saturated with water. This water, in turn, would be under pressure and would lubricate the rock, forcing apart the cracks and reducing the friction that was preventing the fault from slipping. With enough lubrication, the fault would give way and the main earthquake would take place.

The theory was magnificent in that it explained a wide range of observations, and promised a firm basis for predicting earthquakes. Was there a period of seismic quiescence before a large tremor, followed by foreshocks? The quiescence would result from the dilatancy hardening; the foreshocks would mean that the cracks, increasingly well lubricated, were beginning to give way. Were there changes in levels of wells, or swellings and bulges in the fault zone, as had preceded the San Fernando and Niigata tremors? These were the obvious result of the dilatant swelling of rock far below. As Amos Nur had shown, dilatancy would also produce changes in seismic-wave velocities, which now could stand alongside the other changes predicted by Scholtz's theory. And the theory scored a particular triumph in explaining the unusual fact that radioactive radon gas had been detected in earthquake zones. Radon forms from the radioactive decay of uranium, which is present in all common rocks. Yet radon disappears very swiftly, with a half-life of 3.8 days; that is, half the radon decays into other atoms during that time. Thus it must escape from its parent rock very soon after it has formed. If dilatancy had fissured the rock with numerous cracks, the radon would have a route to the surface.

Furthermore, by linking these phenomena to a common cause, the dilatancy theory encouraged the hope that these effects might now be systematically studied and developed as earthquake precursors. Geodetic uplifts might turn up through repeated leveling surveys. Instrumented water wells, recording groundwater level and radon content, would also help. But the mainstay of prediction would be the good old seismograph, which could send its data over phone lines to a central computer for analysis. Seismographs might show not only seismic quiescence or a resumption of low-level quake activity, but the new phenomenon of changes in the velocity of seismic waves.

All this brought dazzling hope. Seismologists might observe precursors as if they were symptoms in a patient, then issue a diagnosis as the symptoms changed. In turn, the changes might follow predictable patterns that could be learned through experience. Earthquake prediction might eventually resemble weather prediction. The quakes would not be like solar eclipses, which can be predicted centuries in advance to the second, but these seismic forecasts would no longer be the province of fortune-tellers and soothsayers.

The dilatancy theory was a brilliant thing, as potentially important as the theory of plate tectonics itself. But there was a catch: dilatancy required large amounts of strain within rocks before it would set in, and such large strains did not appear to exist within earthquake zones. At its maximum stress, a rock would fracture and break. At about half this stress, dilatancy would begin to set in, swelling the rock amid a proliferation of cracks. But most geophysicists believed that faults would give way and produce an earthquake if the rocks on either side of them were stressed to as little as one-tenth of their breaking strain. This suggested that the buildup of stress along a fault would trigger a quake long before it could reach the point of beginning to produce dilatancy.

The dilatancy theory was not just a pretty piece of speculation. There appeared to be real data to support it, from earthquakes in Tadzhikistan and at Blue Mountain Lake, and in the precursors to the San Fernando quake. Still, a lot would depend on whether further tests would continue to support dilatancy. If they did, geophysicists would have to reconcile themselves to the likelihood that they were wrong about the stresses in fault zones. But if new data put dilatancy under challenge, it might quickly sink. Amid this apparent discrepancy—one-tenth of the rocks' breaking strain to produce a quake, versus one-half of this strain to produce dilatancy—the burden of proof was on the advocates of dilatancy to show, by new data, that their views were likely to be correct.

The most convincing data lay in the claims that the velocities of seismic waves had changed just before the occurrence of quakes. This data had come from seismograms, which people were inclined to trust, and Amos Nur had explained the changes as a consequence of dilatancy. But at Berkeley, Tom McEvilly, the thesis adviser for Karen McNally, had doubts about the data: "I was skeptical of the claims of changes in earthquake-wave velocities," he states. "I had worked with the travel times of waves from a lot of earthquakes, and one thing that impressed me was the stability of Mother Earth. I hadn't been seeing changes of 15 percent in velocity, which the Soviets and others had claimed." He set out to examine Amos Nur's theory of seis-

Air Force photo taken from 60,000 feet above Los Angeles. North of the city are the San Gabriel Mountains; at the top of the photo is the Mojave Desert. The San Andreas Fault is the line between the mountains and the desert. (*Courtesy of U. S. Geological Survey*)

After the 1906 fire, San Francisco resembled a city bombed out in World War II. *(Courtesy of U. S. Geological Survey)*

The San Francisco fire of 1906. *(Courtesy of U. S. Geological Survey)*

(LEFT) Decline and fall: San Francisco's city hall following the great earthquake and fire. *(Courtesy of U. S. Geological Survey)*

Offset in a streambed where it crosses the San Andreas Fault.
(Photo by Robert Wallace, courtesy of U. S. Geological Survey)

Main trace of the San Andreas Fault in the Carrizo Plain. *(Photo by Robert Wallace, courtesy of U. S. Geological Survey)*

(LEFT) Donalee Thomason with a satellite transmitter for seismic instruments, near Parkfield, California. *(Photo by the author)*

(RIGHT) Duane Hamann with his laser, used for precise measurement of distances along a part of the San Andreas. Changes in these measurements give clues to the behavior of the fault at depth. *(Photo by the author)*

(OPPOSITE TOP) The San Jacinto Fault. At the bottom of a trench, fourteen feet down, graduate student Carol Prentice of Caltech points to a slight break in the soil. This is the main trace of the dangerous fault. *(Photo by the author)*

(OPPOSITE BOTTOM) Kerry Sieh within one of his trenches. *(Courtesy of U. S. Geological Survey*

Tumbled houses and trees near Anchorage, Alaska, following the great earthquake of 1964. Similar damage can be expected from the coming southern California quake. *(Courtesy of U. S. Geological Survey)*

Destruction along a main avenue in Anchorage, Alaska, following the great quake of 1964. *(Courtesy of U. S. Geological Survey)*

Light-colored patches are sandblows in fields of the central Mississippi Valley, still clearly visible long after the great New Madrid earthquakes of 1811–12. *(Courtesy of U. S. Geological Survey)*

(OPPOSITE, TOP) Collapsed overpass at the interchange of the Golden State and Foothill freeways following the 1971 San Fernando earthquake. *(Photo by Leslie Youd, courtesy of U. S. Geological Survey)*

(OPPOSITE, BOTTOM) Interior of a house wrecked in the 1971 San Fernando quake. *(Photo by Leslie Youd, courtesy of U. S. Geological Survey)*

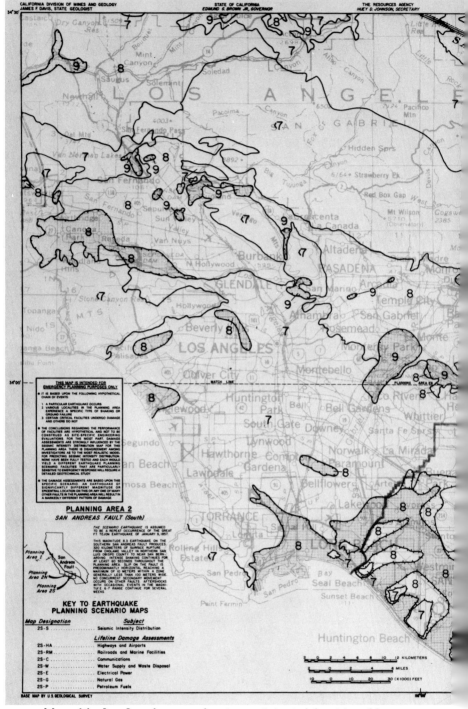

Map of the Los Angeles area showing anticipated densities of the
shaking, along with areas of expected ground failure following a

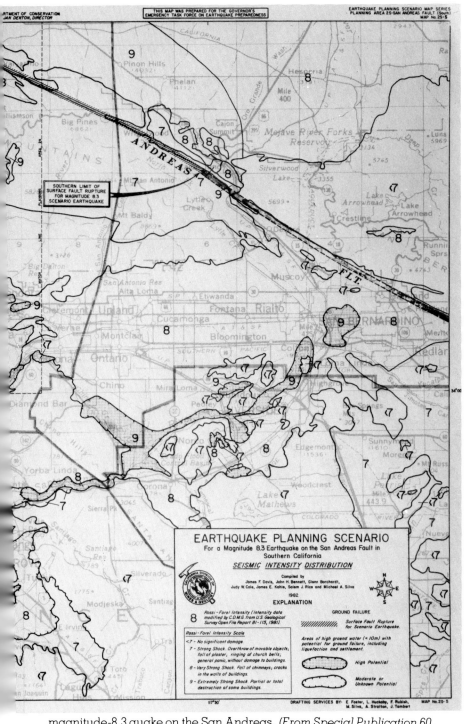

magnitude-8.3 quake on the San Andreas. (From Special Publication 60, California Division of Mines and Geology, Sacramento)

Destroyed buildings at Coalinga, California, following the magnitude-6.5 quake of 1983. *(Courtesy of U. S. Geological Survey)*

Future death trap? Royce Hall at UCLA is one of a large number of state buildings that could collapse in the coming California earthquake. *(Photo by the author)*

mic waves, which was a key part of the dilatancy theory, using something new: dynamite blasts in rock quarries.

As early as 1960, Berkeley seismologists had set up a network of seven seismographs, each one housed in a four-by-four-foot concrete hut, with a telephone line attached. Year after year, these instruments had been sending their signals. As an exercise, students had arranged to use such data to determine accurate times for the quarry blasts. Later they put an instrument only a few miles from one such rock pit, the Natividad Quarry near Salinas, to give particularly precise times for the blasts. Now the seismic traces from these industrial explosions lay in the files of the seismogram library, ready for use in determining precise travel times for pressure waves as they crossed the San Andreas. In McEvilly's words, "It was an experiment just made to be done."

The claims of velocity changes had come from studies of small tremors recorded on seismograms. From these, investigators such as Aggarwal and Whitcomb had been able to estimate the location, time, and magnitude of these tremors. But those very estimates depended on knowing accurately the travel times of their waves. At the same time, those travel times were to be determined using those same tremors. There was enough data to keep the reasoning from being circular, but still there was room for uncertainty. McEvilly's approach, by contrast, put the cart before the horse. Those quarry blasts had amounted to standard sources of earthquake waves, with known locations, times, and energies. Their pressure waves had passed through regions of the San Andreas that had later broken in moderate quakes. And what was better still, there were a dozen years of data available.

The records were all on sixteen-millimeter microfilm. There had been some twenty quakes along the pertinent stretch of the San Andreas, with magnitudes as great as 5.6, between 1961 and 1973. On a great many occasions, pressure waves from the quarry blasts had passed through these quakes' eventual locations, to be recorded on the seismographs. The detonations, sixty-eight in all during those years, stood out clearly. "We could even see the locations of the explosions in the quarry, as they moved to different sites," McEvilly says. And when he had analyzed all the data—it took him about a year—what did he see? "Nothing," he answers. "No effects, within an accuracy of about one percent." The pressure waves had shown no perceptible slowdowns.

This was a bad setback to the dilatancy theory of earthquakes, and it wasn't the only one. "The bottom fell out when the observations were called into question," McEvilly relates. Whitcomb's data, dealing with the San Fernando quake, were examined and failed to hold up. "The story on San Fernando fell apart," is how Amos Nur puts it. "That was the biggest story, and it was a very severe blow." It turned out that a certain psychology had been at work on investigators examining the seismograms. Small tremors, which had been the basis for many of the claims, were hard to time accurately. They often did not stand out clearly, yet they often were the only sources of data available. Then seismologists who knew what they were looking for—slowdowns in these tremors' pressure waves—had unconsciously made the measurements in ways that would support their hopes. It was a case of misinterpreting doubtful data while hoping to see the dilatancy. Not all the data had been so handled; Aggarwal's, at Blue Mountain Lake, still held up. But that might well be a special case, perhaps an area where new faults were forming in unbroken rock, rather than a representative of fault zones generally.

Dilatancy thus offered far less than a sweeping paradigm for seismology. The important feature of such theories was that they stood up in the presence of further study, with confidence in them being strengthened by newer results. Indeed, increasing accuracy in measurement had often been an important factor in heightening confidence in new theories. Such increases in accuracy had been the key to the discovery that the earth travels around the sun rather than vice versa; centuries later, further observational improvements had vindicated Einstein's revolutionary theory of relativity. But now, in seismology, the reverse was happening. These improvements in the ability to draw conclusions from seismograms—the use of quarry-blast data by McEvilly, the recognition of the psychological factor, which could then be allowed for or corrected—had refuted rather than supported the dilatancy theory of earthquakes.

Dilatancy still was real. After all, it had been observed and studied in labs. But there was good reason to doubt that it applied to extensive stretches of rock within a fault zone. At most, it might apply to small, highly strained rocky patches, which would be the last to hold back the quake and whose breaking would trigger it. This was bad news for those people who were seeking earthquake precursors. Major tremors still might be preceded by geodetic uplifts and bulges, by seismic quiescence or foreshocks, even by changes in water-well levels and radon content. But there now would be no systematic way to link these changes to a developing earthquake. They would appear, or fail to appear, through mechanisms more complex and less well understood than simple dilatancy. Sometimes such precursors would suffice for a warning. At other times, in hit-or-miss fashion, they would not.

Yet while the dilatancy theory was badly deflated by 1974, there was hope. Simply by looking for precursors, even without having a clear picture of why they were there, it might be possible to predict a temblor. A casual event at Thanksgiving that year made this look like an idea worth pursuing. Around Hollister, California, east of Monterey, an array of sensitive magnetometers had been put in place in 1973 and operated for a year. Their data was analyzed the following November. Marked changes were seen in the local magnetism of the earth between two of the magnetometers.

More compelling evidence came at the same time from a network of tiltmeters. These were like carpenters' levels, except the bubble was in mercury, not water, and there were electrodes around it. By amplifying the signals from these electrodes, the levels could detect a slope equivalent to lifting up one end of the United States by as little as one inch. The instruments near Hollister showed that in addition to the magnetic changes there were also significant changes in the land's tilt. The changes occurred over an area large enough to suggest that if a quake took place there, it would be larger than magnitude 4.

The tilt data were in hand by the evening of Wednesday, November 27. There was a meeting then of the Pick and Hammer Club, a group of earth scientists in the Bay Area. A member of the group described the data from the magnetometers and tiltmeters as "the sort one would expect to see before a quake." He and his colleagues believed that if there was indeed to be a tremor, it would occur soon. "Maybe tomorrow," suggested Jack Healy, who was from the USGS. A day later the quake indeed rocked the town of Hollister, magnitude 5.2, and Healy found that he had instantly become a local celebrity. What was more, he and his associates faced a sobering realization. If the data processing had been carried out as little as a week earlier, the USGS could have made a formal prediction and warned the public authorities.

Two months later, in China, the prospects for earthquake prediction reached towering heights indeed. At the city of Haicheng in Manchuria, the local authorities gave a disaster warning and saved the people from a quake of magnitude 7.3.

There was irony in the Chinese approach to seismology: it had taken shape during the Cultural Revolution, a decade-long upheaval that had badly damaged much of that country's science and education. The approach was that science must advance by "walking on two legs," the first "leg" being the toiling masses, the second being the expertise of professional scientists. Still, with distinguished professors being routinely sent to "learn from the peasants" by shoveling night soil on collective farms, there was little doubt which leg Chairman Mao preferred.

But in seismology, at least, the involvement of the common people made sense. They could report unusual events to local "earthquake brigades," which often included scientists who could judge whether these reports might be significant. Since major quakes could strike throughout much of the country, it also made sense to have the seismologists out in the provinces, not clustered in Beijing.

As early as 1970, the State Seismological Bureau had singled out Liaoning Province, which includes Haicheng, as a region susceptible to large quakes. By June 1974 there was an increase in the rate of deformation at the surface, as measured by leveling surveys. There also were changes in the local magnetism of the earth. On that basis, the bureau warned that a large quake was likely in the next year or two. With that, thousands of amateur observers began to assist the professional seismologists, expanding the network of instruments.

In November the rate of surface deformation proved to be increasing. The ground along one of the main faults was found to be rising rapidly on one side while falling on the other. During December, nearby farms and communes reported that their animals were acting strangely, and that their water wells were bubbling and changing levels. Radon was detected in the groundwater. On December 20, the area's residents were warned that a large quake was imminent. For two nights the people slept outside in the snow. Nothing happened; the earthquake prediction proved to be a false alarm.

During that December and early January of 1975, there were reports that hibernating snakes, which are cold-blooded, had crawled out of their holes and frozen. At about that time, the bureau reviewed the evidence and decided that a Big One was due after all. Its scientists issued a short-term prediction, stating that it was expected during the next six months. On February 1 a tiny quake occurred, of magnitude less than 1, followed the next day by several more. They were occurring in an area that had not previously reported any tremors; this was suspicious. By now some 70 percent of the wells being monitored were reporting changes in level, with more than twenty becoming artesian, spouting water from the ground.

During the evening of February 3, the local quakes grew in size and began to come in a rapid-fire sequence, increasing above magnitude 3 by midnight. They topped magnitude 4 the next morning, then dropped off. At 10:00 A.M. the Liaoning Provincial Seismological Bureau issued a prediction that a major quake would strike in the next day or two. In Haicheng, the city authorities ordered the people to evacuate en masse from buildings into tent cities and similar shelters. Cars, trucks, and buses were removed from garages and parked out in the open. Emergency squads mobilized and prepared to give assistance. And as the day wore on, with the foreshocks continuing, local authorities received a number of new reports of strange animal behavior.

At eight that morning, there had been an emergency meeting at a local commune. Twenty piglets, born a few months earlier, had been found in the pigsty, crying wildly. More than half had had their tails bitten off and eaten by other pigs, with one of the stumps bleeding profusely. The manager of the commune's earthquake office had looked into this, had decided the pigs had been frightened by precursors of the coming quake, then had made a prediction that a Big One was due. Following the meeting, the commune's leaders began to prepare for such a quake.

That afternoon, a frog was found to have left the hole where it had been hibernating. Elsewhere, sheep cried for most of the day. A number of rats that were not afraid of people were found in a hallway. Deer in a stable were very frightened and unquiet. An old horse and a mule refused to enter their corral; when they were forced in, they broke away.

A dog barked at the air as if it had discovered something,

and scratched at the ground. Three rabbits kept by a family refused to enter their cages, and their ears stood up as if they were listening to something. A goose flew up on a wall and cried oddly for several minutes. A cat's fur stood on end; it ran away with its tail high in the air.

Toward evening, several such events served to warn people of an imminent quake. A keeper noticed seventeen normally quiet pigs climbing the wall of their pen and smashing against the gate. He passed the news to his local earthquake office, which warned nearby families and made preparations for a major temblor. A small bull ran wildly about a village, snorting loudly. A village leader then recalled the earlier quake predictions, and called all the people out of their homes. A dog that had given birth to puppies picked up the pups in her mouth and ran against the door, trying to open it so she could take them outside. The owner thought this was strange and remembered that an earthquake had been predicted. He followed his dog outside into the winter evening.

Four or five minutes later, at 7:36 P.M., the main shock struck with a magnitude of 7.3.

Haicheng had not been evacuated, but city authorities had showed movies outdoors, to encourage people to stay out of their homes and other buildings. The unreinforced brick-and-mortar construction quickly crumbled as the tremor destroyed or severely damaged some 90 percent of the city's structures. Yet among its population of ninety thousand, few if any were killed or injured. Frank Press of MIT, the dean of America's earth scientists, called the prediction at Haicheng ''one of the major events in the history of geophysics.''

The Chinese were highly encouraged as well, and the succeeding months would offer new possibilities for further predictions. Anomalous changes soon appeared in well-water levels in regions north of Beijing, as well as in the water's radon content. Did these observations mean anything? Near the city of Songpan in Sichuan Province, east of Tibet, there was a swarm of quakes, with individual tremors being as strong as magnitude 5. In November 1975, the Sichuan Provincial Seismological Bureau held its usual annual meeting to prepare a report to the governor. This annual report stated that it was likely that the Songpan area, as well as some other places in the province, would have quakes larger than magnitude 6 during the first half of 1976.

North of Beijing there was no prediction of a major quake, but there was a general apprehension that one might be coming. In April 1976, a temblor of magnitude 6.5 struck northwest of that city. The seismologists believed it had been foretold by the changes in radon content and water-well levels, and they relaxed. They were caught off guard in May, when a closely spaced pair of shocks, magnitude 6.9, hit Longling in Yunnan province, close to the Burma border. The official public warning came with only twenty-five minutes to spare, as foreshocks rattled the area. This showed how a major quake could strike without warning.

Meanwhile, in the wake of the November report in Sichuan, "watch brigades" had set up instruments in the Songpan area. Based on their reports, the Sichuan bureau decided that the big quake would probably be somewhat larger than magnitude 6, and farther south than Songpan. Some of the reports had come in from a different area, prompting the shift. Also, since the first half of 1976 was nearly over, they adjusted their prediction of the quake for the second half of the year.

Then, without warning, a great earthquake struck the city of Tangshan, a hundred miles east of Beijing, early in the morning of July 27. It was of magnitude 8.0 on the Richter scale and 7.5 on the seismic-moment scale, making it one of the major tremors of this century. "It definitely hit them by surprise," declares Lucile Jones, a seismologist who has traveled extensively in China. Tragically, there had been no foreshocks or other imminent precursors. The earlier quake of magnitude 6.5 had been over a hundred miles away, and had only acted to confuse the seismologists. The death toll was 240,000, making Tangshan one of the great disasters in history.

In the wake of Tangshan there was general panic in the country. Perhaps half the population took to living outdoors in the summer weather. Every province issued an earthquake prediction, more in fear than from evidence. The State Seismological Bureau then sent out teams to evaluate these projections, and retracted most of them, with a significant exception: the one for Sichuan. Near Songpan, the authorities wanted to decide whether to issue an imminent prediction. The governor of the province moved into the seismological bureau and camped out near the scientists' desks as they were making the decision, placing them under immense political pressure.

On August 12, that bureau issued the imminent prediction. The quake would be of magnitude 7 or more, "within a very short period of time," along some part of the 250-mile-long fault called Longmenchang, "Dragon Gate Mountain." The first major shock struck four days later, magnitude 7.2. It was followed by quakes of magnitude 6.7 and 7.2, on August 21 and 23. These three tremors struck not on the Longmenchang, but on the nearby Huya ("Tiger's Teeth") fault, thirty miles away at its closest point. The original prediction of November 1975 had given the correct location; the subsequent shift in this position, south of Songpan, had been a mistake. Still, nearly everyone was living outdoors anyway. It was said that in the nearby city of Chengdu, almost the only people still indoors were the seismologists.

"The seismologists have been told to predict earthquakes, period," said one China expert who declined to be identified. "They know about as much as we do, which isn't a whole lot. So they do it by having a lot of false alarms," as at Haicheng in December 1974. "All these things are political there. The provincial seismological bureau is a political organization; its head is a politician." Thus, the nuances of scientific methodology sometimes have received short shrift.

One young seismologist was sent to Tangshan after its

quake. Her superiors had more political pull and succeeded in dodging that assignment. Everyone was in trouble for having failed to predict the main quake, but she didn't have the political clout and so was responsible for figuring out if there would be large aftershocks and when they would come. After several months, she declared there would probably be no more events of magnitude 6 or larger. Her boss said, "Are you sure?" She replied, "There probably won't be any more." He said, " 'Probably' isn't good enough. Yes or no?" Put on the spot, she finally said, "No." Through the following year she waited in fear that another temblor of magnitude 6 would come along. Fortunately, none did.

Meanwhile, in a final irony, Chairman Mao died on September 9. His premier, Chou En-lai, had died the previous April. They had supported China's earthquake-prediction efforts, not only to save lives, but also to fight superstitions and "reactionary myths" among the people. Prime among these was the belief that great quakes heralded the passing of a dynasty, just as comets in medieval Europe had been taken as signs foretelling the deaths of kings. For Mao and Chou to die during those major tremors made 1976 the Chinese counterpart to 1066, the year the appearance of Halley's Comet coincided with the passing of Edward the Confessor, followed by the deaths in battle of Norway's King Harald and Harold II of England. In 1976, then, it was as if the ways of the old China had shown their force in a direct rebuke to the leaders of the new.

As the Chinese events became known, the question arose in California: Could animals predict earthquakes? The reports of animal precursors, prior to the Haicheng quake, had been sufficiently compelling for the question to merit serious attention. It was not necessary to think of magic powers; the Haicheng area had been racked by foreshocks, disturbances that could well have sufficed to upset a number of animals. But it was possible that some species were sensitive to earthquake precursors that seismologists had overlooked. If this proved true, it would open up a new line of research

aimed at detecting these precursors with sensitive instruments, thereby going the animals one better.

The USGS therefore funded three experiments. In one,
researchers from UCLA set groups of kangaroo rats and
pocket mice, in cages and burrows, directly on the San
Andreas Fault, thirty miles north of Palm Springs. A swarm
of quakes struck on March 15, 1979, the three strongest
being of magnitude 5. "Just prior to the swarm, we did have
one or two of the pocket mice run above ground at a time
when they are usually in their underground cages," said
Robert Lindberg, a research leader. "But that could have
been attributed to the warmer weather we were experiencing." Indeed, nothing in the creatures' behavior gave the
scientists reason to believe that they were responding to the
impending tremors. "We couldn't prove if the animals could
or could not predict earthquakes," Lindberg added.

In a separate experiment, at the University of California at
Davis, investigators carried out careful interviews of pet
owners and animal handlers, in the days just after a quake.
Had these people noticed anything unusual in their animals'
behavior, just prior to the tremor? In at least one instance,
they had indeed.

At Willits, California, near the northern coast, there was a
magnitude 4.7 shaker in 1977. Out of fifty households interviewed, seventeen reported unusual behavior. An Arabian
gelding became nervous and kicked the sides of its stall. A
cat paced and fidgeted during his usual nap time. A Dober-
man pinscher whined excitedly, put her head passively on
her owner's lap, then did these things repeatedly. Still, most
animals did no such things. Even in the stalls near the gelding, the other horses behaved normally in the hours before
the quake. Moreover, the Davis researchers found that prior
to a larger quake in Montana in 1978, magnitude 4.9, only
one person of thirty-five interviewed noted any unusual behavior. This same pattern, of few if any out-of-the-ordinary
animal activities, also held for three other quakes studied by
the group from Davis. They concluded that a few animals,

within some species, show unusual behavior before some earthquakes, but that the vast majority are unresponsive.

Much the same result emerged from the third study, conducted by two investigators from SRI International, which is just down the street from the USGS, a few blocks away from Stanford University. By putting up notices in post offices, the SRI researchers succeeded in recruiting some 1,700 volunteers living within California's seismically active areas. They were invited to call a toll-free hot line if they ever saw a pet or other animal acting in strange ways.

Over a four-year period, thirteen tremors of magnitude 4 or higher occurred close to the pertinent areas. By running through the telephone records, which noted the place and time of each call, it was easy to tell if any quake had been preceded by an unusual number of reports. In at least one case, the result was dramatic. On March 3, 1981, at 2:45 A.M., the town of Fremont near Oakland had felt a temblor of magnitude 4.3. Within the previous thirty days, twenty-one hot-line calls had come in from the surrounding area, whereas the expected rate was only one call. In six other cases there had been enough animal reports to be statistically significant, which is a catch-phrase that means, "We don't know what's going on, but we see something that looks like it might be interesting." The remaining six quakes, out of those thirteen, showed no unusual upsurge in phone calls. But there was no clear pattern in any of this. As with other precursors, animal behavior was very much a hit-or-miss thing, and probably less reliable than reliance on purely physical data. In short, although it was not without value, it could not be relied on in earthquake-prediction efforts.

Thus, within the span of a few years, seismologists had received a double dose of bad news. First the dilatancy theory, with its promise of a major advance in understanding quakes and their precursors, had proven to be incorrect. Then, amid the hope that at least the precursors themselves would prove to be useful, it had developed that this was true only for some earthquakes, along some faults. These precursors had given hours or days of warning at Haicheng and Songpan, a mere half-hour at Longling—and no warning at all at Tangshan, the deadliest of all. And all these faults had been watched closely by people who were prepared to take the chance of issuing a false alarm rather than miss predicting the quake.

Indeed, America's seismologists also soon realized how much they didn't know, for California was taken by complete surprise and struck by a set of tremors that fell amid arrays of instruments.

On August 6, 1979, a tremor of magnitude 5.9 hit near Coyote Lake, California, in hilly country southeast of San Jose. It fell on the Calaveras fault, an offshoot of the San Andreas, amid seismograph arrays operated by Berkeley and, separately, by the USGS. There were no significant foreshocks, not even microquakes of magnitude less than 3, similar to those Karen McNally had seen in Oaxaca the previous fall. Nor did any clear patterns emerge from reports of unusual animal behavior. There were a few calls to the hot line of SRI International, but the change was no more than marginal. Geodetic tilts and changes in the magnetic field of the earth, which had signaled the 1974 tremor at Hollister in time for the meeting of the Pick and Hammer Club, also were absent.

"We clearly were not overwhelmed by short-term precursors," declared Robert Wesson, a USGS manager of earthquake studies. Indeed, the one possible precursor was identified only by a careful search after the quake, and it was quite enigmatic. Over twenty miles from the epicenter, a spring showed a surge in its flow. Clearly, then, a quake of potentially damaging size could strike in a reasonably well instrumented area, without betraying its imminence. "There's so much we don't know," Wesson added.

Ten weeks later, on October 15, a shaker of magnitude 6.6 struck the Imperial Valley, east of San Diego and not far from the location of a destructive 1940 quake of magnitude 7.1. Three miles away was an electric power plant. The quake ruptured some water lines and bent a few steel supports, but the plant was back in operation only five hours later. The local County Services Building was not so fortunate, even though it was only ten years old and had been built to meet earthquake codes. It featured five upper stories supported by columns of reinforced concrete, above an open first floor. In a quake, the building would resemble a heavy box held up by wobbly stilts. Of the twenty-four columns, only four crumbled and gave way, but that was enough for the $3-million structure to be written off as a total loss.

Clarence Allen of Caltech had been watching the Imperial Fault, an offshoot of the San Andreas where the quake was centered. He had installed a set of creepmeters spanning the fault. These featured piers anchored on either side, with a wire stretched between them and weighted to draw it taut. An electrical gauge then could measure to an accuracy of 0.1 millimeter any pull on the wire produced by motion along the fault. Creep, a quake-free sliding or slippage of rock along a fault, had often been discussed as a possible short-term precursor. The idea was that the fault would give a little, without producing a quake, before rupturing in the main shock.

One of Allen's creepmeters was inoperative at the time of the tremor. Two others had their wires yanked out by its force, while another somehow made it through. But as he later put it, "we have a good record of what was happening in the hours and days before the quake. And there's not a clue of anything strange going on. No creep—and the instruments were recording every two seconds."

On January 28, 1980, another unpredicted quake rattled Livermore, California, forty miles east of San Francisco. It struck at one of the nation's leading centers for physics research, the Lawrence Livermore Laboratory. The quake was magnitude 5.8 on the Richter scale.

In one large building, a welder was on top of a steel vessel, fifty feet above the floor, when his whole world started to shake. He was in a harness, and he thought he'd been paralyzed, because he couldn't move. A quarter-mile away, the world's largest laser was knocked off its supports. Amid the rolling and swaying, its two-hundred-ton steel frame sheared some of the bolts that held it to the floor and rocked out of position. As one of the laser researchers described it, "The building looked like a bomb blast had gone off inside. The fluorescent lights in the ceiling fell in; all the partitions in the offices were turned over sideways. We went in there, and the place looked worse than a building trashed by vandals. The ceilings were strewn all over."

Those three quakes occurred within six months; then California was relatively quiet for more than three years. It did not last. On May 2, 1983, the town of Coalinga, in central California, was heavily damaged by a shock of magnitude 6.5. If you had come off the freeway and driven into town, you might have seen a big cylindrical oil tank whose contents had spilled out, coloring one side of it black. Its steel plates had buckled, showing daylight through the gaps. A similar tank that held molasses for use as cattle feed had split open. The dark, gooey stuff had formed a lake, and an adjacent stack of baled hay had tumbled in. Presumably the livestock found the combination delicious.

A number of modern buildings escaped unharmed. Among them was the one-story structure housing the Elks Club, its life-size statue of an elk continuing to stand unperturbed on the roof. The county sheriff's office and a motel across the street were also undamaged. But in the center of town a number of old houses and other structures were devastated. A wood-frame home with a porch had shifted more than a foot off its foundation. Close by, the top front wall of a brick house had simply collapsed, two bedrooms and the wallpapered walls exposed for all to see. In a similar fashion, storefronts collapsed, covering the sidewalk with rubble of brick and timber. The roof and front wall of another large building fell in, forming a massive pile of broken brick and smashing in the roof of a big Ford. Total damage was $33 million, but fortunately no lives were lost.

Interestingly, this tremor fell within a Mogi doughnut, a

type of pattern found by Tokyo's Kiyoo Mogi in the late 1960s when he was discovering seismic quiescence. The doughnut was a ring of moderate-size earthquakes surrounding a quiescent zone; the eventual Coalinga quake later filled the doughnut's center. Such a ringlike pattern of quakes of magnitude 5 had been seen in China, and assisted in making the six-month predictions of the 1976 Songpan temblor of magnitude 7.2. Near Coalinga the doughnut had begun to form in 1975, as tremors of magnitude 4 and 5 began to circle the town. There were four such quakes, the last one coming in October 1982.

Could this doughnut have predicted the Coalinga quake? There was no short-term warning immediately prior to the main shock. Jerry Eaton of the USGS showed later that there were no foreshocks larger than magnitude 1.5. In the opinion of Clarence Allen, "if you asked any seismologist in California the day before that quake what was the most likely place for a magnitude 6.5 event, I don't think any of them would have picked Coalinga." He sighed at a mention of the Mogi doughnut. "There are so many Mogi doughnuts, we have yet to learn how to make use of them. We're not even sure exactly what fault Coalinga occurred on. It had not been identified as an active fault. At the time, could we have identified that doughnut as particularly dangerous?"

Nearly a year later, Morgan Hill, a town south of San Jose, was struck. Again the Calaveras fault was the culprit, with the quake breaking a section directly to the northwest of the 1979 Coyote Lake tremor. The new quake hit on April 24, 1984, doing $7.5 million in damage and reaching magnitude 6.1. Significantly, there had been a forecast or partial prediction. In a 1980 paper, William Bakun of the USGS had written that a "shock comparable in size to the 1979 Coyote Lake main shock" had occurred near Morgan Hill in 1911, and "might also occur" along the same length of fault in the future.

This amounted to two-thirds of a prediction, since Bakun had specified the location and magnitude, but not the time.

But Bakun had buried his comments inside his paper, in what was nearly a casual aside. It had come to light only because Hiroo Kanamori had an uncanny talent for spotting occasional nuggets of gold within the massive stacks of seismological publications that were filling library shelves. When the Morgan Hill quake struck in 1984, Kanamori soon had the four-year-old paper in hand. He told his colleagues, "Gee, this must be the quake that Bakun predicted." A mutual friend passed news of this to Bakun, who went back and reread his own paper. "I'd forgotten I'd put that in," he confesses. "It's difficult for me to claim that one, since I didn't know at first what Hiroo was talking about."

As with Coyote Lake, this earthquake fell within the Berkeley and USGS networks of seismographs. And again there were no useful precursors. A geodetic baseline straddled the fault, thirty-two kilometers long. Its length had been measured repeatedly with lasers, and any change might show that the region surrounding the fault was undergoing creep. The line had been measured both eight days before and one day before the quake, to an accuracy of seven millimeters; neither measurement showed significant change. Two tiny foreshocks occurred, one of magnitude 0.7, nearly eighteen hours before the main tremor, the other of magnitude 0.4, some three hours before it. But these were quite in keeping with the seismic activity of the area, which had shown more than 150 earthquakes of magnitude 1.0 or more along the eventual rupture zone, during the preceding year.

Why had earthquake prediction proved to be so elusive? The reason was that there was so little about a quake that was regular and predictable. A fault might sit quietly for decades or even centuries, with nothing more than an occasional modest-sized quake. Then, with no warning and in the space of a minute, all hell could break loose. What had caused the quake? What had shaken it loose? What had happened to the fault to produce a difference? There was no clear way to know. Seismology, like any physical science, relied on studies of cause and effect. The effect—the earthquake—was obvious. But the cause too often was so subtle as to elude detection.

That was what had stymied further progress in earthquake prediction. It still was possible to use historical records to identify seismic gaps, where quakes appeared overdue. Seismic quiescence also remained useful as a means of picking out those gaps that were likely to experience their quakes within the next few years. But in China as well as in California, the next step—the detailed study of faults that were known to be potentially dangerous—had failed to give a reliable means of narrowing the prediction by making more accurate the anticipated time of the quake's occurrence. The hope had been that once a hazardous stretch of fault had been identified, as by the seismic-gap method, it would show precursors that would give warning of the quake's increasing imminence. That had indeed happened at Haicheng, but this success was the only one of its kind.

Thus, seismologists had been left to ask the most basic of questions: Is there a physical basis, even in principle, for predicting quakes? The way to study this issue would be to find a fault that was likely to break within the next few years, put many instruments nearby, and watch them closely. That would at least amount to making observations that were subtler and more sensitive, capable perhaps of detecting precursors that the earlier efforts had missed. Unfortunately, to find such a fault was the same as predicting its quake in the first place. For to know that a quake is due soon is to predict it.

Fortunately, there proved to be at least one place in the world where the earthquakes turned out to be sufficiently regular to encourage such an approach. This was the town of Parkfield, in the hills of central California, southeast of Monterey.

6

PARKFIELD

The wind blows ceaselessly in central California's Cholame Valley. A few flattened dark green oaks stand starkly against the hills, which are pale green during the winter and spring, arid yellow-brown the rest of the year. The main road is a single lane of blacktop winding through rangeland; in places the barbed-wire fencing runs alongside the shoulder, and as you drive you may look a dark red cow in its placid face. The only town in the area is Parkfield, population 34. Even in midday, on its single street, the only sound may be a dog barking some distance away. Farther down the valley, off the main road, there is an abandoned gas station. Water trickles from a rusty pipe; a sign reads BAD WATER—DON'T DRINK. The sign shows a skull and crossbones.

This is earthquake country. The San Andreas runs directly through Parkfield and on down the valley. Since the days of the Gold Rush, or as long as records have been kept, this fault has broken regularly, causing earthquakes that with one exception have struck every twenty-two years, give or take a couple. The first appears to have come on January 9, 1857. There were no Yankees or Mexicans living in the valley then, but from Fort Tejon to San Francisco there were a number of reports of foreshocks preceding the great quake that struck at 8:24 that morning. Working with those old records, Kerry Sieh has pinned down the reports, noting the "predawn," "dawn," and "sunrise" tremors, which were felt about four hours, two hours, and one hour respectively prior to the main shock. Not only does he find good reason to believe they occurred at Parkfield; he also argues that they triggered the main earthquake, which ruptured the San Andreas from the adjacent Carrizo Plain to San Bernardino.

The next Parkfield quake struck on February 2, 1881. A few homesteaders had by then begun to settle the area, and a traveler from Salinas was there. As he later wrote in a letter to his newspaper:

> I left Salinas City January 23 on horseback. Passed through Gonzales, Soledad, up Long Valley to the Peachtree, thence through Slack's Canyon to Imusdale in Cholame Valley. We had seven shocks of earthquakes, the two first very hard ones. At Mr. Charles Montgomery's ranch, William Laurence died suddenly. An inquest was held the next day by Judge Ellsworth, where a verdict was found of death from heart disease. He had been herding sheep, and it was supposed that the fright occasioned by the earthquake was the immediate cause of death.

Two decades passed. The little settlement changed its name from Imusdale to Parkfield, because its solitary oaks gave it the appearance of a park. By the end of the century there were more than a thousand people in the valley, and a voters' list tells us that many were farmers or stock-raisers. A few were cowboys, while others worked as mechanics, laborers, even as miners of cinnabar, mercury ore. There was a schoolteacher—and an artist. Most were Democrats or

Republicans, but there were also a few Socialists and Prohibitionists. It was a frontier community of ranchers, complete with a general store. A letter from one C. W. Wilson, who worked in that store, tells what happened on March 2, 1901:

> Well, Ma, we have had a terrific shaking up down here. Last night at twenty minutes of twelve o'clock there was the heaviest shock of earthquake I have ever felt. My bed was jerked out in the middle of the floor. Nearly all the goods in the store was on the floor in an instant, and the poor old earth trembled and groaned like some person in great agony. . . . Daylight revealed a scene of destruction. Eight cases of eggs near the back door had fallen against it so I could not open it, nor could I get to the other doors for debris piled in the aisles and on the counters. All the chimneys in town were shaken down and the ground is seamed for miles, they tell me. I hope it has not been so bad up where you are and that you are all safe.

Another twenty-one years went by, and on March 10, 1922, it happened again. There were cracks in the ground, along with considerable damage to houses, with one house being thrown from its foundation. At Parkfield and in the Cholame Valley, the chimneys were knocked down, while oil pipelines broke some twenty miles away. The quake was felt feebly as far south as Los Angeles, 180 miles distant.

The next Parkfield tremor came ten years early—not in 1944, as might be expected, but on June 8, 1934. It was the end of the school year, and for the twenty or so children in the one-room schoolhouse, a graduation ceremony was being held at the community center. For one nine-year-old girl, Donalee Ludeke, the day was particularly memorable. There was no electricity in the town, and the ceremony got under way by the light from hanging kerosene lanterns. Then a quake struck with considerable force. The program came to a halt. Someone in the audience said, "The Big One always comes first. Let's get on with the play." The show proceeded, and then seventeen minutes later the main shock came. As Donalee later described it, "I remember being thrown back and forth against the walls of the narrow runway behind one side of the stage. It just seemed the hall was turning upside down there in the darkness for a few seconds. I could hear people screaming and trying to run to the exit, but falling down."

Thirty-four years passed. Electricity finally came to the valley in 1949. Donalee married a rancher, Bill Thomason, and they had a son named Douglas. By the mid-1960s he was a restless teenager. On the afternoon of a hot Monday, June 27, 1966, he said, "This is really Dullsville around here. I wish something would happen, even an earthquake!"

It was a well-timed but ill-chosen wish. A heavy shock struck midway through the evening. Donalee remembered such a foreshock in 1934, and she feared a stronger tremor would soon come. She grabbed some delicate figurines from a cabinet, wrapped them in towels, and placed them in a styrofoam cooler. She then went into the kitchen and stood within an open door, believing that its frame would offer her the best protection.

She was surprised when the main shock came without a rumble. She tried to hang on to the door, and as she looked toward the ceiling she was astonished to see the walls wrench out of shape, then snap back into place. Dust flew everywhere. The kitchen door struck her from the blind side, knocking her down on one knee. She was shocked to see her china cabinet's locked doors burst open. Its colored glassware seemed to shoot straight out and hang in midair for what she believed was more than a second, then it crashed and shattered on the floor. Both fireplaces were going down; boards were popping and cracking; household items were falling and breaking. She glanced at the floor; it appeared to be moving in a circle, and she felt a surge of motion sickness. Just then the electricity went off.

And with a final crash, an upright freezer loaded with four hundred pounds of meat pitched forward onto its face.

Following that shaking, the Thomasons soon set about restoring their home to order. And they warned Douglas never to wish for an earthquake again.

Bill Bakun, the man who would give two-thirds of a prediction for the 1984 Morgan Hill tremor, was on the scene just after this 1966 quake. He was then a graduate student at Berkeley, working with Tom McEvilly. Immediately following that shaker, they went down to Parkfield with two other grad students. "We were in a hurry," Bill remembers. "A magnitude-5 aftershock occurred while we were installing seismographs. We drove into farmers' yards; they'd point to an area removed from traffic and say, 'It wouldn't bother us if you had an instrument over there.'" Following the day's work, they drove to the nearby town of Avenal and had dinner in a bar and grill. McEvilly was on the Berkeley faculty, but he looked so young that he was asked for his ID. Then they needed a place to sleep. There were no motels in the area, and Bill wound up borrowing a sleeping bag from the bartender. They then drove all the way to the coast and ended up spending the night on the beach at Morro Bay. That was his introduction to Parkfield.

Bakun's interest in Parkfield continued. "Whenever you do a research project there are unanswered questions, loose ends that nag at you," he says. "Eventually you get back to them." He became interested in foreshocks—and found that the best record of them was from Parkfield. He also became interested in theories of how quakes would recur along a given stretch of fault. "Always the best data kept coming from the Parkfield earthquakes." He kept on working with McEvilly, and by 1979 they realized that they were on the track of something important.

Careful comparison of the 1934 and 1966 quakes showed that they were virtually identical. The main shock of each was of magnitude 5.6, had begun below a local rise called Middle Mountain, and had ruptured toward the southeast, breaking the same length of fault. The "fault-plane solutions," defining specifically the depth, extent, and location of the broken fault, were the same. In 1934, a magnitude-5.1 foreshock had preceded the main shock by 17 minutes 25 seconds. In 1966 the foreshock had been of the same magnitude and the interval had been 17 minutes 17 seconds.

Could the 1922 tremor give a third member of the set? The available data from Berkeley could not answer this question, but the Parkfield temblors had been strong enough to send their waves across thousands of miles, writing permanent records on the world's seismograms. Bakun and McEvilly wrote to seismic stations that had been operating in 1922 and thus might have the needed data, and found what they wanted in the records from De Bilt in the Netherlands. "You could overlay the seismometer traces from the three quakes," Bakun grins. "When we got the data together, we realized the quakes were exactly the same size." Three tremors, across a span of over forty years, had written traces that matched even in their details.

But if the Parkfield quakes were all of a standard size and type, why were they occurring at such irregular intervals? Kerry Sieh had shown that the 1857 foreshocks had probably come from Parkfield, triggering the great quake. Bakun and McEvilly knew about the tremors of 1901, 1922, 1934, and 1966. But the intervals between these successive events thus were 44, 21, 12, and 32 years, which hardly formed any sort of pattern. Then in 1982 they learned there had been a Parkfield quake in 1881. "This really was critical in recognizing the timing pattern," Bakun asserts. Now the sequence of intervals was 24, 20, 21, 12, and 32 years. There now was a clear pattern: a quake every 22 years, with the 1934 tremor being ten years early. And with that, it was easy to add 22 to 1966 and predict 1988 as the year for the next one.

This has not quite shown the regularity of Halley's Comet, but it is close enough. Parkfield has become recognized as the most predictable stretch of fault in the world.

DBN–EW

1922

1934

1966

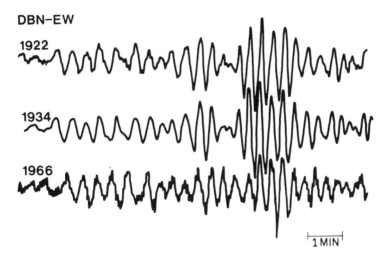

├─1 MIN─┤

DBN–NS

1922

1934

1966

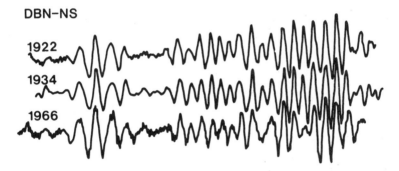

Earthquake traces recorded by seismographs at De Bilt, Netherlands, from Parkfield, California, quakes of 1922, 1934, 1966. Top curves show east-west oscillations; bottom curves are north-south. The extremely close similarity of these seismograms, across more than four decades, show that Parkfield quakes are accurately repeatable in their characteristics. (Courtesy Allan Lindh and William Bakun, U.S. Geological Survey)

Bakun's results, showing this regular behavior, were in hand during 1982. They proved to be the key to a "focused experiment," in which the USGS's seismologists would come to this valley, their trucks and off-road vehicles loaded with sensitive instruments. The goal of this experiment would be to observe the inner workings of the fault in detail, as it strains to the breaking point and finally gives way. The hope is that the data would help to sort out cause and effect, perhaps to learn what triggers an earthquake. But as early as 1978, more from intuition than from data, an independent-minded fellow from the U.S. Geological Survey had already been working to arrange such a focused experiment. He was a colleague of Bakun named Allan Lindh, and he is the man who has led the seismologists to Parkfield.

His life, indeed, has largely been an exercise in independence of mind. During the 1960s he was a hippie in the Haight-Ashbury, then a garbageman driving a truck on what he called "the most beautiful garbage route in the world, up and down the Mendocino coast." He changed tires at a truck stop along the Alaskan Highway, then returned to the Bay Area and took an apprenticeship, to work for several years as what he calls "a real, honest-to-God, house-building carpenter."

In the course of his odyssey, Allan had attended Caltech, Yale, Washington State, Oregon, and the University of Washington. But he had enough credits to receive a degree with as little as a year of concentrated work, and that is what he did. He enrolled at the University of California at Santa Cruz, which had a reputation as a laid-back sort of place. This was about ten years before Karen McNally joined its faculty. He emerged in 1973 with a B.S. in geophysics, and quickly joined the USGS.

The U.S. Geological Survey had grown up as a branch of the Interior Department. It operated three centers, each about the size of a community college, near Washington, D.C., Denver, and San Francisco. Preparing accurate maps was a specialty. One filled an entire wall at a center, at a scale of four miles to the inch, showing all of southern Alaska. Every glacier and inlet appeared in fine detail, as did the roads around Anchorage. Maps drawn to a scale of two thousand feet to the inch would depict all of Monterey Bay, for example, and show individual buildings.

The West Coast center in Menlo Park, near Stanford University, had an additional responsibility. Under a program called Vela Uniform, the Defense Department had made funding available for installing seismograph arrays that could detect underground nuclear tests. The result was the Worldwide Standard Seismograph Network, the first major improvement in global seismology since the work of the Jesuits at the turn of the century. Jerry Eaton, the longtime director at Menlo Park, made good use of the funds and set up a local seismograph network, covering much of California.

Jack Healy, another senior manager and the man who had correctly called the 1974 Hollister quake, was the one who hired Allan. "They decided I looked like a hardworking sort," Allan recalls. "Jack felt very strongly that they needed to hire people like me. He said, 'We've got too many bright guys around here who don't do anything. We need some obnoxious SOBs.' " Not only did he join the USGS; he enrolled at Stanford to work on a Ph.D.

He soon began trying to predict earthquakes. Near Oroville, in the northern Sierra foothills, in August 1975, there was a quake of magnitude 5.5. This was noteworthy; it was a region of very low earthquake activity, which meant that subsequent tremors would surely have a relation to the main shock, rather than stem from other causes. Moreover, Oroville was the location of a major dam and reservoir of the California water system, and there was good reason to believe that the weight of the water could trigger quakes of moderate size. That weight would put stress on a fault, while seepages of water could lubricate it. Allan tried to forecast the occurrence of aftershocks, using the dilatancy theory with its prediction that seismic-wave velocities would change as a precursor.

In the process, he convinced himself and a number of other people that this approach was wrong. "I did some further analysis and showed it was entirely bogus," he declares. "The data didn't stand up under close scrutiny." He wasn't the only one in Menlo Park who felt that way: "Jerry

Eaton thought the velocity changes were a lot of crap. He'd looked at a lot of records; he knew the velocities didn't change that much. And when I finished up the Oroville stuff, I was ready to do something new."

The basis for something new would be Parkfield. Allan had been introduced to its earthquakes as a grad student, while taking a course on strong ground motion. The instructor, David Boore, gave Allan some seismic records and invited him to work them up into a term paper. They were from the 1966 Parkfield tremor, and he wound up choosing that quake as the subject of his Ph.D. dissertation. Working with Boore, he showed that a few miles northwest of the town, the San Andreas took a slight bend in its course, curving by five degrees. That would suffice to isolate the Parkfield section of the fault from the creeping section that lay directly to the northwest, and which was slipping without producing tremors. The 1966 foreshock, magnitude 5.1, had fallen close to that bend, beneath Middle Mountain. It quickly triggered the main shock, magnitude 5.6, which ruptured the fault from Middle Mountain to the southeast, for some twenty miles.

While he was learning these things, his colleagues at the USGS were trying to predict earthquakes, in a desultory fashion. But they were up against a catch-22: to learn to predict quakes, they first would have to succeed in predicting one. With the fall of the dilatancy theory, the best approach would be to go back to square one and get more data. The best data would come from instruments near a stretch of fault that was likely to give way reasonably soon. But to choose such a stretch would be the same as predicting a tremor. Thus, while there was an occasional discussion of developing such a focused effort, no consensus emerged as to how to go about it. To the contrary, the official line was that the USGS would proceed by trying to learn more from the statewide seismograph network put in place by Jerry Eaton, the former director at Menlo Park. That net would have been quite useful if the dilatancy approach had worked; it would have shown the seismic-wave velocity changes all over California. But with the collapse of dilatancy, continued reliance upon that network was open to challenge.

Things came to a head in 1978. "One day we had a meeting," Allan recalls. "Jack Healy and Jerry Eaton, along with the other people who ran the place, were reviewing plans for the coming year. And being a really obnoxious person, I told them very bluntly what I thought of it. I completely blew my cool, and called them names. Jack Healy said, 'If you're so smart, why don't you think of something better to do!' I was being young and arrogant; he was being old and defensive. I stomped out of the room, went back to my office, and did just that. Naturally, I picked the place I knew quite a bit about."

He proposed to run a focused experiment at Parkfield. There was danger in this; the USGS was not lavishly funded, and such a proposal amounted to putting all its eggs in one basket. The Big One could, for example, strike at under-instrumented Los Angeles while the seismological jewels of the Survey sat in the middle of nowhere, waiting for a quake that didn't happen. That would make congressmen and journalists unhappy.

Nevertheless, Lindh persisted. As he describes his efforts, "I'm a better talker than a writer, and I spent a lot of time jawboning people in the halls. A lot of my energy went into talking to people for three or four years. It was plain old science as usual. You write papers, you give seminars, you talk to friends. Some of them believe you, some don't; but they keep hearing the same story. After a while some of them even decide they want to get involved."

The idea was to set up a physics lab around the fault, measuring as many things as possible, and carefully note the phenomena leading up to the next quake. Early on, he received $250,000 in funding from Barry Raleigh, a director at the USGS. "He was interested in new ideas," Allan says. "He was running the Survey a little less autocratically than usual, which was a good thing, because I was just an energetic young person in the right place at the right time." Allan also showed unusual skill in the use of his funds. Ordinarily he would have tried to set up his own operation, with a staff and a set of equipment directly funded under his budget.

But that wasn't what he did. He used his grant as seed money, to cajole other people into working at Parkfield. "Money can keep people's attention," was his attitude. "They'll talk to you longer and more seriously if you have some." A number of other researchers were arranging to install instruments along various faults. Allan's strategy was to offer extra money if the investigators agreed to run their experiments at Parkfield—not as a bribe, but as additional funding to support those scientists' research. In this fashion he secured the use of equipment that was both expensive and of unique design.

At the Carnegie Institution, near Washington, D.C., physicists Selwyn Sacks and D. W. Evertson had invented an instrument called a *dilatometer*. It amounted to a long, oil-filled cylinder and was lowered down a hole to a depth of hundreds of feet, then cemented in place. Small stresses within the surrounding rock would press on the oil, squeezing detectable amounts into a small measuring chamber with a change in strain as small as ten parts per trillion. Sacks wanted to use dilatometers near San Juan Bautista, northeast of Monterey, where the creeping section of the San Andreas gives way to a locked and potentially dangerous section. Allan kicked in with a little extra funding and persuaded him to do it at Parkfield.

The same persuasiveness would be needed to install the instruments on what was, after all, privately owned land. "Our budget is tight," Allan notes. "For instance, we have almost a thousand seismometers in California, all on private property. We don't pay anyone a dime. If they charged us even a nominal sum per seismometer, it would bankrupt us. We rely on goodwill. What people ask from us is copies of our papers, or of the figures we're drafting." The local people are quite interested in the fault that runs so close to their homes, and are usually glad to help. Still, for the dilatometers, holes had to be drilled to considerable depths, using big drilling rigs that disrupted the land for weeks or months. However, it proved possible to reach an understanding with the landowners once Allan's colleagues had located appropriate sites.

What sort of rocks would be suitable? "Good rocks! That's a rock that when you drill a hole in it, the hole stays open. When you drill close to the San Andreas, the rocks are very seriously degraded. Lots of times you might drill a hole, pull out the stem—and the hole collapses. The good rocks will at least stay open long enough to let you put an instrument in. We lower a bucket of cement and dump it in a puddle at the bottom. Then, very rapidly, we bring the bucket back out and run the dilatometer down—a $20,000 instrument on a cable, with one-quarter-inch clearance. It settles in very gently, and the cement is a special type that expands a bit when it hardens." The fit then is especially tight, and the hole is easily filled with concrete to the top. Five hundred or a thousand feet below, the oil-filled cylinder then is in place. And twice a day, as the moon and sun ride overhead, our planet flexes in earth tides. They resemble the tides of the ocean but are far weaker, for they take place in solid rock. Yet the dilatometers readily respond, accurately reading a change in strain of ten parts in a billion from these tides. These earth tides represent a predictable and known effect that produces a well-defined measurement, to show that the instruments are working properly.

Another prize catch has been a laser system for distance measurements, developed by Larry Slater of the University of Colorado. These measurements determine the length of geodetic baselines, with an accuracy of a millimeter in ten kilometers. Such baselines, crossing the fault, serve to detect small motions within the earth, with these motions producing the measured changes. The accuracy is ten times that of surveyors' instruments—and there is no need for tripods and telescopes, or for a survey crew. Instead, all that is needed is to aim the laser at a reflector several miles away, with the path from laser to reflector serving as a baseline. Precise electronics measure the time it takes the light to fly to the reflector and bounce back to the laser; and this time, multiplied by the speed of light, gives the distance.

For an accuracy of a millimeter in distance, this measurement of time must be accurate to three-trillionths of a second. At this level of accuracy, even changes in the weather can produce a noticeable error. The air along the baseline slows the light slightly, for the speed of light is slower in air than in a vacuum. This slowing varies with weather conditions such as temperature and pressure. But the amount of slowing differs measurably at different wavelengths or colors of light. Thus the laser system uses two lasers, one producing red light, the other blue. The system makes separate measurements of the time-of-flight for the light of each color. The difference between these measurements determines the change in the speed of light produced by the atmosphere. This change then serves as an adjustment, giving the true distance to the reflector and hence the baseline length.

Allan has high regard for the data. "Do not be seduced by signals that have lots of changes in them," he warns. "In the seventies, some people argued against the program of making geodetic measurements. The signals never changed, they said—how could you use them to predict earthquakes? We want things that change a lot, so we can find precursors! And they made such arguments with straight faces. But all they could hope for was weak statistical correlations of the changes with the occurrence of earthquakes. They didn't have a physical theory to explain or predict, or even a solid observational base."

These weak statistical correlations were what Karen McNally had studied as a grad student at Berkeley. She had looked at the sequences of foreshocks that had preceded magnitude-5 quakes on a section of the San Andreas, hoping they would form a pattern that would repeat itself often enough to be useful as a precursor. She had put together elaborate mathematical procedures for studying the data and seeking to show that it had statistical significance, that there were correlations that were occurring too often to be due to chance, and that therefore might reflect an unknown cause-and-effect relationship. But the correlations she found proved to be weak, the patterns appearing in hit-or-miss fashion. The same had been true of statistical studies of animal behavior as a precursor.

"We graduated from that in the late seventies. For instance, this geodetic data, which measures strain, is real data. And you have to build on real signals, not on changes that turn out to be random. We're measuring the earth. We are getting solid information on how the earthquake machine really works."

The laser measures slip occurring at the surface, within the faulted area. From the data the seismologists can also determine the slip occurring at depths of many kilometers within the fault itself. If a certain movement takes place far below, it will change the pattern of surface measurements along survey lines. A somewhat more complex procedure, called *inverse theory,* turns this around. From the measurements made in the surveys, it becomes possible to calculate the patterns of slippage at depth.

For instance, suppose some slip is occurring at the surface, but at a rate much less than 3.4 centimeters per year, the long-term average rate that Kerry Sieh found for the motion along the San Andreas. One way to explain this is to propose that a large patch of rock at the fault is locked in place. The patch runs for a certain number of miles, running over a certain range of depths within the earth. How might a seismologist test such an idea?

The answer is to start by trying to guess these lengths and depths, then calculating the pattern of slip that would result at the surface. This calculation will differ from the actual one, because of the guesswork. But by comparing the calculated amounts of slip to the observed ones, it becomes possible to make corrections to those initial guesses, coming up with a new and more accurate set of estimates for those lengths and depths of the locked patch. One then repeats the procedure, calculating the surface slip that such a patch would produce, comparing it anew with the true measurements, and making a further set of corrections. Eventually this process gives a description of that patch whose calculated slip matches closely to what has been observed. At that point it is possible to say that we think we know where the fault has locked. This procedure is the inverse theory.

At the USGS, down the hall from Bakun and Lindh, their colleague Paul Segall carries out these calculations. When I visited him he pulled out a chart marked in patterns of gray, brown, and red. It showed the slippage on the San Andreas near Parkfield to a depth of twenty kilometers. Any slippage could delay the expected quake, by releasing strain along the fault. At great depths, the chart showed a uniform red: the fault was giving way and sliding or yielding easily, rather than building up stress. But at lesser depths, the chart showed a nearly uniform dark color.

"We find that the slip at the depths of the earthquakes, three to ten kilometers, does not match the surface slip," he declared. "It's not moving at all. The slip is restricted to a thin surface layer, one to two kilometers thick. Below fifteen kilometers, the fault shifts at thirty-three millimeters per year. Between these depths it's completely locked. The fault is not moving at all." From three to fifteen kilometers down, then, the fault is steadily building up strain, rather than yielding. This means it can be expected to break suddenly, and on schedule, in the next Parkfield quake, which may strike in 1988.

The USGS has devised a sequence of three-day alerts, rated from level "e" to level "a." Level e represents the normal situation, where there is only one chance in ten thousand that the 1966 event will repeat within the next three days. Depending on the instrument readings, the warnings ratchet upward: a chance of 1 to 3 percent at level d, 3 to 11 percent at level c, 11 to 37 percent for b, and more than 37 percent for level a. This highest level also demands that the USGS send a warning to the California Office of Emergency Services. Also, this system gives a clear measure of success in the game of prediction. A successful quake prediction would mean that the 1966 tremor recurs during an alert of level a, or, at worst, of level b. If that happens, says Allan, "we will be overjoyed." By contrast, if it strikes during a level-d phase or even at level e, that would take everyone by surprise, like at Coyote Lake, Coalinga, Morgan Hill, and the other disappointments of recent years.

The system has already faced its first test. Early in June 1986, a seismometer array picked up a swarm of microquakes beneath Middle Mountain—the epicenter of the 1934 and 1966 temblors. That triggered a level-d alert on June 8. Then, on June 13, another buttress of the system, the creepmeter array, triggered a second level-d alert. It had detected one and one-quarter millimeters of creep within a single week. Two days later, each of two instrumented water wells also were heard from, and their responses raised the alert level to c. As Bakun puts it, "There wasn't anyone who didn't think it might be the start of a repeat of the '66 earthquake."

Allan has a different recollection: "It was fun, because all the powers that be were at a conference in Japan at the time. So we didn't have to deal with the bureaucrats—I mean my friends and my boss. That helps a lot. It makes a difference in the deliberations when the people are nearby who sign the paychecks and write the performance evaluations. Everybody then tries hard not to be wrong; you don't have the relaxed, free flow of ideas. I've teased the bigwigs by saying that the next time we have a level-d alert, we'll give them all tickets to Japan and send them a telegram each day."

He and his colleagues had to deal with a number of questions: What is the data? Do we believe it, through cross-checking? Can we fit it together in a single model or theory?

On June 16 they decided that the observations could be explained if a patch of fault three kilometers long and extending from one to four kilometers in depth had slipped by a centimeter. "That's when we really sort of got excited," Allan continues. "It all fit the idea of a slipping patch that, by good fortune, was right below the two-color laser." Over the next few days the alert wound down as no new signals appeared, and things soon were back to normal. The events of those days had amounted to a dry run, a practice session that had given them experience for use in the real thing.

How will that quake develop? What will it be like? The key point to watch will be Middle Mountain, which is known as the *preparation zone,* the place where earthquakes begin. Close by, notes Allan, small tremors have been striking every thirty-nine to forty-one months since 1971, almost like a clock ticking. The last one, magnitude 3, took place in May 1985 and was the largest beneath Middle Mountain since 1982. The next one is due in August 1988. It could be the trigger that sets off the main shock.

When a quake hits along a short stretch of fault, it relieves some of the built-up stress, but passes the stress onward, further loading other fault sections. Thus, such a small tremor could give the final push to the tightly strained rocks in the preparation zone. That would swiftly bring a larger quake, a repetition of the 1934 and 1966 foreshocks, magnitude 5.1.

In the Parkfield area, as well as through the rest of California, the USGS's seismometers are connected by phone lines to a computer system. Its microchips would quickly pick out the newest and strongest shakings, calculate their magnitude and location, and display the data on terminals. From their similarity to foreshocks of previous decades, they could be recognized immediately as a warning that the next mainshock is perhaps seventeen minutes away. After all, in both 1934 and 1966, this was the time elapsing between foreshock and mainshock. "That would send us to looking at the dilatometers and creepmeters," says Bakun. The warning time would be sufficient to alert seismologists, who could watch their instruments as the main fault broke.

Seventeen minutes after the foreshock, the main quake, of magnitude 5.6, would begin. A small patch of locked fault, several kilometers deep, would slip under the strain from that recent foreshock. The slipping would spread and widen as rocks on either side of the San Andreas, strained beyond what they could bear, slid past each other while violently grinding against one another from the pressure deep in the earth. A wave of sliding would race outward from the hypo-center, the starting point of the quake, traveling along the fault at speeds of several kilometers per second. Whatever this wave's destination, tightly locked rocks would loosen and give way, adding their energy to the building quake.

"The fault has a definite personality," writes Donalee Thomason, the rancher's wife who has spent most of her life in Parkfield. "One moment it is a capricious child; the next, a sinister adult gleefully exploding into action and hoping to scare the wits out of the fainthearted." The shocks from this latest quake indeed will strike with considerable force at the surface.

Chimneys and water tanks may topple; some walls will crack; a pipeline or two may rupture. Fortunately the damage will not be great, for Parkfield is a remote spot, and the area's sturdy wood-frame homes stand up well even to severe shaking. Then the seismic waves will spread around the world. In Europe, Japan, and elsewhere, sensitive instruments will record the tremor as these waves cross continents and oceans, weakening with distance yet remaining readily discernible.

The break in the fault will begin in the northwest and spread quickly to the southeast, in the direction of Los Angeles. Farther up the San Andreas is the creeping section, which is under little strain; the quake will stop there. If the 1988 event is a typical one, it will rupture the fault only over a length of about twenty miles. At that distance from Middle Mountain is another rise, Gold Hill. Here the San Andreas sidesteps like a freeway detour, being offset from a straight line by about a mile. This jog in its trace ordinarily is enough to bring the fault-line break to a halt, ending the quake. But it is just possible that the 1988 affair will be no ordinary tremor.

"A problem that has bothered seismologists is how earthquakes stop," declares Bakun. There appear to be barriers along the fault line that confine them, like the San Andreas's five-degree bend to the northwest of Parkfield, and its jog at Gold Hill. But a big quake can gather momentum and break through the barriers. "It gets up a head of steam," is how he describes it. The result could then come uncomfortably close to a repeat of the great quake of 1857, which Bakun describes as "perhaps a Parkfield earthquake that got away."

When Kerry Sieh was near Cholame, in the country of the Grants and Twisselmans, he found some three-and-a-half-meter offsets along the fault. Evidently the San Andreas had slipped by that amount in 1857. With the fault building up strain at about 3.4 centimeters per year, it would have been ready to break anew by about 1960. It stood the shock of 1966, but the next time it might fail. If so, the next Parkfield quake might shake the stretch of fault southeast of the Cholame Valley, extending the tremor, whose total magnitude might approach 7.

Farther to the southeast is the Carrizo Plain. Here Kerry's offsets were nine and ten meters, with a repeat time of nearly three hundred years. Thus there is every reason to believe this stretch will hold fast. The Carrizo should stand as a strongly locked stretch for the foreseeable future. Yet it is only by good fortune that this is so. For if the last Carrizo quake had been three hundred years ago, like the last one near the Salton Sea, or if the Carrizo offsets had proven to be three and a half rather than nine and a half meters, there would be good cause to fear that the next Parkfield quake might run away. It might rupture the entire southern part of the San Andreas, from the creeping section to the Mexican border, in a catastrophe vaster than either 1857 or 1906. The Carrizo may be a dry, desolate, little-noticed part of California, but it may well be the margin that saves Los Angeles and keeps the next Parkfield tremor from escalating into the Big One.

Such is the advancing state of our understanding. As Allan Lindh puts it, "All sciences go from black magic to alchemy to chemistry. You do go through that intermediate stage, where laws of cause and effect begin to be formulated but things haven't come together yet. Earthquake prediction went through the black-magic stage in the 1950s; Charles Richter was quoted as saying that only charlatans talked about predicting quakes. By the mid-1970s we were well into our alchemy phase, and dilatancy was our phlogiston." (Phlogiston was an eighteenth-century theory that sought to explain combustion and the smelting of metals at a time when oxygen had not been discovered.) "Parkfield indicates the end of the alchemical approaches."

What will come next? He has already prepared a map showing the likelihood of major quakes along key stretches of California's faults. Significantly, he sees the Mojave section of the San Andreas as most dangerous. It extends to the north of Los Angeles, and he declares it has a 40-percent chance of giving way during the next thirty years, producing a tremor of magnitude 7.5 to 8. He bases this on Kerry's findings concerning ancient earthquakes along that stretch. "He recited the dates from memory," Allan recalls. "I wrote them on a scrap of paper, then did the analysis to get the probabilities for the Mojave." Two investigators at New York's Lamont-Doherty Observatory had done much the same thing, but they prepared a lengthy paper full of tables and statistical diagrams. Allan did it differently: "I drew a map. Then the newspapers got hold of it and it started to get publicity, and people said I'd better cover my ass. So I wrote up a few pages, stuck them in front of the map, and put it out as an Open-File Report," that is, a paper published within the U.S. Geological Survey.

Following the next Parkfield quake, then, he hopes the effort will expand to set up similar instrument arrays along the southern margin of the Mojave Desert. "After Parkfield, that's our next best shot," he asserts. "It would be much larger. Even a magnitude-7 would do some damage in the L.A. area. A 7.5 would do major damage." Thus, if the Big One is to be predicted, it may happen through a major effort that builds on the Parkfield experience, and that leads to the issuance of a level-a alert a day or two in advance. The unlikely village of Parkfield is important. It may be the testing ground where the prospect of serious earthquake prediction will emerge and take shape.

Yet across its sere brown hills, there is no sign that anything unusual is happening there. Quietly, steadily, the fault does its work, its strains and minor shakings recorded in small, remote electronic arrays set into the ground. A dirt road through a barley field leads to the site of a barn that stood for two generations. A three-foot length of white drill pipe protrudes from a well, capped with plastic. Close by is a post with a radio transmitter, to send the well's data to Menlo Park. And a few miles away on a hillside there is a small green enclosure on a concrete base, set in scrubby pine, locoweed, and purple owl's-eye. It looks like a carryall for a pickup truck, but encloses a downhole seismometer.

Indeed, the only daily event that is at all dramatic or noteworthy occurs when the local instrument-tender takes measurements with the two-color laser. He is Duane Hamann, the teacher in Parkfield's elementary school, one of the few one-room schoolhouses left in the state. When he operates the laser, he swivels it around like a naval deck gun. He points the laser at each of sixteen reflectors set upon faraway hillsides and fields, sighting carefully as he watches for the strong reflection that shows his beams have found their target.

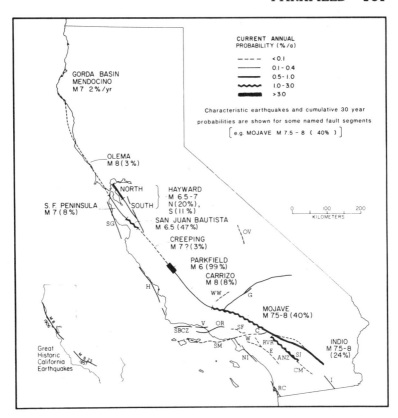

Map by Allan Lindh showing the probabilities of quakes along sections of the San Andreas. For example, in the Mojave sector there is a 40-percent chance of a quake of magnitude 7.5 to 8 on the Richter scale during the next thirty years. (Courtesy U.S. Geological Survey)

At night the red and blue laser colors form a well-focused shaft of light. The reflectors, sheltered within wooden huts, are not simple mirrors, but eight-inch astronomical telescopes. If you drive up to Hamann's laser station, which resembles a shed on a hilltop, and aim your headlights at a hillside more than a mile away, the reflector can be easily seen. With the lasers, the effect is penetrating. Standing at an angle away from their rays, you would see no more than a tiny spot of light on the distant hill. But if you shifted your location by a few feet, your head would enter the reflected light—and you would see a dazzling iridescence of red and blue. As Allan Lindh remarks, "It's like the finger of God."

7

THE SHAKING
NEXT TIME

It will be the worst disaster in the United States since the Civil War.

That is the conclusion of the Federal Emergency Management Agency (FEMA), assessing the likely consequences of the coming cataclysmic earthquake in southern California. It will be worse than the Japanese attack on Pearl Harbor, which cost the lives of more than 2,400 fighting Americans. It will be worse than the disaster at Galveston in 1900, the most deadly natural catastrophe to date, when a hurricane and storm surge from the Gulf of Mexico breached the city's seawall and killed some six thousand people. The Big One may kill as few as three thousand if it occurs in the early hours of the morning, when most people are at home and asleep. But it could kill as many as fourteen thousand, if it took place during the late afternoon. Property damage is likely to come to $17 billion or more. By contrast, the most damaging disaster to date was Hurricane Agnes, which struck in 1972, causing $3.5 billion worth of damage. As many as 55,000 Californians may require hospitalization for injuries—and there is no guarantee the hospitals will be there to treat them. Moreover, these estimates are based in part on actual experience. For the Los Angeles area has had a foretaste of the shaking to come, in the San Fernando earthquake of 1971.

Los Angeles in that year differed only slightly from the city that exists today, one of the main differences being that real-estate prices have gone up fivefold since then, with mortgage rates increasing as well. The downtown skyline lacked a few of its current skyscrapers, but otherwise it looked much the same. Except for a few short, recently built stretches, the region's freeway system also was in place.

The quake came just after six o'clock on the morning of February 9. On a nearly deserted extent of Interstate 5, close to the town of Sylmar, by the northern mountains, two middle-aged telephone installers were in a pickup truck. They were about to drive beneath a towering connector road, part of an interchange with the Foothill Freeway. The two men never made it. At that moment the nearby San Gabriel Fault lurched and shook, toppling that overcrossing, which broke into pieces like a row of tumbled dominoes and fell onto the lanes below. One of its concrete slabs fell directly onto the pickup, crushing it flat and killing the men instantly.

Not far away was the Van Norman Dam, holding back a hundred-foot wall of water. Its custodian, whose home was immediately adjacent, awoke at the first shakings. "It was thumpin' and jumpin' and knocked everything out of our kitchen," he later stated. He ran outside for a look at the dam's concrete face, 1,100 feet long—and saw that it was collapsing into the reservoir. Along the crest, the concrete roadway had split and slid directly into the water. With the face of this dam gone, all that was left was its earthfill core, an embankment of mere rock and dirt. A stiff wind raised choppy waves, and huge blocks of earth began to break away. The water was only a few feet below the crest of what was left of the dam—and five hundred feet above the thickly settled valley floor below. The city's Department of Water and Power hurriedly sent sandbag crews to the scene, and began releasing water into a flood-control channel, lowering the reservoir level and easing the strain.

A few miles away, on the other side of Sylmar, stood the Veterans Administration Hospital. Two of its principal buildings dated to 1926, but had been judged so sturdy that they had been renovated rather than replaced. Only six months earlier they had passed an engineering inspection. These two structures, three and four stories in height, now held most of the hospital's heart patients, as well as others who were being treated for tuberculosis and emphysema. At the first jolt, both buildings collapsed into piles of rubble. A chaplain on his way to visit patients was thrown to the ground by the force of the quake. "When I looked up," he told a news reporter, "in that same instant, the building fell. Just like that, it fell. In a single second. Thank God I wasn't in it."

Forty-one people lost their lives. One nurse was found dead, her skull crushed against a concrete pillar. Another victim had died with his hands shielding his face. Rescuers soon were at work amid the ruins with crowbars, cutting torches, jackhammers, and a bulldozer. Ronald Reagan, then governor of California, also came to the scene and climbed atop the broken heap. He heard someone call out below him, told firemen to dig at that spot, and watched as they pulled out an injured survivor. The rescuers continued cutting through the thick concrete slabs that had recently been the hospital's floors and roofs.

A mile to the east, the Olive View Hospital also gave way. Three people died as the buildings buckled; they continued to stand, but at noticeable angles from the vertical. The main structures, including an 850-bed unit of six stories, had been completed only the previous fall. "They took a direct hit," stated a county engineer as he declared it a total loss. "The force of the impact was so great, light standards were lying in the street." A surgical resident, sleeping on the top floor, told what it had been like: "I heard this tremendous noise— really tremendous. I later found that it was the dayroom wing. The whole thing toppled over. The noise lasted at least thirty seconds, perhaps a minute. Things were falling; my room was a shambles. Then I could hear people screaming."

For people in their homes it was much the same. Paul and Betty More, starting the day in their farm-style house in Sylmar, were expecting to leave for their morning commute into downtown Los Angeles. He was barefoot and wearing a bathrobe as he sat in the kitchen drinking coffee, while she proceeded to fry an egg. Then the quake hit. Betty fell to the floor, screaming as broken glasses and dishes tumbled about her. The interior of the house was reduced to a trash heap. The same was true in many other homes. Water damage also was common, as swimming pools sloshed into houses, while windows shattered and broken glass flew about. "We looked up our insurance," said one woman, "and we're covered for the glass breakage."

That tremor, known as the San Fernando quake, took fifty-eight lives and caused half a billion dollars in damage. It could have easily been worse; if the dam had failed, its waters might have killed hundreds more. Yet it was in no way to be compared with the quakes of 1857 and 1906. It measured only 6.5 on the Richter scale, whereas those earlier temblors had been close to 8.3, making them sixty times more severe. As a result, the damage was restricted to an area a few miles across. Fifteen miles away, in Altadena, Charles Richter was at home when it struck. He ran through his shaking house to the seismograph in his living room, but found that the instrument was being rattled too strongly to give a useful reading. Richter's damage was limited to books and bric-a-brac being knocked off shelves. The few miles between Altadena and San Fernando had been enough to save him from more serious harm.

Yet if the San Fernando quake counted as no more than

moderate, what will the coming Los Angeles quake be like? To begin with, it is important to remember that the major San Andreas tremor is not the most destructive earthquake that is likely to hit southern California, given time. That distinction belongs to an eventual quake of magnitude 7.5 along the Newport-Inglewood fault. This fault begins at the edge of the Pacific close to the wealthy Orange County community of Newport Beach, then runs along the coast to the northwest through Long Beach, continuing across the center of Los Angeles to Inglewood, north of the airport.

A major Newport-Inglewood quake would be at least one and a half times as deadly as the largest anticipated San Andreas tremor. If it strikes at 2:30 A.M., according to the FEMA estimates, it will leave 4,000 dead and 18,000 needing hospitalization, compared with 3,000 and 12,000 for the San Andreas shaker. If it hits in late afternoon, the dead are likely to number 23,000 and the badly injured 91,000, compared with 14,000 and 55,000 for the San Andreas case. Moreover, such a Newport-Inglewood disaster would produce a total property loss of $69 billion, an estimate that could easily be on the low side. This is four times as much damage as would result from the San Andreas. The reason is that the Newport-Inglewood cuts directly through the most populous and heavily built-up areas of the city, in contrast to the San Andreas, which runs through mountain and desert country to the north and east.

This downtown fault is not considered in imminent danger of breaking, so far as we know. According to FEMA, there is only one chance in a thousand that such a Newport-Inglewood quake will strike in any given year, compared with a twenty- to fifty-fold larger probability for a great San Andreas tremor. The Newport-Inglewood fault broke in 1933, producing the damaging Long Beach quake that killed 115 people. It is widely believed that this relieved the strain—though the northern portion of that fault, running through the main part of Los Angeles northwest of Long Beach, took no part in that earthquake and thus may yet be dangerous.

And there are other potentially worrisome faults: the Whittier, ten miles east of downtown; the Raymond, which runs through Pasadena; the Santa Monica, near that city; and the Cucamonga, near San Bernardino. Any of these might bring a repeat of the 1971 San Fernando quake, having a magnitude around 6.5 and producing a great deal of damage by striking within a built-up area. Indeed, the 1987 shaking, killing three and causing $358 million in damage, was of magnitude 5.9 and broke a fault quite close to the Whittier.

Nevertheless, life will bear only so many worries. The California Department of Conservation, which has sponsored the most detailed development of scenarios for the coming major quake, has kept its eye on the Big One: the San Andreas tremor. A 1982 report, *Earthquake Planning Scenario for a Magnitude 8.3 Earthquake on the San Andreas Fault in Southern California,* sets forth a lengthy list of freeways, electric power stations, natural-gas pipelines, and other facilities where the damage is likely to be greatest. Complete with a set of detailed maps, this report—Special Publication 60—also shows where homes and other buildings are likely to be in greatest danger.*

This scenario is based on facts of the 1857 earthquake, which wasted much of its force in the open country well to the northwest of Los Angeles, in areas such as the Carrizo Plain. The Big One actually is likely to strike closer to home, breaking the long-dormant section of fault that lies southeast of San Bernardino. That will make the quake's damage even worse than in this scenario, particularly in those eastern areas. But even without that extra fillip, districts up to fifty miles from the San Andreas will face widespread damage. In these areas the soil is loose or the water table is high, increasing the likelihood of ground failure. They include much of Long Beach and adjacent parts of Orange County

---

*The report is available for eight dollars from the Division of Mines and Geology, 1416 Ninth Street (Room 1341), Sacramento, CA 95814.

from Cypress to Costa Mesa; districts within the floodplain of the Santa Ana River northeastward toward San Bernardino; an area extending approximately from Pomona to Monterey Park and southwest to Pico Rivera; much of the southern San Fernando Valley; and the low-lying region around Oxnard, well to the west, extending northeastward along the Santa Clara River past Fillmore.

In these areas, much waterlogged earth will turn into a porridge resembling quicksand. The driving pressures of the seismic shocks will force the groundwater between the points of contact of the fine grains of sand or alluvium that make up the local soil, so that the water will act as a lubricant. As a result, many homes and buildings will tilt or settle into the earth for some distance, or even topple over. In this way the 1964 Niigata, Japan, tremor destroyed several ten-story apartment buildings that had met the best seismic standards. They fell over onto their sides as the ground liquefied; people walked to safety by making their way along the walls. Such soils may also produce sandblows, miniature volcanoes of mud and water that erupt when the quake compresses the local groundwater, forcing it to burst through the surface to a height of several feet.

The 1985 Mexico City quake showed further danger in such soils. The downtown area had been built on the former bed of Lake Texcoco. Its sediments, soft and waterlogged, now shook like a bowl of Jell-O, responding particularly strongly to undulations that swayed once every two seconds or so. This two-second period of the motion proved particularly deadly, for many of the medium-rise buildings had a natural tendency to move with just such a frequency. These buildings thus were like metronomes, with the seismic shakings giving them additional pushes that accelerated the structures' oscillations. With the lakebed amplifying the two-second seismic waves, and with the buildings amplifying their motion in response, close to one-fourth of all structures of nine to fifteen stories sustained severe damage or collapsed.

As in Mexico City, such loose soil will increase the shaking, typically to intensity VII or more on the Modified Mercalli scale. Well-built, ordinary buildings of substantial construction will sustain breaks in walls, ceilings, and chimneys, with the damage being considerably worse in poorly built or badly designed structures. Windows will shatter; furniture and belongings will fall over or fly about, and the interiors of most homes will be left in shambles. Nor will such forms of destruction limit themselves to low-lying or alluvial areas. Within a broad swath of territory, from San Bernardino through Pasadena and on through the populous San Fernando Valley, homeowners will face entirely similar miseries.

What about earthquake insurance? Say you have a home that would sell for $150,000. Deducting the price of the land, the replacement value of the house might be $120,-000. Earthquake insurance would cover you for the cost of damages, minus a deductible of up to 10 percent of this replacement value, or, in this case, $12,000. The cost of the likely damage would probably be less than that. The Big One will probably trash your interior and break the wallboard; perhaps a ceiling or two will fall in. But it is not likely to produce major structural damage. The prospect is that the foundation and frames will stand, rather than give way. For this reason, Kerry Sieh, who lives only seven miles from the San Andreas, carries no earthquake insurance. He anticipates his losses to fall within the deductible.

Still, Kerry lives on solid ground near Lake Arrowhead in the mountains. For those living in the low-lying and alluvial areas, the situation may be much riskier. Earl Schwartz, an engineering manager for the city of Los Angeles, puts it bluntly: "If you're in an area of major ground failure, there's not going to be much left of your house." He adds that "if you don't have any equity in your home and something happens to it, it's basically going to be the bank's problem, because you can just walk away from it." But if you do have such equity and want to protect it, then Councilman Al Bernson puts it differently: "I would say that such people should have all the insurance they can get."

Standard homeowner policies do not protect against the risk of earthquake. But California law requires that home insurance firms offer earthquake coverage as an option, for an additional cost. It cannot be refused to a homeowner merely because he lives in an area of high groundwater, and the rates can be quite reasonable. For instance, my town of Fountain Valley stands on low ground within the floodplain of the Santa Ana River. It is listed as a prime area where ground failure may occur, and I worry about a big sandblow breaking through my foundation, which could leave the house a total loss. Allstate has offered to sell me earthquake insurance at an annual premium of $167. That would provide $111,000 in coverage, subject to a deductible of $11,100, and it could make the difference between seeing my home destroyed and seeing it rebuilt.

What about downtown Los Angeles? Here the greatest danger will be from older buildings, many of unreinforced masonry. A 1973 survey, commissioned in the wake of the San Fernando quake, found that some four hundred such structures might collapse, littering the streets with 44,000 tons of debris. "We have some buildings in the older section of town," remarks Schwartz, "Main Street, Spring Street, Broadway. You can see pretty clearly that they were built in 1910 or 1920. They generally were not designed to resist earthquakes." "I would assume that most of the unreinforced brick and masonry buildings in the vicinity would come down," adds Councilman Bernson. "We could probably anticipate a large number of deaths and injuries, mostly from collapsing buildings. The potential of the force generated in an 8.3 is tremendous." Indeed, a 1986 survey for the National Science Foundation projects that 1,660 structures will be damaged beyond repair, with another 1,320 demanding major repair. The only solace is that when the Newport-Inglewood breaks, it will be much worse: 33,000 structures destroyed beyond repair and 22,000 needing major work, out of a total stock of 700,000 buildings within the city.

Next to their homes, the most prized possessions of Angelenos are their cars. While damage to homes will rank as the most serious threat to personal safety, the general collapse of the freeway system will stand as the next major problem. Even in the best of times, the freeways are vulnerable. A motorist changing a tire on the shoulder may bring traffic to a near-halt, as rubberneckers slow for a look. A truck accident can snarl traffic for hours across much of the city.

The 1971 San Fernando quake gave an indication of the severe problems that southern California can expect. Portions of four freeways—the San Diego, Golden State, Antelope Valley, and Foothill—were shut down within the northeast San Fernando Valley. Moreover, with the threat of the Van Norman dam failure, a number of major surface streets also were closed. Traffic jams resulted, on an unprecedented scale. As one highway patrol inspector declared, "I think we can picture traffic backed up from five to ten miles in certain areas. I think we can picture delays anywhere from one to five hours."

At 11:00 A.M. the day after that quake, when traffic in the westbound lanes on the Ventura Freeway was light and moving at full speed, the four eastbound lanes were at a standstill. The delays were running up to three hours, and the highway patrol reported that the freeway was "hopelessly jammed" as far west as Woodland Hills, halfway down the valley. Even where it could move, the traffic was sluggish to glacial. Many motorists, frustrated from long waits on the freeway, made their way to off-ramps—only to find that the surface streets were just as jammed. Other drivers, impatient with lengthy delays at the traffic lights on such streets, went up the on-ramps to find that the freeway was no improvement.

Such conditions are what the *Earthquake Planning Scenario* describes as "route[s] open subject to delays and detours." That crisis will beset virtually every freeway north of a line from Riverside westward, across the northern border of Orange County, through Whittier, Downey, and on to the airport. Within this region, which amounts to the northern half of the greater Los Angeles metropolitan area, the state of the Ventura Freeway in 1971 will be the norm. In addition, along some fifty stretches of road, physical damage will simply cut the route altogether for as long as it takes the work crews to clear the wreckage.

This list of fifty includes all the principal roadways linking Los Angeles to northern California, as well as to the rest of the nation. Highway 101, the main coastal route, will be blocked by fallen overpasses. For the Pacific Coast Highway, the main alternative, closures will result from heavy landslides in the Malibu area, where the road cuts along the base of the steep Santa Monica Mountains.

To the north, the Golden State Freeway, Interstate 5, will sustain a number of heavy blows. The rupture of the fault will produce severe damage where that freeway crosses the San Andreas, near Gorman, while landslides in Grapevine Canyon will add to the blockage. Parts of the Golden State rest on landfill, masses of rock, and earth dumped into place and graded to form a foundation. Some of these fills will slump, producing still more damage. Much the same thing will take place along parts of Interstates 10 and 15, the principal highways leading to Phoenix and Las Vegas. In particular, the tall interchange linking these freeways near San Bernardino is likely to collapse. Numerous other interchanges will also fall, including those joining the Golden State to the Hollywood and Antelope Valley freeways. Another main east-west route, Highway 60, also will be blocked, and its bridge over the Santa Ana River, north of Riverside, will probably fail.

For some days, then, essentially the only way out of the Los Angeles area will be the San Diego Freeway to the south. There will be clear driving to and from that city, but if the earthquake breaks the San Andreas well to the southeast, then San Diego may be isolated as well. Interstate 8, its main link to Arizona, may be cut amid falling overpasses and physical rupture from the sliding of the fault.

Railroads, too, will be blocked. The coastal route of the Southern Pacific, entering the Los Angeles area from the north by way of Ventura, will be closed for at least five days by landslides and the collapse of highway overpasses. To the northeast, the main lines of the Santa Fe, Union Pacific, and Southern Pacific all run through Cajon Canyon northwest of San Bernardino, alongside Interstate 15. Landslides and the slumping of rockfill foundations will put all these routes out of service. Moreover, it is hard to gain access into this canyon with heavy equipment, so the railroads will not be functioning for a month or more. And to the south, at Colton, the collapse of the Interstate 10 and 15 interchange will close the route of the Southern Pacific running alongside Interstate 10 and eastward to Arizona. That same railroad line will also break near Palmdale, where it crosses the San Andreas, completing the near-isolation of the Los Angeles area from the rest of the country.

Meanwhile, millions of people will be trying to call friends and relatives. If they get a dial tone at all, most of them will hear the announcement, "We're sorry, all lines are temporarily busy." Even emergency services will have a great deal of trouble getting through. Police, fire, and medical agencies can often gain priority in use of the phone network, but in large parts of greater Los Angeles, three days after the main quake, such services will still be able to put through only one-quarter of their attempted calls. Still, that will be an improvement over the first day, when fewer than one call in ten may go through.

Water systems will present overwhelming problems. These may take the most deadly form imaginable: the failure of a major dam. If you drive north on Interstate 5 to Castaic, just before the highway goes into the mountains, an immense flat-topped embankment of earth, a mile long and more than three hundred feet high, can be seen on the right, near Lake Hughes Road. This is Castaic Dam. It holds 350,-000 acre-feet of water, enough to flood fifty square miles to a depth of ten feet. No one expects it to give way; but no one expected the Van Norman dam to come close to collapsing in the much less severe 1971 tremor. If Castaic Dam goes, it could kill some fifteen thousand people while leaving 143,000 homeless.

Now proceed farther along I-5, up the long grade and into the Angeles National Forest. A few miles beyond the top of that grade, shadowed by tall Cobblestone Mountain, there is a spectacular view of Pyramid Lake. White wakes of power boats cross its waters as green pines cling to the steep slopes that rim its shore. And to the far left, barely visible, is the flat-topped Pyramid Dam, nearly four hundred feet tall. If it should go, the lake will send its 179,000 acre-feet of water surging downstream across the lowlands east of Ventura, destroying the town of Oxnard. The loss could equal that from a failure of Castaic. And still farther back in the hills, well off the main highway, is the attractive Bouquet Canyon, the site of another major dam. If it gives way, the toll will be 8,300 potential deaths, with 121,000 left homeless.

Even if the dams manage to hold up, that certainly will not be true for the aqueducts. Their importance is emphasized by the work of William Mulholland, for whom the elegant Mulholland Drive near Beverly Hills is named. He was city water commissioner in the early decades of this century. He found a route that would bring water from hundreds of miles away to the city, and built the first major aqueduct. GLORIOUS MOUNTAIN RIVER NOW FLOWS TO LOS ANGELES' GATES read the front page of the *Los Angeles Times* when that pathbreaking work was completed in 1913, adding that the water promised "good health, great wealth, long life and plenteous prosperity." Indeed, without such aqueducts, the local water supply would support a southern California population only a fraction of its present size.

The threat of earthquakes to such systems was dramatized

in a quake east of San Diego in 1940, magnitude 7.1. In the town of Imperial, the municipal water tanks collapsed. Water and irrigation facilities were knocked out; large irrigation canals were breached, and the water poured through the breaks, cutting holes twenty feet wide, to spill uselessly into the desert. This brought extensive crop losses along with a serious water shortage. Drinking water had to be sent into the area by railroad tank cars, but at least the rails were still in service.

Today, three large aqueducts supply the Los Angeles region. One follows Mulholland's original route from the Sierras. It crosses the San Andreas in a tunnel some 250 feet below the surface, making repairs difficult as well as highly hazardous in the midst of the continuing threat of aftershocks. Another, running from northern California, has a branch that closely parallels the fault for over sixty miles, crossing it at two locations near Palmdale. A second branch also crosses this fault, and these great channels will all rupture and go out of service for three to six months. If the earthquake strikes farther to the southeast, then a third aqueduct, which runs from near Riverside eastward to the Colorado River, will also be out. For months, then, greater Los Angeles will be cut off from its main water supplies.

"There's no question that if the Big One comes, there will be severe damage," declares Richard Clemmer, the engineer in charge of planning at the Metropolitan Water District. He remembers 1977, when two dry years in succession brought water rationing to the Bay Area. "The worst spot was Marin County, where they had a shortfall of 60 percent. Marin is a fairly well-to-do area. I was up in Sacramento and a very well-dressed woman was in the lobby of my hotel, and we got to chatting. She said, 'I live in Marin County, and we have a car pool. I gather all my neighbors' clothes and drive over from Marin to Sacramento, where they have plenty of water. I wash the clothes in the laundromat and then I drive back. Next week it's one of my neighbors' turn.' She had a big station wagon; she could afford the gas. Gas was almost easier to get than water.

"It was really tough times in Marin. You didn't plant your favorite petunias, or if you did, they died. These people were really hurting. They literally put plugs in the bottom of their showers, scooped the water out with buckets, and carried it out to try to keep their trees alive. They were flushing the toilet only once a day. People said, 'If it's brown, flush it down; if it's yellow, let it mellow.' Restaurants stopped serving glasses of water. During the drought, the city of Los Angeles passed an ordinance that if you used too much water, they'd give you a warning. If you kept it up, they'd put a constriction in your water meter, to physically restrict your flow. You'd turn on your shower and just get a little dribble. Turn on your sink and it would take forever to fill up your cooking pot."

The city will be left with more than just the water in its pipes. A considerable amount is on hand in local reservoirs and storage facilities, and with strict rationing, at least a hundred days' supply should survive the shaking. Emergency pipelines will also help; such a line took up a lane of the Golden Gate Bridge in 1977, easing the thirst of Marin County. Still, at least in the days immediately following the disaster, the cutting of the aqueducts will be the lesser of the problems facing many areas. Water mains will break at some 1,200 different places.

Moreover, half of the sewage treatment and pumping plants will be out. These offer only a limited ability to store untreated waste water, which will thus have to be discharged with nothing more than emergency chlorination to reduce the health hazard. The disruption of the sewers will cause part of their normal flow to proceed through the streets as well as in open channels. In other places, raw sewage will overflow through manholes and run through the common road gutters. Many household sewer connections will break or become plugged, leaving people unable to use the toilets even if these have water and are otherwise undamaged. With raw sewage spilling out of its normal conduits, it will pollute many waterways, as well as rivers, harbors, and beaches. Anyone who ventures near such open bodies of water, then, will face a considerable health hazard.

There will also be a loss of half the available electrical power. To some degree this will result from damage to a few of the generating plants, which either rely on hydropower from the aqueduct system or are located along the coast near Long Beach. These may be damaged by ground failure in areas where the soil can liquefy. But the largest such losses will stem from the destruction of power lines where they cross the San Andreas in mountainous country. These lines bring huge blocks of electrical energy from major generating plants in Arizona, Utah, and other places in the West. Their steel towers will collapse from the quake, as well as from landslides on steep canyon slopes.

Even the 1971 quake brought major damage to this system. It struck at the Pacific Intertie, an 846-mile array of power lines capable of shunting huge flows of current along the West Coast, linking Los Angeles to such projects as the Bonneville and Grand Coulee dams, as well as to nuclear plants like Rancho Seco near Sacramento. That tremor also shattered equipment at a major substation or power-conversion center near Sylmar, where this electricity was distributed through the municipal power mains. It raised the likelihood of a crippling electric shortage in warm weather, when thousands of people would be using their air conditioners.

The Big One is likely to knock out eight such substations, many of which are as significant as was the one at Sylmar in 1971. It is likely to take a week before even one major transmission line can be restored to service. Even the surviving power plants within the region may not be able to do much, because there will be a great deal of damage to local power lines. Underground mains will pull apart in areas of ground failure; power poles along streets will break where buildings collapse against them. With all this, the best that anyone may hope for is that power will be off completely for two or three days. When it is restored, it will be on an emergency basis—which means that the available electricity will be spread among different districts through rotation, with each area in turn having its power cut off for an hour, several times a day.

Across vast areas, then, people will be left without lights. There will be no radio or television, except for battery-operated portables. There will be cold as well as dark; most home-heating systems rely on electricity, particularly in forced-air furnaces. Refrigerators will be out, as well as kitchen ranges. Gasoline will be available sporadically or not at all, since it takes electricity to operate the pumps, and long lines may form at the stations that are open even temporarily. The loss of power, along with the disruption of the phone system, will make it unlikely that people will be able to draw emergency cash from the banks' automated tellers. Supermarkets also will close due to the power outages, leaving people with few outlets for getting fresh food.

And on top of all these hardships, there will be major fire hazards. Natural-gas lines will break in some 1,500 places. Gas pipelines also will break where they cross the San Andreas or pass through areas of ground failure. The same will be true for oil pipelines—and Los Angeles is among the nation's leading petroleum centers, with widespread facilities for production, refining, storage, and transport. The resulting threat of fire will be particularly sharp if the Big One strikes during a time of warm, dry weather. Many oil and gasoline lines pass through the areas near Long Beach and the port of San Pedro, where the threat of breakage is particularly high because of the prospect of soil liquefaction. Leaking fuels might spill into the harbor and ignite, burning even as they float on the water. That happened in the 1964 Alaskan earthquake.

Many modern pipelines are equipped with automatic shutoff valves, which would close off the line if they sensed the drop in pressure that would accompany a break. But the pipelines in the port area are old, and few are so equipped. If a major fire were to break out in that district, it could get out of hand with help from the wind. Most Los Angeles–area roofs are of wood-shingle construction and can catch fire easily. The combination of ground failure near Long Beach, rupture of old oil lines, widespread breaks in water mains, and a hot and windy day thus could combine to produce a far greater catastrophe. It was fire, after all, rather than earth-quake, that caused most of the destruction in the catas-trophes in San Francisco in 1906 and Tokyo in 1923.

Even without condemning Los Angeles to the flame, the Big One certainly will earn its reputation as the worst disas-ter in this country since the Civil War. Nearly half the homes and buildings will face damage. Fifty thousand people will be left homeless for extended periods, even if all the dams hold and there is no major fire. One-sixth of the hospitals will be unusable in Los Angeles, with this proportion rising past three-fifths in Riverside County and approaching three-quarters in San Bernardino County. A third of a million people, by contrast, may be injured enough to need first aid, if not more extensive treatment.

The Big One, in short, will overwhelm existing abilities to cope with disaster. There will be not one but a combination of large-scale losses, any of which by itself could cripple the region: breakdown of the freeways, blockage of the rail-roads, overload of the phone system, widespread damage to the sewage system, disruption of the water supply, severe shortages of electric power, and substantial fire hazards from petroleum and natural-gas pipelines. All these together will strain the region's emergency services well beyond the point of breakdown. It will be several days, at least, before the main aftershocks cease to rumble, the freeways are cleared, a semblance of power is restored, and the people who need help can begin to see the assurance that it is at hand.

What can anyone do about it?

The answer is that everyone should expect to camp out in his or her home for at least three days, getting along with supplies on hand.

"Camp out" is the proper term, for if you live in an earthquake zone, you should expect to get along precisely as if you were off in the wilds. For instance, water will be either unavailable or of doubtful purity, and it will be necessary to keep a store on hand. It helps to begin by appreciating that even under the worst circumstances, some water will remain in the household. The hot water heater will be quite important; unless someone has taken a bath in the minutes before the quake hits, there should be thirty to sixty gallons of fresh, drinkable water within it, ready to tap by opening a small faucet at the base. There is water in the pipes of a two-story home; open a faucet on the top floor to equalize the pressure, then drain it from another tap on the ground floor. And toilet tanks—not the bowls—will contain drinkable water, if the tanks are free of algae and the water is clear rather than blue with chemicals.

Breaks in the water mains, together with widespread flows of raw sewage, will raise the risk that city water will be contaminated. Thus, you should look for your main cutoff valve—it is most likely set beneath a small concrete slab alongside the water meter—and learn to shut it off. Beyond this, each person in the household will need up to four quarts per day just for drinking and the preparation of food. For a one-week reserve supply, then, a family of four would need some fourteen gallons, with none left over for bathing or washing. Get a few five-gallon plastic bottles of water, and keep them in the garage where they'll be safe.

Then there is the problem of getting along without electricity. There may be damage to your home's wiring, which could produce a short circuit and start a fire. Find out where the main fuse or circuit breaker is located—close to the electric meter, probably—and go through the exercise of shutting down all your household power, so you'll know how to do it when the Big One hits. Now you can start to plan for life without this power. Buy a couple of flashlights and put them in the cars. Then put a couple of boxes of candles, along with a lantern or two, in the garage along with the bottled water.

Food will be a problem. The insulation in your refrigerator

and freezer will keep things cold and fresh for at least a day and quite probably longer. If items are cool to the touch, they're okay. Finish off the perishables first—milk, meat, eggs—with cereals or packaged foods kept for later. Even though you may keep a fair amount of food on hand in the cupboards, however, much of it will probably be spilled and scattered from the force of the quake. That means you'll need an emergency reserve for at least several days, along with paper plates and cups.

Again, imagine you are preparing for a lengthy camping trip. What foods do you like, and how can you buy and store them so that they'll keep? Choose such items as granola, canned fruits and vegetables, tuna, macaroni and cheese, powdered drinks. Many packaged foods will keep for a long time, and you should store a variety of them. Food can be a big boost to morale, and if your family can continue to enjoy some of its favorite dishes, it will be easier to face the problems and look toward better times.

How can you cook these things? A fireplace is an obvious possibility, but if the flue is damaged, hot gases could set the roof aflame. If there is any damage at all to the chimney, use a hibachi, barbecue, or brazier, and in any case, make sure you have an adequate supply of wood or charcoal on hand. Check that there is good ventilation; burning charcoal gives off carbon monoxide. Portable stoves, which burn Sterno, propane, or white gas, are another solution.

What about sanitation, with sewer mains out of service? Build a latrine the army way, by digging a slit trench in the back yard. It should be two to three feet deep. Keep a shovel on hand, along with a supply of disinfectant or powdered lime. Every time anyone uses the latrine, the waste should be covered with a thin layer of lime. A similar trench can serve for burial of household garbage.

As with the electricity, water supply, or telephone, you will not be able to rely on your natural-gas service. Leaks in the gas pipes could prove to be a serious fire hazard. This means that again you'll need to practice with the shutoff valve, which is located on the gas meter. A wrench will turn this valve to the "off" position, which is horizontal. Then, for warmth, you can rely on longjohns, heavy blankets, and perhaps a tent and a set of sleeping bags. Many homes will be in a condition of little damage, or will be "damaged but habitable"—windows broken, wallboard and stucco cracked, but with little or no harm to the basic structure. Cleaning up the rooms and sleeping in your own beds— albeit under heavier blankets than usual—again will boost everyone's spirits.

Still, there may be cuts or other injuries to care for. Take a trip out to the shopping mall while it's still standing, and buy a good first-aid kit. It will look less like a little blue box and more like a foldout container for fishing tackle, but it could make the difference between a modest inconvenience and a serious infection. And while you're at it, stop by the local Red Cross and pick up a copy of their first-aid handbook. Ask them if they have a thirty-two-page guide that describes what to do before the Big One: *Earthquake Preparedness*, by Libby Lafferty, published by CHES of California, P.O. Box 1026, La Canada, CA 91011; telephone (818) 952-5483. The advice in that booklet, which is far more extensive than what you are now reading, would enable you to cope with anything short of the great San Francisco fire.

All this means that a half-day's worth of shopping—camping gear, charcoal and lime, extra food and water, household tools—can make a real difference. Psychologically, you will face the quake with genuine preparation. This will be quite the opposite of denying its likelihood, or hoping that it will somehow not be too bad.

You can do even more with a visit to the hardware store. "An 8.3 is a tremendous earthquake, really a monster," remarks Los Angeles Councilman Al Bernson, the seismic expert in City Hall. "Anything in your home that isn't secured will come down or tip over—refrigerators, water heaters—and there will be a tremendous potential for injuries." You can secure them using brackets with bolts driven into the wall studs. Or if these studs are in inconvenient locations or can't be found, use plumber's tape, which is a strong steel strip, and secure it in place with Molly bolts, which hold tightly through wallboard or plywood. Protecting the water heater in this way will also secure much of your home's emergency water supply. Put latches on cabinet doors; use bolted flanges for heavy furniture, including dressers and bookcases. On open shelves, guardrails will help keep items from falling off.

A few days' worth of work around the house can protect your belongings from flying about and being destroyed. In fact, if you live in an older home, you can prevent it from sliding off its foundation. Most homes built since 1940 are reasonably well anchored, but houses built earlier often merely sit loosely on their concrete-slab foundations. By installing expansion bolts, you can firmly attach the wood frame to the concrete.

For a great many people, the Big One will be, emphatically, a devastating disaster. Many will panic at the outset, then grow increasingly desperate as their needs mount and help is not at hand. Others will face the threat of fire or flood and will be evacuated, to sleep on cots in refugee centers. There will be tens or even hundreds of thousands of people in serious trouble, with their homes gone or with major injuries that demand hospitalization. Tom Tobin, executive director of California's Seismic Safety Commission, has stated that "if a major earthquake occurred in Los Angeles, two thousand students would die at UCLA alone." That campus is full of lovely old buildings such as the twin-towered Royce Hall, constructed of unreinforced brick and masonry at a time when no one had heard of seismic safety standards.

But the vast majority of Angelenos will face nothing so terrifying. Most people can help themselves greatly with a day's worth of shopping, followed by a handyman's job of bolting down the furniture and appliances. Those who do these things can anticipate that the Big One will be more a substantial inconvenience than a horrifying catastrophe. Such people can take charge of their lives in the days following this earthquake. They will protect their belongings, rather than face the need to repair or replace them at their own expense. These people will maintain a semblance of normal life in the days after the quake. And they will greet the arrival of emergency services and the restoration of utilities not as if they were ropes tossed to a drowning man, but as the reappearance of welcome friends.

8

AFTERSHOCKS

It is rare for any single earthquake, particularly one of moderate size such as magnitude 6, to change the way seismologists approach their subject. There simply have been too many such quakes, pored over by working scientists and their graduate students, for the study of any particular one to offer many surprises. Seismic catalogs list hundreds of well-documented magnitude-6 quakes, each one being much the same as the next. But the Whittier quake of 1987, magnitude 5.9, was different. It showed that the seismic hazard in Los Angeles, even at this late date, still has been underestimated. The risk of quakes is greater than had been believed. The reason is demonstrated by the work of two geologists, Jay Namson and Thom Davis. They have shown that deep beneath the city lies a network of previously unknown active faults, and the Whittier quake has confirmed their danger.

Namson works for Arco Oil and Gas; Davis is a consulting geologist with long experience in the oil industry. For a

212

number of years they have been taking advantage of the fact that that industry's wells yield not just petroleum, but geological data. When roustabouts drill a well, they bring up fragments of rock cut by the drill bit. A geologist, studying these fragments, notes the type of rock and the depth, thus producing a "well log," a record of the formations pierced by the borehole.

Such logs are vital; they may show that the borehole is going down through sandstone or shale, porous sedimentary rock that can trap oil or gas. The recovered samples may indeed be black with oil, showing that it is time to stop drilling and start pumping. Or they may show that the drill has reached granite, basement rock that never holds oil, and which thus demonstrates that this is a dry hole. But beginning in the early 1980s, Namson and Davis began to do more. Working from collections of well logs, rather than from any single one, they undertook to develop maps of the subsurface rock formations, following the dips and folds of particular beds of shale or other types of rock. Arco gladly supported this work, because oil and gas tend to collect within particular types of folds. These subsurface maps, then, might give valuable clues as to where to drill next.

Then in early May of 1983 came the Coalinga earthquake in central California, magnitude 6.5. Very soon it became apparent that a good deal of data was available for this quake. Its location or epicenter was known from the seismograms; it lay beneath a broad, low, and hilly rise called the Coalinga Anticline. The nature of the quake was also known. Arrays of seismographs, sensitive to the direction of the recorded waves, had shown that that quake must have taken place along a *thrust fault,* a sloping ramp of rock deep within the earth. Thus, rather than one rock mass sliding past another, in the fashion of a San Andreas quake, the moving mass had slid up the ramp.

Nevertheless, there was a mystery: where, precisely, was the fault? Seismologists were familiar with quakes of this magnitude, and even much larger ones, that had occurred on thrust faults. But always, before, the faults had reached the surface, breaking the land in a noticeable cut that could readily be studied. It thus was a surprise when the Coalinga quake proved to involve no such visible fault. It was also worrisome; a quake of that size could do a good deal of damage in a city such as Los Angeles, and if its fault was hidden in this way, there would be no warning, no way to assess the hazard. This mystery was what led Caltech's Clarence Allen to say, a year later, "We're not even sure what fault Coalinga occurred on."

Namson and Davis, however, had something new: the well logs from exploratory oil drilling in the Coalinga area. Such logs are generally closely held, treated as if they were classified information, because they contain the records of what an oil company has learned from its drilling. As a result, few working seismologists have access to this data. However, the Coalinga area had been drilled rather extensively and its oil-bearing potential was well understood, which led Namson and Davis to hope that Arco would release data from its well logs for use in searching for the missing fault. They soon won the support of Robert Hirsch, Arco's vice-president for exploratory drilling, who had been a research physicist in his younger years and who readily appreciated what these geologists hoped to do.

What they hoped to do, indeed, was to use the well logs, along with maps of the surface topography, to locate deeply buried thrust faults that ran far below ground level. To appreciate what is involved, think of a thrust fault as a sloping ramp several miles long and as much as ten miles beneath the surface. A massive block of bedrock rests upon this ramp and can move under tectonic forces, producing an earthquake. Shallow layers of rock, lying on top of this block, have bent and folded to form hills, just as carpeting in the living room would do if it was pushed upward by a moving slab of broken foundation. The presence of the hills, along with subsurface maps developed by using well-log data, then show the location of that thrust fault.

These geologists could do even more: they could determine just how active the fault had been, and how long it might be until the next Coalinga quake of similar size. They did this by taking advantage of the fact that layers of rock generally do not lie at uniform depths, like piled-up blankets. Instead they tilt, and reach the surface at various places. Other geologists, mapping the rock formations of California over past decades, have carried out extensive field explorations, chipping off fragments and studying them with care. This work has led not only to detailed descriptions of these formations, but to determinations of their ages, based, for instance, on the fossils they contain. The subsurface maps of Namson and Davis showed specifically how the beds of rock ran downward from the surface to form the great blocks that had broken and slid along the thrust fault. With this, they could say that rock of certain ages had broken in certain patterns, representing a record of the fault's history.

"We compiled all the data into a single model," says Namson. "It explained the origin of the Coalinga Anticline as well as of the Coalinga earthquake." This model was based on the past motions of a block of the Tulare Formation, a pebbly and coarse-grained sandstone containing clay from ancient lakebeds, and whose fossils were distinctly those of land rather than marine animals. From studies of these fossils, as well as from age determinations based on the decay of trace radioactive elements, the lower parts of the Tulare Formation were known to be about 3 million years old. The moving block, from the subsurface maps, proved to have slid a distance of 5.5 kilometers in this time, along the length of the ramplike thrust fault, while pushing upward a distance of 2.5 kilometers.

The rest was easy. Leveling surveys, carried out after the Coalinga earthquake, showed that the local hills had risen some 0.8 meters. That subsurface block, in turn, was rising at an average rate of 0.8 millimeters per year, since it had gone up by 2.5 kilometers in 3 million years. The Coalinga

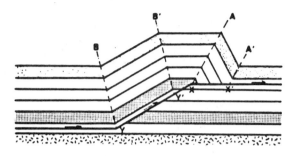

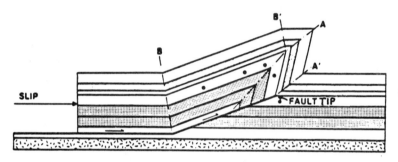

Development of hills through folding of rock formations along a thrust fault. Top, formations move continuously along a ramplike fault. Bottom, formations fold along a "blind fault," which terminates at a fault tip some distance below the surface. (After Namson and Davis)

quake thus had accounted for one thousand years' worth of this average rate. That time interval, a thousand years, then would be the expected time before another Coalinga quake of similar size, magnitude 6.5. Namson and Davis, in short, had mapped and characterized their fault, which was miles underground and completely buried, with the same sort of detail that seismologists were accustomed to seeing in the faults they could study at the surface.

These geologists' colleagues were quick to appreciate the significance of their work. Ross Stein, a seismologist with the USGS, wrote that "apparently folds provide as good an indication of earthquake sources as do faults." Such folds in the earth's surface—hills or basinlike depressions—indeed would point to the existence of deeply buried faults. Sometimes the folds would be eroded, showing little change in elevation at the surface, yet would still leave their marks in the undulations of subsurface formations. "You could practically go around California," Stein added, "and wherever you find an old oil field, you're probably in the vicinity of an active fold. If the folds were not there, the oil would not have been trapped."

Indeed, following the success at Coalinga, it was clear that the next step for Thom Davis would be to use the same techniques to study the buried thrust faults of Los Angeles. Again it was a matter of using well-log data in a judicious way, along with geologic data from observations at the surface. Early on, his attention was drawn to the Elysian Hills, south of Glendale, which had the advantage of being located near his home. He recognized these hills as the sort of folded terrain that was likely to hide a buried thrust fault. He proceeded to map this fault, proposing that it ran westward from a spot north of Whittier, connecting up with a known fault that ran along the seacoast west of Santa Monica. That fault had broken twice in recent years, in the 1973 Point Mugu quake, which struck east of Ventura, magnitude 5.9, and in the 1979 Malibu tremor, magnitude 5.0. Davis then proposed that the Elysian Hills might be uplifted by Coalinga-size quakes. If so, they would strike with an average interval of "about 125 to 225 years," as he wrote in a paper. Here was a clear suggestion that the Whittier area, which includes the Elysian Hills, was at risk from a damaging quake along a thrust fault.

It struck on the morning of October 1, 1987, magnitude 5.9. Although it made national headlines, the death toll was surprisingly low, only three people being killed. One was a man working at the bottom of a deep trench, which caved in and buried him. Another victim fell headfirst from a second-story window onto concrete. The third was a college student, killed when a concrete block dislodged from a parking ramp and fell directly upon her. In contrast to the San Fernando quake of 1971, no major buildings fell down, nor was there extensive damage to freeways. Nevertheless, the total damage came to $358 million, much of it uninsured, with more than a thousand people left homeless. It was a sobering reminder of the city's vulnerability to even a moderate quake—if it should happen within a built-up area.

"I had postulated there was an active fault that no one knew about," Davis said later. He had written his paper on this fault in April 1987; it reached print in July. He had not predicted a date for the quake, but had gotten its location and magnitude nearly right. In addition, this was the first time someone had used fold shapes to assert that there was a hidden fault—and that fault had then produced an earthquake. It was a neat reversal of the sequence at Coalinga, where the quake had come first, then the discovery of its buried fault. As Davis put it, "Traditional methods of evaluating seismic risk don't pick this up. You have earthquake sources you didn't know about."

Still, his work left a question: Why should those buried faults exist, and what risk do they pose? He has not been shy about coming forth with explanations; indeed, they have been a major part of his work. As he sees it, everything hangs on the characteristics of the San Andreas Fault—but not in the way that one might expect.

The San Andreas bends. If it were straight, then all the coastal lands to its west could slide northwestward in a reasonably straightforward way. That is how it is along most of the world's similar faults, which cross the country like enormous incisions. But the San Andreas takes a great bend to the west, along a line a hundred miles north of Los Angeles. It is not clear why that bend should be there; perhaps the fault has had to deviate around the Sierra Nevada, whose thick and mountainous formations would be hard to break.

But because that bend exists, the coastal lands cannot slide along the fault so straightforwardly. They tend to hang up in their motions, piling their rock formations in thick layers that are riven by faults. Much of this piling-up is seen in the Transverse Ranges, which are remarkable among the mountains of the United States. Most ranges in this country run approximately north and south, reflecting the stresses within this continent as it has moved slowly to the westward during the past 200 million years. But the Transverse mountains run east and west. Like a fold in some enormous carpet, they have been pushed up along the southern edge of that great San Andreas bend, where the northwestward movement of Baja California has squeezed the rock formations while that bend has pinned them in place.

The Transverse Ranges, indeed, feature some of the most spectacular and well-known sights in southern California. They begin as the Santa Ynez range near Santa Barbara, where President Reagan has his ranch, then march eastward in pine-covered splendor only a short distance inland from the coast. The Channel Islands in the Pacific, whose serrated cliffs glow in a late-afternoon sun, have also been pushed up from the ocean in this fashion. Northwest of Los Angeles, the Transverse peaks form a broad band of mountains, forty miles across.

Close to the city, this range takes the form of the Santa Susana and Santa Monica mountains, which mark out the San Fernando Valley. The Santa Monicas, which run to the coast at Malibu, fall away in sharp cliffs crowding closely against Pacific Coast Highway, with Mulholland Drive running along the crest. Beverly Hills, too, nestles close to those mountains, as do the movie stars' homes in Coldwater, Laurel, and Benedict canyons; thus the Transverse Ranges enter our popular culture.

There is a modest gap near Burbank; then these mountains begin anew as the San Gabriels, steep and dramatic, rising sharply from the uplands of Pasadena, extending again for many miles inland. To the east the San Gabriels merge into the San Bernardino Mountains, towering and snow-capped, peaking in the 11,500-foot Mount San Gorgonio. Here too are the lake and ski resorts: Big Bear, Lake Arrowhead, Mountain High, Snow Summit, Crestline, Idyllwild. Finally, near Palm Springs—over two hundred miles east of Santa Barbara—the Transverse Ranges peter out into the low-lying Little San Bernardinos and the Indio Hills, and lose themselves within the vastness of the desert.

All these mountains have been thrust up through compression, from the pressure of Baja California pushing against the unyielding bend in the San Andreas. All have risen as great rocky blocks shifting along thrust faults. Along the base of the mountains, these faults frequently reach the surface, where their activity can be studied. In this fashion, Caltech's Clarence Allen has found that portions of the San Gabriels still are vigorously rising, along faults that have been active in the relatively recent past. The San Fernando earthquake of 1971 took place in this same fashion, along a fault that also reaches to the surface; and that quake uplifted the local mountains by as much as seven feet.

All this was known and appreciated for a number of years before Davis began his work. His contribution has been to show that the thrust faults, rather than merely running along the base of the mountains, extend in a hidden network beneath the entire city. Indeed, these faults are the reason the city exists. If those faults were not there, the site of Los Angeles would lie beneath the Pacific Ocean.

As he has reconstructed the area's history, 3 million years ago the city's location was a bay, a shallow arm of the sea. It reached from Santa Ana in Orange County northward past Pasadena, where the early San Gabriel Mountains already existed but were much lower. Throughout this extensive region there were occasional islands, while the coastal shores showed hills and slopes, but little in the way of steep mountains running to the sea. Had there been Spanish explorers in those days, they might have regarded Los Angeles as we view Monterey Bay today; but the low-lying islands in this southern bay, green and covered with trees, very likely would have made the views even more attractive than at Monterey.

This situation did not last, however. Baja California, pressing up from the south, raised the land beneath this bay just as it pushed up the San Gabriels and the rest of the Transverse Ranges. Great rocky blocks moved along the buried thrust faults, and the site of Los Angeles slowly rose above sea level. As these blocks shifted, they produced earthquakes. The result is that, rather than such quakes causing the city to tumble into the Pacific, they have been the means whereby it has emerged.

Today, because of this, you may stand atop the hills of the Palos Verdes Peninsula, the southwesternmost part of Los Angeles, and if the smog is clear you may look across the city to the crest of the San Gabriels. That distance today is sixty-two miles. But Davis, in his reconstruction of the region's geological history, has carried out an analysis that is equivalent to laying a string along the intervening distance, across each fold and ridge and hill, then stretching this string to full length, thus measuring the extent of the ancient bay that rose from the sea. This distance, he finds, is eighty-four miles. Three million years ago, as a result, the distance from what is now Palos Verdes to the San Gabriels was twenty-two miles greater. As a result, Los Angeles has been compressing, being squeezed from south to north, at a rate of twenty-two miles in 3 million years, or 1.2 centimeters per year. This is what drives earthquakes such as the one at Whittier.

That is a fairly considerable rate. It is over five times faster than the rate at Coalinga, and some one-third the average rate of movement along the San Andreas itself. It also is some sixteen times faster than the rate along the Newport-Inglewood fault, as determined by several independent surveys; the Newport-Inglewood cuts directly across Los Angeles and is viewed as capable of producing a quake of magnitude 7.5, with a repeat time of about a thousand years. This compression of the Los Angeles region is sufficient to give rise to damaging quakes every decade or two. The question then is, how severe can they be?

To answer this, Davis notes that one of the most powerful California quakes on record—the 1952 Tehachapi earthquake, magnitude 7.7—very likely was due to movement along a thrust fault. That quake is usually regarded as having occurred on the White Wolf fault, an offshoot of the Garlock fault that marks the northern edge of the Mojave Desert. But the White Wolf is a rather minor rupture, unlikely to sustain so major a tremor. Also, Davis notes, "the amount of surface movement was very small, which is unsettling." By contrast, Bear Mountain in the Tehachapis, the tallest one nearby, went up an additional three feet as a result of that quake. To Davis, all this means that the White Wolf activity was secondary, with the main part of the tremor occurring as a thrust event. And Bear Mountain is only about a hundred miles from Los Angeles. This would mean that in the region of this city, thrust quakes as large as 7.7 can occur, which would be quite shattering if one were to strike the downtown.

Nor was this 1952 quake a mere fluke. Davis also points to the 1927 Point Arguello tremor, magnitude 7.3. "That one's been reworked," he declares. That is, its seismic data have been reevaluated in recent research. "It's definitely a thrust event." It took place at the western end of the Transverse Ranges, and thus also stands as part of the overall picture of Los Angeles–area seismicity. Indeed, as Davis sees it, "you have the great San Andreas earthquakes of 1906 and 1857. Everything else of consequence, except the 1933 Long Beach event, which was on the Newport-Inglewood, took place on a thrust fault."

All of this means that Los Angeles appears to face a third class of dangerous earthquakes. The looming prospect of a great San Andreas quake still remains as the dominant threat; it still counts as the Big One, and represents the first and most dangerous class. The second class involves rare but powerful quakes along the known faults that run through downtown, particularly the Newport-Inglewood. Though such a quake could do even more damage than a San Andreas tremor, its repeat time is sufficiently long—a thousand years—to be much less worrisome.

But now Davis's work raises the likelihood of a new class of quakes, from motion along the deeply buried thrust faults that run beneath the city. The worst of these could well exceed magnitude 7, with the risk being considerably higher than that of the Newport-Inglewood. This third class thus offers an intermediate level of hazard, less than that of the San Andreas, but nevertheless rather more than had previously been anticipated, based on what was known about the downtown faults. It means that regardless of what happens along the San Andreas, a repetition of the 1971 San Fernando quake, in a different part of the city, stands high on the list of future prospects. And even though such a quake will fall short of being the Big One, still it will be bad enough. No one who experienced that 1971 quake would care to do so again; yet it appears to be inevitable.

Moreover, the work of Davis is no more than a small part of an upsurge in seismological work that has flourished during the past fifteen years. This work, pursued in many areas outside California, has given an increasingly clear picture of the nationwide earthquake hazards. It has become increasingly clear that regions thought to be safe, cities and states that have been earthquake-free, actually face a substantial hazard and have been living on borrowed time. The Pacific Northwest is a prime example; its hazard has become apparent only within the past couple of years. This risk, in turn, arises from recent discoveries concerning a long-vanished region of the Pacific seafloor known as the Farallon Plate.

The Spanish word *farallon* means "a small rocky island in the sea." It gives a name to the Farallon Islands, some thirty miles off San Francisco. They are pinnacles of granite rising sharply from the continental shelf, the gently sloping seafloor close to the coast. These islets are set amid a solitude of crashing waves and crying seabirds. Their steep cliffs discourage adventurers from coming ashore, leaving them nearly as remote as if they were in mid-ocean. But they have given their names to, and stand as monuments to, this vanished section of ocean floor that once was among the largest of our world's continuous features. When Magellan struggled from Cape Horn to Guam, a voyage of thirteen thousand miles and ninety-eight days that reduced his crew to eating rats and shoe-leather, his ships were tracing what, 140 million years ago, had been the southern boundary of this Farallon Plate.

During this time, virtually the whole of this plate has been slowly thrust under the western edge of the Americas, sinking in time to depths of hundreds of miles. There, some of its rocky material has melted in the heat, slowly rising toward the surface to erupt as volcanoes. For many eons this plate pushed its way beneath what is now the West Coast, its materials softening and rising to form the Sierras and even the Rockies, far inland. At one time there were twenty-three volcanoes in Colorado, all fed by material from the underthrusting Farallon Plate, depositing a total of fourteen thousand cubic miles of new rock. What is more, that plate has left its mark along the entire length of the Americas. There are extensive mountain ranges in Alaska and western Canada; that is the work of this plate, for those mountains formed like the ones in Colorado. The Andes today stand as a major and continuous wall; that too is a legacy of this immense slab of seafloor. The formation of central America, as a rocky bridge of land linking the continents, is another legacy, for it too has formed from eruptions of material derived from this deep-thrusting slab.

A remnant of this ancestral plate exists today as the Cocos Plate, off the coast of Mexico and Central America. It is advancing from the Pacific beneath those lands, where its molten rock has thrust up such volcanoes as Popocatepetl and Ixtacíhuatl. It also produces frequent and devastating earthquakes: Managua, Nicaragua, in 1972, which killed 6,000 people; Guatemala in 1976, 22,700 dead; Mexico City in 1985, 10,000 killed. And there was also the major quake of 1978, for which Karen McNally was on the scene in Oaxaca. That too was the work of this Cocos Plate, a fragment of the ancient Farallon.

And another fragment is still in existence as well. It is called the Juan de Fuca Plate, and lies directly off the coast of the Pacific Northwest. The San Andreas Fault forms part of this plate's southern boundary, running out to sea from Cape Mendocino in northern California. This plate too has raised its full share of volcanoes, and it is no coincidence that the southernmost of them, California's Mount Lassen, lies almost directly east of Cape Mendocino. Then, continuing northward, one finds such peaks as Mount Shasta, Mount Rainier—and Mount St. Helens. All have been fed with magma that melted at great depths from the underthrusting Juan de Fuca Plate, and all have been active in recent times. For this plate continues to move, building up strain as friction holds part of it back. It is advancing in the direction of Seattle, Tacoma, and Vancouver. In time these cities will experience an earthquake as severe as any in Central America.

How can we know such things? How has it been possible to determine the motions of these plates today, let alone to say what they were over the past hundred million years and more? The answer lies in the action of the earth's magnetic field. When old plate moves, it opens up a gap along one edge. Magma wells up along this line, and it contains small iron particles resembling compass needles. These align with the earth's magnetism and point north. Then, as the magma freezes, the iron is trapped in place, in a permanent orientation. The newly forming rock, along the edge of the plate, thus lies in long windrows with a characteristic magnetism.

It is part of the story of plate tectonics that studies of this magnetism, within a variety of rocks, disclosed the surprising fact that the earth's magnetic field has not always

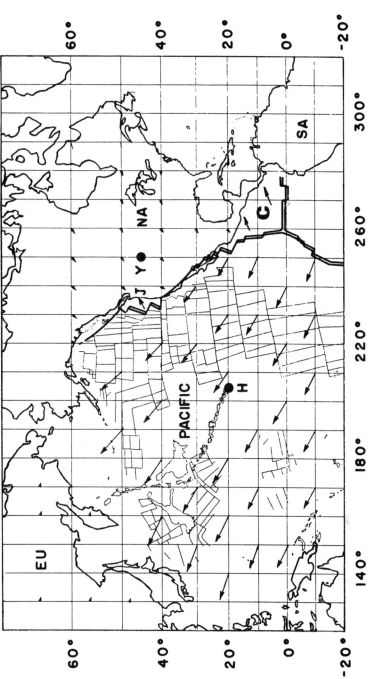

Motions of tectonic plates; arrows indicate speed and direction. H and Y are fixed points, currently at the locations of Hawaii and Yellowstone. EU is the Eurasian plate; NA the North American; SA the South American; C the Cocos Plate; J the Juan de Fuca Plate, off the Pacific Northwest. (After Engebretsen, et al., courtesy U.S. Geological Survey)

pointed north. It has shown reversals; there have been eras when it pointed south, leaving a trace in old rock that is readily detected with a magnetometer. Furthermore, these magnetized stones—basalts, for the most part—contain small quantities of radioactive elements that have decayed over millions of years. As with carbon 14, then, it has been possible to determine the rocks' ages, and thus to show how the earth's magnetic field has reversed in time. A continuous sequence of ages amid a rock collection, youngest to oldest, can be matched with a similar sequence of magnetic variations.

That has made it easy to determine the ages of rocks of the seafloor. As new plate forms from the upwelling magma, it acts like tape in a cassette recorder, which picks up a varying magnetism when it passes the recording head. The "tape" is the moving plate of seafloor; the "recording head" is the earth's magnetic field, which lines up the iron particles in the magma. The reversals of this field show up on the seafloor as long stripes of rock, all of nearly the same age, all lying next to one another, and each stripe showing a characteristic magnetism indicative of its age. All of this means that to show the age of seafloor rocks, it is not necessary to recover samples with dredges and drills, which would be costly and tedious. Instead, it has merely been necessary to tow a sensitive magnetometer across the ocean. The record of the rock magnetism thus indicates its age.

The magnetometer shows that rock of a certain age exists at a particular location. The place where it formed is known; it is the edge of the plate, marked by a line of volcanoes to show that here is where the magma wells up. Knowing the distance to that edge from the particular location, as well as the age, it is then possible to say that the rock in this place has moved through this distance in that time. The speed of the plate's movement, as well as its direction, then are known. That is how we know that the Cocos Plate is moving toward Central America, producing its volcanoes and earthquakes. That is how it has been possible to learn of the Farallon Plate, from studies of Pacific seafloor rock up to 140 million years old. And in the same fashion it has been possible to learn of the danger from the Juan de Fuca Plate off Seattle.

Quite recently, even more compelling evidence has come forth to show that the plates move in certain directions and at certain speeds. This has involved not geology but radio astronomy. It has become possible for two distant radio telescopes to observe the same quasars, intensely energetic starlike objects whose distances march outward to the edges of the universe. Quasars emit radio waves, which arrive at slightly different times at different observatories, because these waves travel over different distances to reach the radio telescopes. Using atomic clocks of exquisite precision, these arrival times can be compared with sufficient accuracy to determine the distance between these telescopes to within a few millimeters. It is like applying on a scale of continents the laser-ranging technique that precisely measures slip along the San Andreas Fault near Parkfield.

By repeating those measurements in successive years, it has very recently become possible to tell how the plates are moving. Hawaii, for instance, which rides the Pacific Plate, is on a course to the northwest at 8.3 centimeters per year, in the direction of Japan. The whole of North America is also moving westward, but more slowly; the distance from the United States to Europe is increasing at about 1.7 centimeters per year. Significantly, these rates and directions are very nearly the same as those found by using magnetic measurements of the seafloor.

These radio-telescope results came out during the spring of 1987. At nearly the same time, several geologists were coming forward with specific warnings about the hazard from the Juan de Fuca. From magnetic measurements, this plate is known to be moving onshore at about four centimeters per year. No major quake has occurred in the past two centuries, since the coming of the first settlers; thus there is a minimum of eight meters of strain in the rocks, ready for release in a great quake. Two USGS geologists, Tom Heaton and Stephen Hartzell, made detailed comparisons of the local geology with that of other seismically active areas. They concluded that from this comparison, the coastal Northwest closely resembles the coasts of Chile, Japan, and Colombia, all of which have experienced great quakes in this century. Writing in *Science,* these scientists declared that the eastern edge of the Juan de Fuca Plate represents a seismic gap, a length of fault where a quake is expected or overdue. This gap runs from Cape Mendocino to the north of Vancouver Island, a distance of 750 miles. To relieve the seismic strain in this gap, they declared, "a sequence of several great earthquakes (magnitude 8) or a giant earthquake (magnitude 9) would be necessary."

Another geologist, Brian Atwater, has added to this warning. Like Kerry Sieh, he has taken the view that information on the earthquake hazards of the region is to be found within the sediments deposited over the past several thousand years. He has worked in marshy inlets and estuaries—and has found six occasions in the last seven thousand years when the tidelands dropped suddenly by several feet into the sea, drowning the plant life and forming layers of peat. Between these layers are beds of mud, which built up in the shallows that resulted from these drops. This mud covered the peat, piled up to the surface of the water, and allowed plants to grow anew. Such alternating beds, showing plant remains—the peat—interlayered with mud, exist in similar estuaries of Chile and Alaska. Great quakes strike those coasts and cause the land to drop suddenly by a few feet, in just the manner that would form such deposits. Atwater concludes that where he has been working, along the coast of Washington State, these layerings were formed from similar quakes. There have thus been six great earthquakes in those seven thousand years, near Seattle.

No one has yet found a date for the most recent one, but

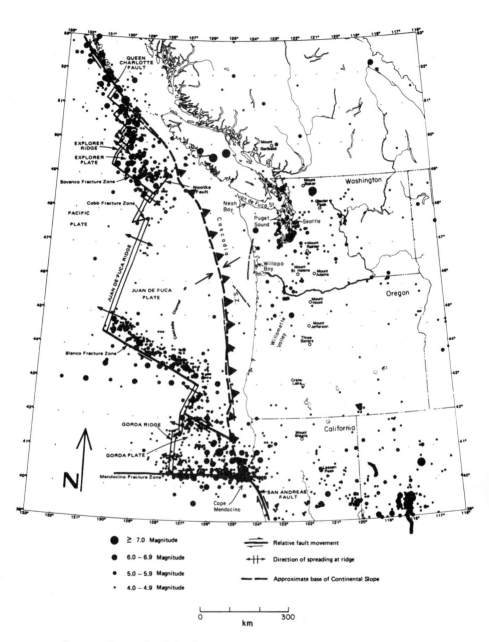

Seismic hazards of the Pacific Northwest. (After Heaton and Hartzell, courtesy U.S. Geological Survey)

when the next one comes, it may bring its own peculiar horror: a seismic sea wave. Coastal earthquakes often raise such waves, which can sweep inland and cause vast destruction. Moreover, adjacent to Vancouver Island, the coastline is indented with numerous fjords. The combination of a quake, a great wave, and a fjord could perhaps bring a repetition of what could have been an immense tragedy in 1958, in southern Alaska.

Lituya Bay indents that coast deeply, a natural harbor where a thousand ships could anchor with ease. A spit or sandbar, thickly wooded with pines and northern aspens, extends across its mouth like a breakwater. Low hills and rolling coastland ride inland for several miles, strewn with gemlike blue lakes, carpeted with dense green forest. At the bay's head rise mountains, their rocky and snow-strewn flanks rising steeply into the overhanging clouds. A low, green island lies amid the bay. So favorable is this island, so lush the land, that if Alaska were populous, the island might stand as a northern Manhattan, with the bay as an Alaskan version of San Francisco.

On the evening of July 9, 1958, the local fault known as the Fairweather, which resembles the San Andreas, broke and shifted by twenty-four feet. At the head of the bay a mountainside broke loose in a vast avalanche as 90 million tons of rock split off, plunging into the deep water of an adjacent fjord. Between two headlands at the side of the fjord there appeared an explosion of spray, amid which were large blocks of ice, all surging higher than the headlands themselves.

From beneath the spray there emerged a wave of unbelievable height. It stretched from one side of the bay to the other and quickly swept over both headlands, flicking away millions of trees, instantly denuding the forested mountainsides. To the left the wave reached a height of 1,720 feet, tall enough to inundate totally the Sears Tower in Chicago, or the World Trade Center in New York. If Lituya Bay had been the location of a city, it would have been washed away at a stroke.

The prospect of great Pacific Northwest quakes, then, stands alongside what may well be a melancholy sequence of California earthquakes, which are likely to follow the major San Andreas tremor in southern California. Across the decades there will be others. The Newport-Inglewood will rupture, or some other downtown fault, and again Los Angeles will be crippled. Also, the northern faults will give way: the Hayward and Calaveras in the Bay Area, then the San Andreas itself once again, where it passes close to San Francisco. There will be another great shaking of the city, as well as other destructive temblors elsewhere in the state, for that is the nature of California. With each shock, the West Coast will be imprinted more and more emphatically in the public mind as the place where such disasters are unavoidable.

It is not, however, the only place. Americans must understand that major quakes can strike any region of the country. They are not limited to California or the West. To the contrary, tremors elsewhere can be stronger than those of the West Coast; they can be damaging over larger areas, and can be comparatively more destructive when striking at eastern cities that are entirely unprepared. The only solace is that major quakes occur less frequently outside California. In the long run this may be slight solace, for the total damage of these eastern quakes may exceed the losses from their West Coast counterparts.

Indeed, by far the heaviest and most severe earthquakes known to have occurred in North America took place not along the San Andreas, but in the heart of the Mississippi Valley. So strong were these quakes that an *aftershock* of one of them was very nearly as powerful as the 1906 San Francisco shaking. These tremors took place during the winter of 1811–12. That was far too early for them to leave an impression in the modern public mind. But it is sufficiently recent that it has been possible to reconstruct them from

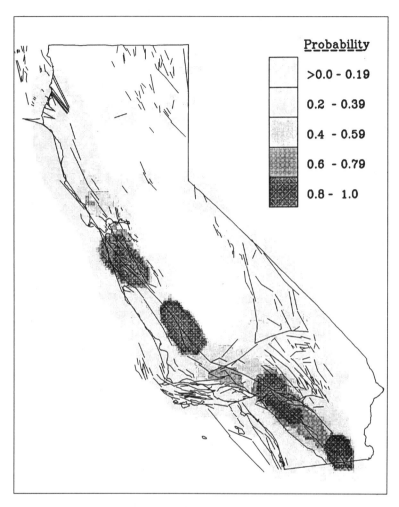

Map by Steve Wesnousky, showing probabilities of damage from earthquakes during the next fifty years. (Courtesy California Institute of Technology)

contemporary accounts in their full horror, and to set them forth as a warning. For when they recur—as they will—these quakes may devastate much of the central United States.

They struck not far from the Mississippi, about midway between St. Louis and Memphis. The riverbanks were almost entirely unsettled in 1811. In places where it had recently changed its course, the river bottom was thick with solidly braced willows and cottonwoods. Towns were sparse; one of the few in the area was the Missouri village of New Madrid. The people there pronounce the name New MAD-rid, just as nearby Cairo, Illinois, is pronounced KAY-ro. New Madrid was the place where the earthquakes took place.

The first of them struck with great force early in the morning of December 16, and was followed by a number of severe aftershocks. A New Orleans man, William L. Pierce, was close to the epicenter at that moment, on a voyage by flatboat from Pittsburgh. He described his experiences in a lengthy letter to the New York *Evening Post*, which the newspaper printed on February 11, 1812:

> Precisely at 2 o'clock on Monday morning, the 16th instant, we were all alarmed by the violent and convulsive agitation of the boats. The idea of an earthquake then suggested itself to my mind, and this idea was confirmed by a second shock, and two others in immediate succession. These continued for the space of eight minutes. . . . A few yards from the spot where we lay, the body of a large oak was snapped in two. . . .
>
> During the first four shocks, tremendous and uninterrupted explosions, resembling a discharge of artillery, were heard from the opposite shore; at the time I imputed them to the falling of the river banks. This fifth shock explained the real cause. Wherever the veins of the earthquake ran, there was a volcanic discharge of combustible matter to a great height, as incessant rumbling was heard below, and the bed of the river was

excessively agitated, whilst the water assumed a turbid and boiling appearance—near our boat a spout of confined air, breaking its way through the waters, burst forth, and with a loud report discharged mud, sticks, &c, from the river's bed, at least thirty feet above the surface. . . . Large trees, which had lain for ages at the bottom of the river, were shot up in thousands of instances, some with their roots uppermost and their tops planted; others were hurled into the air; many again were only loosened, and floated upon the surface. Here the earth, river, &c torn with furious convulsions, opened in huge trenches, whose deep jaws were instantaneously closed; there through a thousand vents sulphureous streams gushed from its very bowels, leaving vast and almost unfathomable caverns. Every where nature itself seemed tottering on the verge of dissolution. . . .

Although these quakes were far from the settled sections of the country, they produced damage over an enormous geographical extent. Buildings of stone and masonry were severely damaged up to 150 miles away. Chimneys fell down in Nashville, Louisville, and Cincinnati; much of the east coast felt a perceptible motion of the ground, while church bells rang from the vibrations, and pendulum clocks stopped, as far off as Savannah, Charleston, Raleigh, Norfolk, and Washington, D.C.

That was only the beginning. On January 23 came another tremor, almost as strong, followed by its own train of aftershocks. And two weeks later, on February 7, came the most violent earthquake in the series. It cracked walls in brick buildings as far away as Savannah, Georgia, throwing down a chimney in Richmond, Virginia. In Washington, D.C., it awakened many people just after 4:00 A.M., and a correspondent at the House of Representatives reported that "it continued upwards of two minutes, unaccompanied by any noise." In the words of a Connecticut newspaper, "The extent of territory which has been shaken, nearly at the same time, is astonishing—reaching on the Atlantic coast from Connecticut to Georgia and from the shores of the ocean inland to the State of Ohio.''

And with that, these great earthquakes soon vanished from general knowledge. Few lives had been lost in the sparsely settled frontier that was then the Mississippi. As the 1857 California quake came before mass communications and so did not leave its mark on the public consciousness, so it was with the 1811–12 earthquakes. A handful of articles appeared in magazines and other publications during the nineteenth century. A particularly lengthy discussion came out of the U.S. Geological Survey on the hundredth anniversary, in 1912, but for the most part, that was it. The Mississippi Valley grew to become the nation's heartland. Still almost no one was aware that that river's waters had been ruffled by anything larger than its steamboats.

The man who took the lead in changing this state of ignorance was Otto Nuttli, a seismologist at St. Louis University. He was a local boy who had graduated from that university. St. Louis University was an old Catholic institution where the Jesuits helped to establish the modern science of seismology, early in this century. The New Madrid earthquakes were among the things Nuttli learned about in a combination of local and professional folklore; but they did not concern him at first. What did interest him was a quake in south-central Illinois in November 1968, magnitude 5.3. Though no more than moderate by California standards, it was the strongest quake in the region in this century, and was felt in parts of twenty-three states, causing a fair amount of damage.

There were a number of seismographic stations throughout the Midwest, and Nuttli set out to use their records to determine that tremor's magnitude on the Richter scale. Using the procedure introduced by Richter and his colleague Beno Gutenberg, Nuttli focused his attention on seismograms that had been recorded at various distances from the epicenter. He soon found that the Richter scale didn't work; the conclusions drawn from those seismograms were wildly inconsistent. The farther a station had been from the epicenter, the stronger the quake appeared to have been, for the Richter magnitude kept increasing.

He looked at records for other Midwestern quakes—there had been two of magnitude close to 5 in 1965, for instance—and found the same inconsistency. Clearly, something was very wrong. But it proved to be a fairly simple problem. The Richter scale had been based on the assumption that the intensity of shaking falls off or attenuates at a certain rate, as one travels from the epicenter. That attenuation rate had been set from studies of California quakes. But in the Midwest there was less such fall-off; a quake could retain more of its strength for longer distances. Allowing for this, Nuttli could develop a consistent measurement of the magnitudes of Midwestern tremors.

Now he was in a position to go back and reexamine the records of the old New Madrid quakes. One of the main things he wanted was an isoseismal map, a chart showing how the felt intensity diminishes with distance. This was the same sort of map that Kerry Sieh had compiled for the 1857 quake, on the basis of contemporary records. "It was the most natural thing in the world," Nuttli states. No one had put such a map together, because no one had ever compiled the old and scattered records that had been published at the time. But Nuttli had an advantage: a reference book called *Newspapers on Microfilm.* It listed not only the old publications that might prove useful, but also where they could be found. "I just looked for newspapers dating to 1811," he recalls, "then tried to order them and look at them. The *Louisiana Gazette* was on microfilm in the St. Louis public library. For the other ones, I wrote to other libraries.

"The hardest problem was to keep my attention on the earthquakes," he adds. "It was a time when Napoleon was marching across Europe, a time just before the War of 1812. There were Indian scalpings, raids on settlers in the Midwest, runaway slaves—'a hundred-dollar reward for the return of my black female slave, age such-and-such.' " He could match up the published reports of the earthquakes' effects with the standard descriptions given by the Modified Mercalli scale. Thus, in Washington, the tremors were "felt by nearly everyone; many awakened." That amounted to intensity V. In Cincinnati, by contrast, there were a number of reports of fallen chimneys, which raised the shaking to intensity VII. And since these intensities could be used to estimate the true sizes of those tremors, Nuttli was able to propose what had been their magnitudes on the Richter scale, even though there had been no seismic instruments at the time.

His conclusions were startling. The December 16, 1811, quake had been of magnitude 8.5 or 8.6, making it up to twice as powerful as the worst in California. Its largest aftershock had rated at 8.2, very close to the 8.3 of California's earthquakes of 1857 and 1906. The shock of January 23, 1812, had been less powerful, at 8.4. But the main quake of February 7, which even at the time had been described as the "hard shock," went all the way up to 8.7 or 8.8—as much as three times the force of the California shakings.

Even more surprising was the extent of area in which those New Madrid tremors had caused damage or had been noticeably felt. The 1857 San Andreas rupture had touched San Diego relatively lightly, and had not been reported east of the Colorado River. Similarly, the 1906 San Francisco earthquake had largely spent its force west of the Sierras. But the December 16 New Madrid quake, which was by far the best documented, had been many times more far-reaching. Nuttli's Mercalli-intensity zones could tell the tale:

VI: Felt by all; many frightened and run outdoors. Some heavy furniture moved; a few instances of fallen plaster or damaged chimneys. Such shakings were felt from Chicago nearly as far south as New Orleans, and from the central Carolinas westward to the eventual sites of Oklahoma City and Dallas.

VII: *Everybody runs outdoors. Damage . . . slight to moderate in well-built ordinary structures, considerable in poorly built or badly designed structures. Some chimneys broken.* The zone of such intensities included Springfield, Illinois, Cincinnati, Ohio, and Chattanooga, Tennessee, as well as Jackson, Mississippi, then extended west to the Oklahoma line.

VIII: *Damage slight in specially designed brick structures; considerable in ordinary substantial buildings, with partial collapse; great in poorly built structures. Panel walls thrown out of frame structures. Fall of chimneys, factory stacks, columns, monuments, walls. Heavy furniture overturned. Sand and mud ejected in small amounts.* This was what happened within a football-shaped region 400 miles long and 170 wide, extending from Evansville, Indiana, to Greenville, Mississippi.

IX: *Damage considerable in specially designed masonry structures; well-designed frame structures thrown out of plumb; great in substantial masonry buildings, with partial collapse. Buildings shifted off foundations. Ground cracked conspicuously. Underground pipes broken.* At this level of destruction, the football-shaped area measured 260 by 100 miles. It included Memphis, Tennessee, Cape Girardeau, Missouri, and Paducah, Kentucky.

All this meant there was a great deal more to learn. Where were the faults that had produced such shakings? And when might it happen again? William Stauder, a colleague of Nuttli's, got some funds from the USGS, then set up an array of seismographs in the region between St. Louis and Memphis, hoping to spot small, recurring quakes that might help him locate the faults. And Davis Russ, a young seismologist at the USGS office outside Washington in Reston, Virginia, proceeded to ride herd over a group of experts as they set

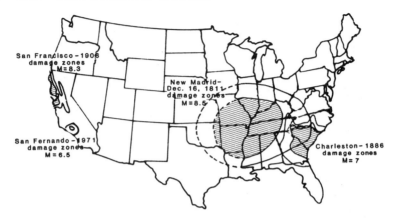

Damage zones from noteworthy earthquakes. Outer curves represent regions where people were badly frightened, with some damage to buildings (Modified Mercalli intensity VI). Inner hatched areas show regions of significant damage. The New Madrid quakes were only slightly greater than the San Francisco tremor of 1906, but affected much wider areas. (After Robert Hamilton, U.S. Geological Survey)

out to study the Mississippi Valley using the full range of techniques of modern seismology.

"With earthquakes," says Russ, "the major thing is to determine how the ground has been deformed. We knew that a lot of the traditional approaches we'd been using in California, such as mapping along faults, were not going to work in the Mississippi Valley, where there are no major faults exposed at the surface." Thus, an important part of the effort was to send out geologists to make maps of whatever they might see, even if it wasn't a fault, hoping it would prove to be useful. Deep deposits of sediment, laid down amid the wide changes in the river's course, had long since buried the bedrock up to three thousand feet deep. But here and there were rocky outcrops or tilted land formations, which stood as pieces in the puzzle.

The making of such maps is a part of every geologist's

education, from undergraduate days on. At Caltech there is
even a song about it, to the tune of Monty Python's "Lumber-
jack Song," describing a mapmaker's typical adventures ("I
fall down cliffs, I follow cows, I love geology. . . . I take them
tests, I get my D's, I have a 1.3").

In western Tennessee and northwest Arkansas it was very
nearly like that. The effort demanded groups of no more
than two or three people. They would get up before dawn,
meet around 6:00 A.M., and after breakfast they would head
out to some area in a Jeep or a Chevy Blazer. From then on
it was an exercise in meticulous observation. "You'd walk
through and try not to miss any features, observing as you
went," remarks Russ. "You'd take readings with your brun-
ton compass on the orientation of fractures," with that instrument measuring both direction and dip. "You'd look very
carefully at the soil, looking for a cut made by a stream, or
a bluff that exposed some rocks or sediment." The route
would lead across farmers' lands, and it would call for more
than just looking. "You'd be chipping off samples all along,
putting them in small cloth bags that you'd label. You'd be
putting dilute acid on them to see if there was limestone,
comparing them with rock and soil-color charts that you had
with you. You'd be looking through a hand lens, and taking
constant notes in a field notebook. Usually you're carefully
making marks on a map, making pinpricks with a needle
that you circle on the back, with a reference number that's
keyed to a note in your book. Lunch might be a brown bag
or a local luncheonette. Lots of times, that's the most fun,
because you get to meet the people in the area." The geologists who were working in this way might conclude, at the
end of the day, that a particular soil bed had been laid down
following the Ice Age but had since been tilted—perhaps
by an earthquake. That would add one more bit of data to
the emerging picture.

Similar field teams made their way across the farms with
sensitive instruments for measuring variations in the force of
gravity or in the local magnetic field. A deeply buried body

of dense basalt, for instance, would be heavy and might increase the local gravitational pull by a few parts per million. And bedrock showed greater magnetic strength than soil or sediment; if the basement rocks fell away sharply at a fault, for instance, this could show on the magnetometers. Further, it was possible, using a technique resembling sonar, to probe directly into the earth to depths of several miles.

The technique was *seismic reflection profiling,* and it had been used extensively by the oil industry to seek out deep oil-rich formations. A survey group would come down a two-lane country road, painting marks on the asphalt. The marks would indicate where the trucks of the seismic crew would stop for various purposes later in the week.

This crew would then make its way in a procession. First would come a stake-sided truck carrying ten or so roustabouts called "jug hustlers." They would set out the "jugs" or geophones, sensitive microphones for picking up vibrations from the earth, looking like cylindrical pints of ice cream. Each had a spike to assure good contact with the ground. They were painted bright red or blue, to stand out in the fields, and had wires attached. These would lead to the "doghouse," an instrumented van or small truck fitted with banks of instruments, including data recorders.

At that point there would be an array of geophones set in a field, linked by wires to the central doghouse. A vibrator crew would follow, in a heavy vehicle resembling a garbage truck. It featured a hydraulically operated pad that would come down, pushing the truck off the pavement. Pistons run by air compressors then would pump a heavy vibration into the ground, which would penetrate to the deeply buried rock layers, returning to the surface and the geophones. The signals reflected from the rock would run down the wires to the doghouse. Analysis of them would produce the equivalent of an X-ray picture of the bedrock.

By the late 1970s these efforts had yielded five types of data: geological field maps, gravity variations, magnetic-field variations, seismic profiles from the doghouse data, and records of micro-earthquakes from Bill Stauder's array of seismographs. From these findings, a clear and consistent picture emerged of the long-extended aftermath of one of the great upheavals in the geological history of North America.

Perhaps half a billion years ago, possibly longer, a plume of hot rock made its way upward from the deep mantle of the earth, hundreds of miles down. Such plumes exist today, underlying Yellowstone National Park, feeding magma to the volcanoes that have built Hawaii. But this one was potentially far more powerful. It amounted to nothing less than an attempt to break the continent in two.

The attempt failed. The plume was not strong enough, or did not last long enough. Nevertheless, it left its mark. It cracked the deep basement of North America, the permanent bedrock, rifting these formations to depths of forty kilometers. The fractured rocks formed three faults, joined together in a zigzag. That is why there were three major New Madrid earthquakes, as the branches of this fault zone broke in turn. The pattern of the zigzag showed quite clearly in Stauder's small tremors, which represented the continuing grindings and creakings of these deep-running flaws.

The New Madrid faults thus have lain since time out of mind as a zone of weakness in the depths of the midcontinent. The gravity and magnetic data showed this clearly; the bedrock had pulled apart along these lines, slumping to form what amounted to subterranean canyons. And along the line of this slump, the Mississippi River had found its course. There was only this single major river draining the central continent; its existence and its route were due in large part to the work of that ancient plume.

All this means that similar quakes can be expected again in time. Those New Madrid faults are not like the San Andreas, which builds up strain as the Pacific floor drives northwestward, rubbing against North America. But with the Atlantic continuing to widen, pushing our continent irrevocably to the west, its motion will slowly build up new stress along those deeply buried faults.

How soon, then, might a Bigger One occur in the heartland of America? David Russ of the USGS went out to western Tennessee and excavated a set of trenches, using the methods of Kerry Sieh to learn about ancient earthquakes in the region. Otto Nuttli examined the pattern of quakes of different sizes that had occurred along the faults. Seismographic data showed the frequency of tremors of magnitude 2, 3, 4, and so forth. The higher the Richter magnitude, the longer was the average time between successive quakes of that magnitude. This gave a rule with which to estimate the interval between quakes as large as magnitude 8.5. Both methods gave closely similar results. Russ found ancient sandblows and similar disturbances at two earlier levels, showing that there had been a total of three sets of great earthquakes in the past two thousand years. Nuttli, extrapolating from small quakes to large ones, found an interval of six hundred to one thousand years.

If that was all there was to it, we would be justified in not worrying. There is no reason to concern ourselves with a quake, even a great one, that is not expected for four hundred years or more. But while a set of 8.5 earthquakes may well be far off, what of others of lesser magnitude, which would still be damaging? Here the situation is not so sanguine. Nuttli estimates that at present, enough stress has built up along the faults to produce a quake of magnitude 7.6. That is the tremor worth fearing; and it has the potential to strike this very day.

Because it would be a full unit less in magnitude than those of 1811–12, the Mercalli intensities in the cities of the central United States would be a full unit less as well. Moreover, the epicenter would not lie near a large city, but rather in open country marked by only a few small towns, such as New Madrid itself. It is an exceptionally flat and waterlogged country. The tall smokestack of a power plant can be seen from twenty miles away. The Mississippi is lined with swamplands of black muck, where trees in the forests show lighter colors along the bottom twenty feet of their trunks, which are watermarks produced by recent floods. There are few roads and fewer bridges; along one stretch, from southern Illinois to northwestern Tennessee, the only way to get across is by ferry.

At the epicenter, then, such a major quake would produce the same sort of upheavals as in 1811–12, and in country that has been little changed. The description given by William Pierce at that time then would apply as well to this potential present-day quake:

> On Wednesday, in the afternoon, I visited every part of the island where we lay. It was extensive, and partly covered with willow. The earthquake had rent the ground in large and numerous gaps; vast quantities of burnt wood in every stage of alteration, from its primitive nature to stove coal, had been spread over the ground to very considerable distances; frightful and hideous caverns yawned on every side . . . I was gratified with seeing several places where those [volcanolike] spouts which had so much attracted our wonder and attention had arisen; they were generally on the beach; and have left large circular holes in the sand, formed much like a funnel. For a great distance around the orifice, vast quantities of coal have been scattered, many pieces weighing from 15 to 20 lbs. were discharged 160 measured paces— These holes were of various dimensions; one of them I observed most particularly, it was 16 feet in perpendicular depth, and 63 feet in circumference at the mouth.

The "volcanoes," with their discharges of coal, were sandblows, eruptions of mud under pressure within waterlogged soils, carrying with them decaying buried wood and peat. Moreover, there were widespread collapses of the adjacent banks. In Pierce's words, "we passed thousands of

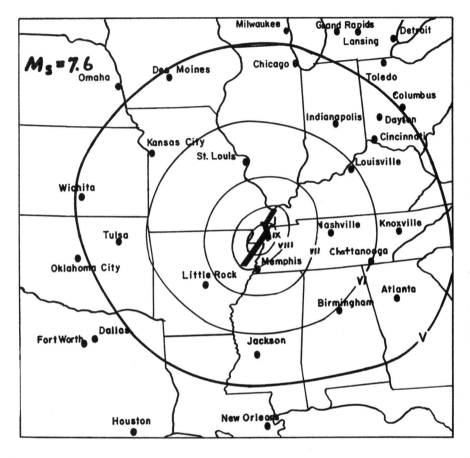

Map by Otto Nuttli showing damage areas, as indicated by zones of various Modified Mercalli intensity, that must be expected from a magnitude-7.6 earthquake on the New Madrid faults. Such a quake could occur today. The zigzag mark at the center is the trace of the New Madrid faults. (Courtesy U.S. Geological Survey)

acres of land which had been cleft from the main shore and tumbled into the water, leaving their growth waving above the surface."

A short distance downriver, this quake would find its first major city in Memphis, which would be as badly damaged as Mexico City in 1985. The downtown district has a number of modern steel-frame buildings, which could well be hard hit. Some tall Mexican buildings sustained their greatest damage in the upper floors. Their flexing had caused them to crack like whips, with the greatest motion at the top. Other structures, set close together, crashed into each other as they rocked back and forth, also causing the top portions to collapse. In a group of five steel-frame high rises, a twenty-one-story building split at the third floor and fell upon an adjacent structure of fourteen stories, bringing it down as well. The two towers collapsed into a heap of rubble nearly as tall as the booms of the diesel shovels that came to clear the wreckage. Less destruction, but in a stranger form, came at the medium-rise Hotel de Carlo. It broke cleanly in the middle, with three upper stories resting in a block upon the lower part of the hotel, canted backward at a twenty-degree angle.

But the greatest danger, in cities as far apart as Nashville, Little Rock, and St. Louis, would be from unreinforced brick buildings, which represent a particularly common type of construction. Here, one could expect many people to find themselves amid calamities similar to one that took place on a sidewalk in front of a store in Imperial, California, during the magnitude-7.1 shaking of 1940.

A young housewife was in a store, carrying two babies. She ran screaming for the street as the building's brick facing began to collapse. A high school girl, Juanita Blevins, ignored her own safety and ran to help, clutching at the woman as she fell beneath the bricks. Then the main fall of masonry buried all four people. Juanita's brother, standing nearby in horror, was unable to save her. He pulled her from the debris and got her to a hospital, where she died twenty minutes later.

That is how it would be in parts of Missouri, Tennessee, Illinois, Kentucky, Mississippi, and Arkansas, within a zone three hundred miles across. And surrounding it would be a still larger ring of damage, reaching such cities as Birmingham, Indianapolis, and Kansas City, along with most of the states in mid-America. Here, large items of furniture, along with kitchen appliances, would topple and crash amid the ruins of home interiors, with plaster cracking and some chimneys toppling. Few houses would experience irreparable damage, but throughout this vast area, the quake would be a horrifying experience for everyone involved.

Such a quake, striking at the heartland, would be triply terrifying. The slow attenuation of its seismic waves, as noted by Nuttli, would spread its damage far more widely than would a similar-sized quake in California. The cities in the path of these waves are full of buildings far older than those of the West Coast and less earthquake-resistant. Moreover, the Midwest simply does not expect earthquakes. Its people are no more prepared for them than Angelenos are ready for floods or tornadoes.

The Mississippi Valley is not the only region east of the Rockies that could sustain major or damaging tremors. Charleston, South Carolina, was hit with a quake of magnitude 7.5 in 1886. It was the same old melancholy story of crashing chimneys, crumbling walls, and panicking people, with some sixty of the townsfolk dead in the debris. More than half of the brick buildings were damaged or destroyed, but this quake was not a disaster at the level of General Sherman's march to the sea, twenty-two years earlier. Only about one structure in sixty was a total loss as a result of the earthquake. Interestingly, some of the oldest mansions, built of masonry, stood up well. These had been constructed from handmade bricks whose rough surfaces gave particularly strong bonds with the mortar. And that mortar was of an unusually good grade, made from the lime of oyster shells.

Newer mortar, imported from the North, had crumbled. Thus, even in 1886, the old workmanship had been the best in quality.

The zone of damage—intensity VII or higher on the Modified Mercalli scale—covered all of South Carolina and extended into central Georgia. Indeed, among the earthquakes of the East, this one stands out as the second most destructive after the New Madrid series. Yet this coastal region has been much more difficult to study than the Mississippi Valley, which has been hard enough when compared to California. Near Charleston, the overlying sediments are ten thousand feet thick. Also, the faults in the area show so little activity, and produce so few quakes, that it has not been possible to map them.

Indeed, what little we know about Charleston-area earthquakes has stemmed in good part from a dead horse. A few years ago, a party of geologists met a farmer who told them that his grandfather had seen a spout of wet sand erupt from the ground in 1886. Such sandblows would offer some of the best evidence of the age and extent of past quakes, but amid the region's frequent rains and lush growth, none survived to be studied. But the farmer knew the location of his granddad's spout because someone had shot a troublesome horse and left the carcass there. Its skeleton served as a marker. After cutting trenches near the bones, geologists from the University of South Carolina were able to see what an ancient sandblow would look like when its soil disturbances showed up in the walls of an excavation.

The obvious next step was to dig more trenches in the region that had shaken in 1886, to look for more sandblows. This turned out to be unnecessary, for the timber growers in the area had done such work. They had cut numerous drainage ditches through the wet pinelands to increase the trees' growth rates. A group from the USGS went to Hollywood, west of Charleston, which had reported numerous sandblows in 1886 and where an extensive drainage-ditch system was in place. They found proof that over the past few thousand years there had been two other major quakes, showing that the 1886 tremor was not unique. To the contrary, such shakings could be expected to recur about every eighteen hundred years.

Now if there is no need to think about a set of great Mississippi quakes in the year 2500, no one should be concerned with a major Charleston event in 3700. Nor is there reason to think of a buildup of strain at Charleston, which could produce a lesser but still powerful and damaging shock. But when we look at the Pacific Northwest, New Madrid, and Charleston together, we see a pattern. We see deeply buried faults, either found only recently or still hidden, with the power of breaking and causing large tremors, entirely without warning. And we are entitled to ask how many more such unmapped and potentially dangerous faults may exist beneath the United States.

A common view is that such faults will produce microquakes, betraying their presence through low-level seismic activity. But there is good reason to believe that this is not always so. In China's Shensi Province in 1556, an earthquake destroyed the city of Sian and killed 800,000 people. As Otto Nuttli describes it, "Right now that area is completely quiescent—not even micro-earthquakes." Near Borah Peak, Idaho, there is a fault that had shown no seismic activity for decades. Trenches dug across it, Kerry Sieh–style, showed that its last major tremor had occurred two thousand years earlier. But it broke in 1983, in a quake of magnitude 7.3. Similarly, there is an Oklahoma feature called the Meers fault, which had been presumed dead for millions of years. Then the geologist Charles Gilbert of Texas A&M found a number of features that were most peculiar for a fault so long inactive. If it was very old, there should have been much more erosion in soft rock than in hard and resistant rock. But the amount of erosion along its length was surprisingly uniform. In fact, this fault had apparently broken in a quake of a magnitude as great as 7.5, again within the last two thousand years.

The recurrence intervals may be very long for such earth-quakes. But if there are enough such faults, and if their quakes strike unexpectedly, sooner or later some city or state will incur serious damage. Indeed, there is increasing reason to believe that virtually the entire basement of the United States, the deep formations that form our nation's permanent bedrock, is fractured and faulted. Surveys made by aircraft, which have mapped changes in local magnetism or the force of gravity, have extended the explorations in the Mississippi Valley to the entire country. These show wide-spread evidence of faults.

Moreover, these faults can be understood in view of our current understanding of North America's geological his-tory. It holds that much of America consists of fragments of terrain that have been assembled along fault lines, often after breaking off from other continents. For instance, hun-dreds of millions of years ago, North America and Africa were separate continents, but 240 million years ago they rafted together and joined. Eighty million years later they separated anew with the opening up of the Atlantic Ocean. Part of Africa stuck to the shores of what is now the southeast-ern United States. In the words of one Carolina geophysi-cist, "When you tell the local Baptists that this is where their land came from, they don't like it."

What is to be done, then, if over time hardly any place in the nation will prove safe from damaging quakes? It is likely that seismology and its branches will emerge as a major new industry to provide warnings, counsel architects and build-ers, and in time perhaps even control the quakes them-selves. Today seismology is an arcane discipline. It is a small, closely knit community of scientists, where everyone knows the people and the gossip. But in earlier decades, the same was true of rocket experts, specialists in nuclear phys-ics, and computer scientists. In time seismology may grow into a high-tech enterprise, just as these other fields have, and this may give us the means to deal with the major quakes of the future.

9

MAN MEETS QUAKE

Tom Heaton of the USGS, who appeared briefly in the last chapter with his warning of a seismic gap near Seattle, is a man who knows how to predict earthquakes. Using modern instruments and computers, he is prepared to festoon a fault with an array of equipment that will give a true warning, without fail. In contrast to the hit-or-miss procedures of other seismologists, his technique will work every time.

He wants to use strong-motion accelerometers, which respond quite effectively to the powerful and prolonged shaking of a major tremor. Such instruments feature a weight supported by springs, with the forces on these springs being measured as the weight oscillates. They show little response to minor and frequent quakes, but when a great quake strikes, they show accelerations that equal or exceed the force of gravity, as their weights rock back and forth. Heaton wants to set a number of them along major faults, linking them to a computer. Its microchips would receive the strong-motion signals, evaluate the size and strength of the gathering quake, and transmit an alert.

The key to this is that in comparison with the speed of electronics, seismic waves travel quite slowly. The P wave, which brings the initial shaking, has a speed of about 5.6 kilometers per second. The more powerful S wave, which usually does the most damage, travels at only 3.4 kilometers per second. In contrast, electronic systems can transmit at nearly the speed of light, which is at least fifty thousand times faster. A city two hundred kilometers distant from a quake's epicenter then could have up to a minute of advance warning of the dangerous S wave. This warning, delivered by signals that outrace the seismic waves, would be Tom Heaton's prediction. Though short, the warning time could protect a great many sensitive systems from being caught unawares.

There would be time for subways and trains to come to a halt, rather than face the danger of derailment. Electronic signs along freeways could flash the message EARTHQUAKE IMMINENT, so that motorists could stop their cars. Computer networks and electric power plants could be protected by opening their circuit breakers to avoid possible damage by the sudden downing of a power line. Valves could shut in oil refineries, offshore drilling platforms, and pipelines, thus easing the risk of fire or spillage. Similarly, chemical plants could gain a measure of protection. Hospitals could start up their emergency electric generators, ensuring the continued operation of life-support equipment. Firemen could get their trucks under way, keeping them from being trapped at their stations and gaining extra seconds that could help bring fires under control.

Even thirty seconds would be enough warning for radio and TV stations to break into their usual programming: "Emergency, emergency. A powerful earthquake will strike Los Angeles within the next few seconds. This is not a test. We repeat: A powerful earthquake is about to strike." This would require computer-activated recordings at the broadcast stations, ready to break instantaneously into the transmissions. It would give people extra seconds to get out of buildings or take cover beneath a desk or a strong table.

The announcement would also reach many motorists who would not be in view of a freeway sign but who would be driving with the radio on.

Such a seismic-warning system could be particularly useful to San Francisco, where the San Andreas runs just west of the city. Thus, while Los Angeles must fear the strong S waves from sections of fault a hundred or more kilometers away, San Francisco could literally be ripped apart by a quake only a few miles from downtown. But if the next such quake is like the one of 1906, it will have its epicenter or place of origin well to the north. The fault then will rupture to the southeast, somewhat like a zipper opening; and this rupture will rip along the fault at a speed of 2.5 kilometers per second. This is slower than the S waves from the epicenter; these waves thus will reach the city first. But they will produce far less damage than the motion along the fault itself, when it strikes the city. If the next San Francisco quake has its start near Cape Mendocino, four hundred kilometers to the north, there would be the opportunity for some two and a half minutes of warning time before the rupture of the fault proceeded as far as the city.

Heaton's proposed arrangement would also be valuable in the Midwest, in the event of another New Madrid earthquake. Here the danger would be from the S waves, since the faults do not run close to a major city. Memphis and St. Louis could have as much as a minute of warning, with more distant cities—Little Rock, Kansas City, Indianapolis, Birmingham—receiving as much as two minutes. That could save a great many lives among the large number of people who live or work in low-rise death traps of unreinforced brick.

Still, a minute of warning is not what most people have in mind when they think of earthquake prediction. The goal continues to be the development of increasingly specific warnings as the quake becomes more imminent. That would allow people much more than the opportunity to get out of a building; they could bolt down their homes and furniture, lay in provisions, even decide whether they wanted to stay around to experience it. And such predictions can only come from continuing work in seismology. Thus, it is appropriate to look at where we stand today, and where we may proceed in the future.

In earthquake prediction, there is an old approach and a new one. The old approach has relied on the seismograph. Its records of quakes from around the world, cataloged and tabulated, have permitted the identification of seismic gaps, places where major tremors are overdue. Similar seismic records cover quakes down to magnitude 4, the limit that can be detected by the worldwide seismic network. These suffice for spotting quiescence, regions where such modest-sized tremors are missing and where a large quake thus may be only a few months or years off.

But when one seeks to gain more specific warnings with the aid of seismographs, things get sticky. Premonitory patterns of quakes have appeared and failed to appear, in hit-or-miss fashion. Foreshocks have preceded many quakes, but often they have been hard to identify, or have come with only minutes to spare before the main shocks. There has been the long-standing hope that seismograms, with their records of small quakes identified after they happen, would give clues to processes within the earth that are building toward a quake that hasn't happened yet. But this hope has not been fulfilled.

That is why the dilatancy theory was so important in the mid-1970s. It held the promise, for a while, that observations made with seismographs indeed would give insight into the earth's processes, and would warn of a gathering earthquake. The idea, again, was that the mainshock would follow a time in which cracks would open in the rocks and groundwater would infiltrate them. These changes were believed to slow the velocities of P waves from distant tremors. Such waves, therefore, passing through the quake-prone region, would show up clearly on seismographs, where their slowings could readily be measured. Had it worked, the dilatancy theory indeed might have allowed scientists to use data from seismographs to peer into the fault zone, with the changes in these P-wave velocities tracing the preparations for the quake. These P-wave slowings turned out not to exist in any useful fashion, but the underlying idea—to use seismographs as instruments with which to infer physical conditions within the fault itself—was well worth pursuing.

That was the old seismology, and most advances in forecasting have been closely linked to its methods. Kerry Sieh's trenches, for instance, amount to prehistoric seismograms, yielding information similar to that of catalogs compiled from earthquake records, and permitting the identification of seismic gaps. Studies of other precursors—rock magnetism, water-well levels, tilts and bulges in the earth, even the behavior of animals—all sought to reinforce the predictive patterns that people hoped would be seen in the seismograms.

This approach continues to be invaluable, but it deserves the name "old seismology" because it gives no new insight into the workings of the earth. It amounts largely to extrapolation, to saying that earthquakes have struck before and will do so again, without being able to tell what is happening physically within the fault zone. If we think of seismograms as recording the heartbeat of such a zone, we could say that the old seismology is like trying to diagnose a patient merely by taking his pulse. What we really want are X rays and samples of blood and tissue.

The new seismology, then, seeks deliberately to develop real information as to what is going on within a fault zone. Here the basic instrument is not the seismograph, but the two-color laser Geodimeter used for precise distance measurements, as at Parkfield. The data from these instruments, suitably processed by computer, indicate how and where the rocks along the fault may shift or move, often without producing an earthquake.

Such subsurface shifts are important. They can relieve stress along one part of the fault, passing this stress on to another part and loading it more strongly. Even when such shifts produce small quakes, often there is little indication as to how they have occurred: How large was the moving patch of rock? How far did it go? But the laser Geodimeter data can show such results plainly, yielding the desired X-ray images.

With this, it will become increasingly possible to map out fault zones in detail. Most faults are jagged and irregular, with numerous protrusions extending into the adjacent rocks to pin them in place. Since these protrusions remain fixed in position during the buildup to a major quake, data from the Geodimeters may serve to identify them and map their positions within the fault, deep under the surface.

Earthquake prediction then may develop as the art of following the loading of strain onto these fixed patches, with the occasional slipping of unlocked parts of the fault stressing them more and more heavily. In time they will fail and give way, sometimes producing foreshocks but at other times not, and they may tend to do this in recognizable sequences. Perhaps it will become possible to say, for example, that twenty-three protrusions, each with a well-defined location, lock the San Andreas in the region north of Los Angeles. Perhaps they slip and give way in a certain order, the weakest first, and when all but seven have gone, the main quake is only twenty-four hours away.

Certainly we are far from being able to draw such conclusions today. But if such protrusions can be identified and mapped, perhaps it will be possible to study them directly. Particularly important would be determinations of the precise amount of strain within their rocks. When we speak today of strain along a fault, we are talking quite loosely. We say, for instance, that a fault is building up strain at three centimeters per year; it is two hundred years since the last quake, so the fault has built up six meters of strain. But that is no more than an average value, distributed over the entire fault. The stress and strain are far greater within the protrusions, but the fault-zone averages do not show how great.

Yet today an experiment is under way east of Los Angeles, showing how such protrusions might be studied.

It is visible from Interstate 15, where that freeway climbs toward the high desert north of San Bernardino. A drilling rig stands in an open field, nineteen stories high, making it one of the largest in the world. The San Andreas runs two miles from this site, and this rig is penetrating the adjacent rocks. The seismologist Mark Zoback of Stanford University is running this experiment, and is making measurements of the stress within these rocks, as the first attempt to determine what forces are pushing at the fault.

To make such a measurement, Zoback's drillers seal off a six-foot section of the hole and pump in water, measuring the pressure as it builds. Suddenly this pressure collapses; the rock has given way and has cracked, draining off some of the water. The drillers have rock samples that have been tested in a lab to determine the stress at which they break. This stress is equal to the sum of the water pressure plus the preexisting stress within the rock; and since the water pressure is known, a simple subtraction gives the measurement of the stress. Moreover, the cracks form in the direction where the stress is greatest, so its orientation as well as its magnitude can be determined readily. This technique is called *hydrofracturing*.

Zoback has found a surprise: there is little stress acting to force the sides of the fault to shift past each other. Instead, most of the stress goes into pushing the two sides tightly together. This is hard to understand if we picture the fault as two smooth and flat faces of rock pressed together. At this late date, with no major quake having struck the area since 1857, such faces would be expected to show considerable strain that has built up in the direction along the fault, tending to push one side past the other. But if we think of the fault as being pinned in place through protrusions, then all we need to consider is that this drill site is not observing a pinned area. If the drill is penetrating an unpinned section, it is easy to imagine that the rock there has slipped and relieved some strain. A future drill hole, which could indeed bore into a protrusion, might indeed find it to be under a good deal of strain in the direction along the fault. And this strain could be measured not only by hydrofracturing, but also with downhole strainmeters such as are already permanently in place at Parkfield.

The hole near San Bernardino is only two kilometers deep, and San Andreas earthquakes may begin at depths up to fifteen kilometers. New deep-drilling technology, however, has brought such depths within reach. The leaders in this effort have been in the Soviet Union, and have bored the world's deepest hole. It is already at a depth below twelve kilometers, and is heading for fifteen.

Their rig stands near Murmansk on the Kola Peninsula, east of Norway. It looks like a milk carton thirty stories tall, set amid the barren flatness of the tundra. Inside this carton are several innovations. The drill pipe is made of aluminum alloy, which is much lighter than conventional steel. This makes it easier to haul the miles-long string of pipe in and out of the hole. This must be done many times during drilling operations, to recover rock samples or to change worn drill bits.

Such bits, diamond-studded for cutting power, are fitted to the bottom end of this string, to bore through the rock. The usual arrangement is that the entire string rotates to turn this bit. But the Soviets have introduced a turbodrill, which spins on its own while the pipe stands stationary. They have done this by using drilling mud, which is essential to every such operation. Mud is pumped down the hole to pressurize its sides and prevent them from collapsing, to cool and lubricate the bit, and to carry away the cuttings of rock that otherwise would clog it. The mud then flows back up through the drill pipe. The Soviets use this mud in yet another way: to spin a turbine that drives the bit in its rotation. That gives more effective control and less wear on the bit than would accrue if they were to try to rotate the entire string.

All of this means that in time it should become possible not only to map the protrusions and other features of a fault, but to bore into them and make measurements. After that, it will be a matter of waiting. It is likely that every fault will have its own characteristic patterns of behavior, which will be seen only through detailed observations with Parkfield-type instrument arrays. As time goes by, our growing experience with earthquakes might indeed allow seismologists to make increasingly accurate forecasts. But true predictive power will probably come only after it has been possible to observe the details of a fault's preparation for a major quake, then to use the record of these details for comparison with the fault's behavior the next time around. A fault will have to go through the complete cycle of straining, breaking, and gathering strain anew for another quake. Only then will it be possible to make the detailed comparisons of the two successive earthquakes and say that we truly understand how that fault works.

For the San Andreas, this is likely to take at least a century; along such stretches as the region near the Salton Sea, it could take till the year 2300. This means that, for a long time, our efforts at earthquake prediction will remain incomplete. Moreover, there is likely to be a gnawing question: Are such predictions really worth the trouble? The limited experience to date suggests that credible predictions are something less than unalloyed blessings.

When Karen McNally went to Mexico in 1978, it was in response to a forecast of a major quake in Oaxaca, based on the finding that it was a region of seismic quiescence within a seismic gap. This prediction was the work of three experienced geophysicists at the University of Texas, and it soon became known outside that specialized community. In Pinotepa, a town on the Mexican coast, the local newspaper reported the consequences:

> After this announcement, there has been a tremendous commotion on the Oaxaca coast, to the point where

many persons are fleeing their homes to emigrate to other towns in Mexico. . . . The psychosis caused by the alarming news has induced them to sell their properties to the highest bidder, thus destroying their homes. . . . At first it was a speculative news item, but so much has been written about it that it has brought damage to all of Oaxaca as well as to the neighboring states of Guerrero, Michoacan, Puebla, and others. . . . Unfortunately, there has been panic, particularly in Pinotepa and nearby coastal towns . . . some local people have already sold their property, and people with money are buying land. . . . One wonders: Who are these people picking up cheap land along the Oaxaca coast?

Eventually the governor of Oaxaca state had to make a special appearance in Pinotepa, to reassure the populace.

Two sociologists, Eugene Haas of the University of Colorado and Dennis Mileti of Colorado State University, have constructed a scenario for a credible quake prediction in California. One version of this scenario begins in July 1988, when the USGS announces that Long Beach has been picked for an intensive study of earthquake precursors. When interviewed by reporters, two well-known seismologists give the reason: Data already exist indicating a 25-percent chance of a major quake in 1991. The newspapers pick up the story, and the TV networks carry it as well.

Within a year, population growth in the Long Beach area slows markedly. Property values fall sharply, new construction stops, and there is considerable unemployment in construction and related industries. Then, in August 1989, the Survey announces a more specific prediction: a 50-percent chance of a quake of magnitude 7 or greater, to strike in September or October of 1991. The California Earthquake Prediction Evaluation Council, whose mission is not to issue predictions but to assess the merits of forecasts made by others, issues a report: This prediction is sound. The news media begin outlining emergency plans. Newspapers carry feature articles on earthquakes, along with maps of the estimated damage areas.

California's state insurance commission bans the sale of new earthquake insurance policies in the areas expected to be hardest hit, to protect the solvency of the companies and the policies currently in force. Taking the insurance commission's cue, banks stop writing new mortgages for the affected areas. Credit tightens for purchasers of appliances and similar items that are likely to be damaged. Many small firms close their doors, while sales-tax revenues drop markedly.

By the fall of 1990 the USGS has further refined its prediction, stating that a quake of magnitude 7.1 to 7.4 will strike in September 1991, with 80-percent probability. By now many people have been laid off and some families are leaving the area. Tax revenues continue to drop, just as public agencies are calling for budget increases to help them prepare for the expected disaster. Unemployment continues to rise; real-estate speculators are busy. The governor of California requests the President to declare a state of emergency.

By the beginning of 1991, one-fourth of all small businesses in Long Beach have closed. Many people are stockpiling emergency supplies. In July, officials urge people to evacuate the high-risk areas, particularly those below dams. A month later, over half the original population has left the area, with one-fifth of these people vowing never to return. Many of those remaining begin to eat, cook, and sleep outdoors. There is fear of looting, and in response to requests from the mayor, the National Guard moves in. A taut air of impending panic and disaster descends over Long Beach, thoroughly disrupting normal life for months. And all this happens before the quake itself occurs.

Such prospects thus suggest that earthquake prediction could cause nearly as many problems as it would solve. If this proves to be true, it may be that we will want to go beyond mere prediction. Our ultimate goal may be to bring earthquakes under control.

So far-reaching a prospect smacks of steering storms and turning off lightning; and if earthquake prediction today lies at the limit of what we may pursue as science, then earthquake control must surely appear as black magic or alchemy. Yet while there is no solid evidence that prediction is physically achievable, there exists a record of a well-controlled experiment showing that earthquakes can be made to start and stop at will, at least in principle. There thus already exists a physical basis for earthquake control. In times to come, this could become a major enterprise.

Earthquake control got its start in 1966. Near Denver, geologists were puzzled by a series of recent local quakes that had no obvious cause. From 1882 to 1962 there had been no quakes in the area strong enough to be felt, but from 1962 to 1966 there were several hundred tremors in the area, with magnitudes of up to 4.3 on the Richter scale. A local consultant, Dave Evans, came up with an explanation. Not far from the city, the army was manufacturing nerve gas at its Rocky Mountain Arsenal, and pumping chemical waste down a deep well. They had been doing this since March 1962. Evans argued that the well was right over a fault and that the wastes were lubricating the fault, allowing it to slip and produce the quakes.

"Dave was quite an imaginative fellow," recalls Jack Healy, a longtime USGS seismologist who was there at the time. "We set out to disprove this." Along with a colleague, Barry Raleigh, he put portable seismographs near the well. "Much to our surprise, the quakes were clustered very near the well. That was a very exciting experience." For the first time there was clear evidence that a man-made activity could trigger the onset of earthquakes.

Raleigh and another geologist, Bill Rubey, then devised a theory to explain what was happening. The basic concept was simple: the pressure of the earth was pushing the sides of faults together, so that they locked in place through friction, allowing the stress to build. But if you pumped water down a borehole at high pressure, it would counterbalance part of the earth's pressure. This would reduce the frictional force that was locking its sides, allowing the fault to slip and produce quakes. Then, if you pumped the water back out, reducing the counterbalancing pressure, the fault again would lock more tightly and the tremors would stop. And these ideas could be tested by experiment.

The key point in the experiment was to test these ideas by pumping waste back out of the hole. But this could not be done. In Raleigh's words, "The chemicals were so noxious, the drillers got sick." Rubey then said he'd heard quakes were occurring around Rangely, in the far northwest of Colorado. That was high plains country, over a mile in elevation.

An oil field was close by; its operator, Chevron Oil, was pumping water deep into the rock formations to force out more petroleum. Healy and Raleigh took their seismographs to study Rangely's tremors. Then Raleigh met with the vice-president of Chevron West, Earl Kipp, who agreed to let them change the pressure deep underground. By using the existing water-injection systems within the field, they attempted to turn the earthquakes on and off. If their ideas were correct, pumping more water into the rocks would trigger new quakes. Pulling this water back out would shut them down.

According to their theory, earthquakes should be triggered in the oil field whenever the water pressure downhole exceeded 3,730 pounds per square inch or 257 times standard atmospheric pressure—257 bars, in their parlance. In October 1969 they raised the downhole pressure from 235 to 275 bars. During the following year, their instruments recorded more than nine hundred tremors within the field. Of these, 367 occurred within one kilometer of the four wells that were injecting the water. Then, in November 1970, those wells were "backflowed," as water was withdrawn. Seismic activity soon dropped from the previous year's average of twenty-eight tremors per month to only about one per month, as the pressure fell from 275 to 203 bars.

The next step was to do it all over again. Healy and Raleigh went out to the Rangely field with a hard-hatted roustabout in tow. They made their way to the water-injection equipment, and the oilman showed them which lever to push. Raleigh then said to Healy, "All right, Jack, let's turn these earthquakes on." And with this, the pressure began to build deep underground.

Late in May of 1971, with the water-injection wells at work, they raised the pressure to 265 bars. Nothing happened; the seismic activity remained at the level of less than one tremor per month. Late in 1972 they raised the pressure a bit more, to 275 bars. The monthly average also rose, but only a little, to six quakes near the injection wells. During the early months of 1973 they raised the pressure a little more, to 280 bars. The monthly average jumped to 26. On May 6 they began to backflow those wells, dropping the pressure. Within one day the quakes ceased, dropping again to only one per month, in formations at some distance from the field.

This evidence showed that the theory of Raleigh and Rubey was correct and could stand as a basis for earthquake control. They had been a little off in their calculation of the critical pressure downhole that would allow the existing stresses within the rocks to produce tremors. That was why the quakes had started not at the predicted 257 bars, but at slightly higher pressures. But the key point was that they had turned them on at all. A slight change across a threshold, from 275 to 280 bars, had sufficed, which was in line with the theory's basic ideas. Writing in *Science*, the seismologists declared that "earthquakes can be controlled wherever we can control the fluid pressure in a fault zone."

Their colleague Jim Dieterich, also at the USGS, soon developed a concept for practical quake control. He appreciated that large and damaging quakes arose when a fault broke along a substantial length. But if the sides of the fault could be pinned in place at frequent intervals, the rupture lengths would be far shorter and the tremors a great deal milder, even though they would take place more often. Thus, Dieterich suggested drilling a number of wells along the length of the San Andreas, spaced several miles apart. To begin, he would pump out groundwater from, say, the even-numbered wells, thus causing the fault to lock more tightly at those locations. He would inject additional water through the odd-numbered wells, encouraging the fault to slip and relieve its strain. Later he would reverse the process, withdrawing water from the odd-numbered installations to pin the fault anew in those places, then injecting water into the even-numbered ones so that their lengths of fault would slip in their turn. Amid these cyclical alternations, the San Andreas would be tamed. Like dams regulating the flow of the Colorado River, these regularly spaced wells would control the release of seismic energy, preventing great quakes just as the dams prevent great floods.

The deep Soviet borehole has recently given new support to this hope. It has been drilled within a thick formation of granite, which the pressures at great depths might have welded into a solid and impermeable mass. But the Soviet drillers have found that as far down as twelve kilometers, the rocks are fractured and cracked, with water circulating through the fissures. This is just what is needed to make earthquake control work. If Murmansk was threatened by an overdue quake, the Soviets might already be working to delay it still further, by pumping out this deep water so as to lock the fault more tightly. And as a bonus, the water contains valuable quantities of dissolved minerals.

Nevertheless, down to the present day, these ideas have remained in limbo. There just have been too many unknowns. Even at Denver, the army's activities had triggered quakes as large as magnitude 5 on the Richter scale, strong enough to crack plaster and break windows. In Raleigh's words, "It's extremely important to study the physical conditions deep within a fault. But if you try to think of any parameter that would be important to know—we don't know it."

And Clarence Allen of Caltech, a former student of Richter and a dean of seismology, has an even more pointed set of views.

"I think these ideas are a lot of fun," he told me, "and someday—a hundred years from now, perhaps—we may actually be controlling quakes, or setting them off on schedule. We have to avoid giving people the impression that this is just around the corner. Perhaps the biggest problem is, there's no obvious way to test this in nature. We can't go out and start drilling holes down the San Andreas, start pumping water, because our lawyers advise against it. It's easy to say, 'Let's pick a fault in a remote area and work on it.' Well, it turns out there are no more remote areas. One of my suggestions was, 'Let's talk about the eastern end of the Garlock fault.'" This major fault marks the northern boundary of the Mojave Desert, running off to the northeast from a junction with the San Andreas.

"It's an active fault," he went on. "Most of it's in the military base out there. But if you really generate a magnitude-7 quake, it's going to have effects far outside that area. And the minute you trigger an earthquake, even though you were not responsible for the tectonic strain that was released—the minute you trigger it there are interesting legal questions as to whether you are liable for every little crack that develops within a thousand miles. Lawyers do tell me that if you trigger an event, you have to accept a certain amount of responsibility.

"I myself could not argue that right now, without understanding the phenomena better, without really knowing what we're doing, we should go out and punch holes down the San Andreas. But it's worthwhile to think about these things. We may be dreaming, to talk about controlling or scheduling earthquakes. But it's not a ridiculous dream." Kerry Sieh adds that if it were to be done at all, the time would be *after* the next major quake, when there will be much less stress within the fault, and thus less chance of something going badly wrong.

The Big One will come in its time, then, and will stand as one of the memorable events of its era. The media will cover it in full, and it may be that a venturesome cameraman will capture the collapse and destruction of tall buildings. Such a scene will be as noteworthy, riveting itself as strongly into the national mind, as the explosion of the space shuttle *Challenger* in 1986. For over 10 million people, the coming California earthquake will stand out as a turning point in their lives. For perhaps half the nation—100 million and more—it will be a matter of having a friend or relative who will be caught up in it.

California has seen its great quakes before, but this one will be different. And there is a place on the coast where this difference presents itself in the most compelling fashion. It is a spot known as the Devil's Jaw, and is only a few miles from Lompoc, close to the southwesternmost corner of California. The Point Arguello earthquake, magnitude 7.3, fell very close to this place in 1927. The damaging Santa Barbara quake, magnitude 6.3, was not far to the east in 1925. And on September 8, 1923, at this location, the U.S. Navy sustained its worst peacetime disaster in history, when nine destroyers ran onto the rocks.

I visited that spot in July 1984, sixty years later. The land falls away sharply at this coast, plunging steeply amid jagged stone into a small cove, white with the rushing foam of the waves, salty with their spray flung by the onshore wind, rhythmically resounding to the sweep and roar of the incoming swells. Close to one group of rocks was the rusted steel that had once been a ship, part of a boiler at one spot, along with some corroded girders and plating close by.

And then I lifted my head and turned to the left. There on a low rise, less than a mile away, loomed the tall, stark, boxlike forms of Space Launch Complex 6, largest of the rocket facilities at Vandenberg Air Force Base. There was a massive, windowless structure hundreds of feet high, with another one close behind, a vast cube. A third such tower, wide and with a high, overhanging top, completed the group. To their rear were the yellow hills of California, retreating into the distance.

The desolate shore of 1923 represents the California of earthquakes past. For the state has been fantastically lucky, until now. In 1812, 1838, 1857, 1872, 1906, 1927, 1940, and 1952 the land was rocked by major tremors of magnitude 7 or greater. Thus they have come about every twenty years. Yet, with the exception of San Francisco in 1906, they all fell in remote and largely uninhabited areas, even though the greatest and most dangerous fault, the San Andreas, runs close to the populous coastal areas.

But this luck will not last. The space-launch complex of today represents the new California, where Los Angeles stands as the nation's second city, where 16 million people will live in the counties of the south coast by century's end. The homes and lives of these people, including Angela's and mine, are on a collision course with the fault. To paraphrase what Napoleon said of China: Let the San Andreas sleep; when she awakens the world will be sorry.

=========== SOURCES

CHAPTER 1: SAN ANDREAS

Hill, Mason L., and Thomas W. Dibblee, Jr. "San Andreas, Garlock, and Big Pine Faults, California." *Bulletin of the Geological Society of America* 64 (April 1953): 443–58.

Readings from Scientific American: Continents Adrift. San Francisco: W. H. Freeman and Company, 1973.

CHAPTER 2: EARTHQUAKES PAST

Agnew, Duncan Carr, and Kerry E. Sieh. "A Documentary Study of the Felt Effects of the Great California Earthquake of 1857." *Bulletin of the Seismological Society of America* 68, no. 6 (December 1978): 1717–29. (Includes compilation on microfiche of contemporary newspaper accounts of this quake.)

Anderson, Don L. "The Seismological Laboratory: Past and Future." *Engineering & Science* 38, no. 1 (October–November 1974): 8–13.

Bronson, William. *The Earth Shook, the Sky Burned.* Garden City: Doubleday, 1959.

Coffmann, Jerry L., and Carl A. von Hake, eds. *Earthquake History of the United States.* U.S. Department of Commerce Publication 41-1. Washington: U.S. Government Printing Office, 1973.

Dictionary of Scientific Biography, vol. 5. New York: Scribner's, 1972.

Gilbert, G. K. "A Theory of the Earthquakes of the Great Basin, with a Practical Application." *American Journal of Science* 27 (January 1884): 49–53.

———. "Earthquake Forecasts." *Science* 29 (January 22, 1909): 121–38.

Goodstein, Judith. "Albert Einstein in California." *Engineering & Science* 42, no. 5 (May–June 1979): 17–19.

Lewis, Oscar. *San Francisco: Mission to Metropolis.* San Diego: Howell-North Books, 1980.

Morris, Charles. *The San Francisco Calamity by Earthquake and Fire.* Secaucus, New Jersey: Citadel Press, 1986.

Sagan, Carl. *Broca's Brain.* New York: Ballantine Books, 1980.

Scheid, Ann. "Interview with Charles F. Richter." California Institute of Technology Oral History Project. Pasadena: Caltech Archives, 1979. Excerpted in *Engineering & Science* 45, no. 4 (March 1982): 24–28.

Thomas, Gordon, and Max Morgan Witts. *The San Francisco Earthquake.* New York: Stein and Day, 1971.

Toppozada, Tousson R., Charles R. Real, and David L. Parke. *Preparation of Isoseismal Maps and Summaries of Reported Effects for Pre-1900 California Earthquakes.* California Division of Mines and Geology, Sacramento, 1981.

Townley, S. D., and M. W. Allen. "Descriptive Catalogue of Earthquakes of the Pacific Coast of the United States: 1769 to 1928." *Bulletin of the Seismological Society of America* 29 (1939): 1–297.

Tyler, Sydney. *San Francisco's Great Disaster.* Philadelphia: P. W. Ziegler Co., 1906.

CHAPTER 3: DIGGINGS

Alexander, George. "Scientist Sees Big Quake on Tejon Pass–Salton Sea Fault." *Los Angeles Times,* 26 September 1984.

Meisling, Kristian E., and Kerry E. Sieh. "Disturbance of Trees by the 1857 Fort Tejon Earthquake, California." *Journal of Geophysical Research* 85 (10 June 1980): 3225-38.

Sieh, Kerry E. "Prehistoric Large Earthquakes Produced by Slip on the San Andreas Fault at Pallett Creek, California." *Journal of Geophysical Research* 83 (10 August 1978): 3907-39.

———. "Is California 'Overdue' for a Great Earthquake?" *Engineering & Science* 44, no. 4 (April 1981): 4-8.

Sieh, Kerry E., and Richard H. Jahns. "Holocene activity of the San Andreas fault at Wallace Creek, California." *Geological Society of America Bulletin* 95 (August 1984): 883-96.

Smith, R. Jeffrey. "A Seismological Shoot-out at Diablo Canyon." *Science* 214 (30 October 1981): 528-29.

CHAPTER 4: PRECURSORS

Aki, Keiiti. "Possibilities of Seismology in the 1980's." *Bulletin of the Seismological Society of America* 70, no. 5 (October 1980): 1969-76.

Anderson, J. G., et al. "Strong Ground Motion from the Michoacan, Mexico, Earthquake." *Science* 233 (5 September 1986): 1043-49.

Castle, Robert O., et al. "Elevation Changes Preceding the San Fernando Earthquake of February 9, 1971." *Geology*, February 1974: 61-66.

Castle, Robert O., J. P. Church, and M. R. Elliott. "Aseismic Uplift in Southern California." *Science* 192 (16 April 1976): 251-53.

Castle, Robert O., and Robert W. Simpson. *An Early-20th-Century Uplift in Southern California: Associations with Seismicity.* Menlo Park, Calif.: U.S. Geological Survey, 1986.

Kanamori, Hiroo. "The Energy Release in Great Earthquakes." *Journal of Geophysical Research* 82, no. 20 (10 July 1977): 2981–87.

———. "The Nature of Seismicity Patterns Before Large Earthquakes." In *Earthquake Prediction—An International Review.* Washington, D.C.: American Geophysical Union, 1981.

Kerr, Richard A. "Earthquake Prediction: Mexican Quake Shows One Way to Look for the Big Ones." *Science* 203 (2 March 1979): 860–62.

———. "Another Successful Quake Forecast." *Science* 203 (16 March 1979): 1091.

———. "Concern Rising About the Next Big Quake." *Science* 207 (15 February 1980): 748–49.

———. "Palmdale Bulge Doubts Now Taken Seriously." *Science* 214 (18 December 1981): 1331–33.

———. "Does California Bulge or Does It Jiggle?" *Science* 219 (11 March 1983): 1205–6.

LeFevre, L. Victoria, and Karen C. McNally. "Stress Distribution and Subduction of Aseismic Ridges in the Middle America Subduction Zone." *Journal of Geophysical Research* 90 (10 May 1985): 4495–4510.

McNally, Karen. "Trapping an Earthquake." *Engineering & Science* 43, no. 2 (November–December 1979): 6–12.

Mogi, Kiyoo. "Recent Earthquake Prediction Research in Japan." *Science* 233 (18 July 1986): 324–30.

Ohtake, Masakazu, Tosimatu Matumoto, and Gary Latham. "Seismicity Gap Near Oaxaca, Southern Mexico, as a Probable Precursor to a Large Earthquake." *Pure and Applied Geophysics* 115 (1977): 375–84.

Overbye, Dennis. "The Earthquake Trapper." *Discover,* July 1981, 48–54.

Shapley, Deborah. "Earthquakes: Los Angeles Prediction Suggests Faults in Federal Policy." *Science* 192 (7 May 1976): 535–37.

CHAPTER 5: SURPRISES

Bakun, William H. "Seismic Activity on the Southern Cala-veras Fault in Central California." *Bulletin of the Seis-mological Society of America* 70, no. 4 (August 1980): 1181–97.

Bowker, Michael. "Can Animals Really Predict Earth-quakes?" *Los Angeles Times,* 1 February 1988.

"Earthquake Prediction Is Coming." *Mosaic* 8, no. 2 (March–April 1977): 2–7.

Hammond, Allen L. "Earthquake Prediction: Progress in California, Hesitation in Washington." *Science* 187 (7 February 1975): 419–20.

Kerr, Richard A. "Prospects for Earthquake Prediction Wane." *Science* 206 (2 November 1979): 542–45.

———. "Quake Prediction by Animals Gaining Respect." *Science* 208 (16 May 1980): 695–96.

———. "How Much Is Too Much When the Earth Quakes?" *Science* 209 (29 August 1980): 1004–7.

———. "Harbingers of the Coalinga Earthquake." *Science* 222 (25 November 1983): 918.

———. "An Encouraging Long-Term Quake 'Forecast.'" *Science* 225 (20 July 1984): 300–301.

McEvilly, T. V., and L. R. Johnson. "Earthquakes of Strike-Slip Type in Central California: Evidence on the Ques-tion of Dilatancy." *Science* 182 (9 November 1973): 581–84.

Meredith, Dennis. "Lessons from the Coalinga Earthquake." *Engineering & Science* 47, no. 2 (November 1983): 6–9.

Nur, Amos. "Dilatancy, Pore Fluids, and Premonitory Varia-tions of t_s/t_p Travel Times." *Bulletin of the Seismological Society of America* 62, no. 5 (October 1972): 1217–22.

Otis, Leon S. *Can Animals Predict Earthquakes?* Menlo Park, Calif.: SRI International, 1982.

Qidong, Deng, et al. "A Preliminary Analysis of Reported Changes in Ground Water and Anomalous Animal Be-

havior Before the 4 February 1975 Haicheng Earth-
quake." In *Earthquake Prediction—An International
Review.* Washington, D.C.: American Geophysical
Union, 1981.

Scholtz, Christopher H., Lynn R. Sykes, and Yash P. Aggarwal. "Earthquake Prediction: A Physical Basis." *Science* 181 (31 August 1973): 803–10.

Shapley, Deborah. "Chinese Earthquakes: The Maoist Approach to Seismology." *Science* 193 (20 August
1976): 656–57.

Whitcomb, J. H., J. E. Garmany, and D. L. Anderson. "Earthquake Prediction: Variation of Seismic Velocities Before
the San Francisco [*sic*] Earthquake." *Science* 180 (11
May 1973): 632–35.

CHAPTER 6: PARKFIELD

Bakun, W. H., and A. G. Lindh. "The Parkfield, California,
Earthquake Prediction Experiment." *Science* 229 (16
August 1985): 619–24.

Bakun, W. H., and T. V. McEvilly. "Earthquakes Near Parkfield, California: Comparing the 1934 and 1966 Sequences." *Science* 205 (28 September 1979):
1375–77.

———. "Recurrence Models and Parkfield, California,
Earthquakes." *Journal of Geophysical Research* 89 (10
May 1984): 3051–58.

Kerr, Richard A. "Stalking the Next Parkfield Earthquake."
Science 223 (6 January 1984): 36–38.

———. "Earthquake Forecast Endorsed." *Science* 228 (19
April 1985): 311.

———. "Parkfield Earthquake Looks to Be on Schedule."
Science 231 (10 January 1986): 116.

———. "Quake Prediction Under Way in Earnest." *Science*
233 (1 August 1986): 520.

Lindh, Allan G. *Preliminary Assessment of Long-Term Probabilities for Large Earthquakes Along Selected Fault Segments of the San Andreas Fault System in California.* U.S. Geological Survey, Open-File Report 83-63, 1983.

Segall, P., and R. Harris. "Slip Deficit on the San Andreas Fault at Parkfield, California, as Revealed by Inversion of Geodetic Data." *Science* 233 (26 September 1986) 1409–13.

Sieh, Kerry E. "Central California Foreshocks of the Great 1857 Earthquake." *Bulletin of the Seismological Society of America* 68, no. 6 (December 1978): 1731–49.

CHAPTER 7: THE SHAKING NEXT TIME

An Assessment of the Consequences and Preparations for a Catastrophic California Earthquake: Findings and Actions Taken. Federal Emergency Management Agency, Washington, D.C., November 1980.

Brownlee, Shannon. "Waiting for the Big One." *Discover,* July 1986: 52–71.

Davis, James F., et al. *Earthquake Planning Scenario for a Magnitude 8.3 Earthquake on the San Andreas Fault in Southern California.* Special Publication 60, California Division of Mines and Geology, Sacramento, 1982.

Kerr, Richard A. "California's Shaking Next Time." *Science* 215 (22 January 1982): 385–87.

———. "Pinning Down the Next Big California Quake." *Science* 230 (25 October 1985): 426–27.

Lafferty, Libby. *Earthquake Preparedness.* CHES of California, La Canada, Calif., 1983.

"Los Angeles: When the Earth Quaked." *Newsweek,* 22 February 1971: 19–23.

Soble, Ronald L. "Study Foresees Vast Damage in Central L.A. in 6.3 Temblor." *Los Angeles Times,* 16 July 1986.

Steinbrugge, Karl V., et al. *Metropolitan San Francisco and Los Angeles Earthquake Loss Studies: 1980 Assessment.* U.S. Geological Survey Open-File Report 81-113, 1981. (Available from U.S. Geological Survey, Denver, Colorado.)

CHAPTER 8: AFTERSHOCKS

Atwater, Brian F. "Evidence for Great Holocene Earthquakes Along the Outer Coast of Washington State." *Science* 236 (22 May 1987): 942–44.

Beck, James L., and John F. Hall. "Engineering Features of the Recent Mexican Earthquake." *Engineering and Science* 44 (January 1986): 2–9.

Coffmann, Jerry L., and Carl A. von Hake, eds. *Earthquake History of the United States.* U.S. Department of Commerce Publication 41-1. Washington: U.S. Government Printing Office, 1973.

Engebretson, David C., Allan Cox, and Richard G. Gordon. *Relative Motions Between Oceanic and Continental Plates in the Pacific Basin.* Special Paper 206, Geological Society of America, 1985.

Heaton, Thomas H., and Stephen H. Hartzell. "Earthquake Hazards on the Cascadia Subduction Zone." *Science* 236 (10 April 1987): 162–68.

Johnson, Arch C. "A Major Earthquake Zone on the Mississippi." *Scientific American* 246 (April 1982): 60–68.

Johnson, Arch C., and Susan J. Nava. "Recurrence Rates and Probability Estimates for the New Madrid Seismic Zone." *Journal of Geophysical Research* 90 (10 July 1985): 6737–53.

Kerr, Richard A. "Assessing the Risk of Eastern U.S. Earthquakes." *Science* 214 (9 October 1981): 169–71.

———. "New Gravity Anomalies Mapped from Old Data." *Science* 215 (5 March 1982): 1220–22.

———. "A New View: First U.S. Magnetic Anomaly Map." *Science* 218 (3 December 1982): 986–87.

———. "Eastern Quakes Pinned Down?" *Science* 227 (25 January 1985): 400.

———. "Unexpected Young Fault Found in Oklahoma." *Science* 227 (8 March 1985): 1187–88.

———. "Continental Drift Nearing Certain Detection." *Science* 229 (6 September 1985): 953–55.

———. "Charleston Quakes Are Large or Widespread." *Science* 233 (12 September 1986): 1154.

———. "Direct Measurements Confirm Plate Tectonics." *Science* 236 (12 June 1987) 1425–26.

Nuttli, Otto W. "The Mississippi Valley Earthquakes of 1811 and 1812: Intensities, Ground Motion and Magnitudes." *Bulletin of the Seismological Society of America* 63, no. 1 (February 1973): 227–48. (Includes compilation on microfiche of contemporary newspaper accounts of these earthquakes.)

Penick, James Lal, Jr. *The New Madrid Earthquakes.* Columbia, Missouri: University of Missouri Press, 1981.

"Quakes in Search of a Theory." *Mosaic* 7, no. 4 (July–August 1976): 2–11.

CHAPTER 9: MAN MEETS QUAKE

"Earthquake Prediction: Is It Better Not to Know?" *Mosaic* 8, no. 2 (March–April 1977): 8–14.

Heaton, Thomas H. "A Model for a Seismic Computerized Alert Network." *Science* 228 (24 May 1985): 987–90.

Kerr, Richard A. "Continental Drilling Heading Deeper." *Science* 224 (29 June 1984): 1418–20. See also "The Deepest Hole in the World," same issue, 1420.

———. "Is the San Andreas Weak at Heart?" *Science* 236 (24 April 1987): 388–89.

Kozlovsky, Yevgeny A. "The World's Deepest Well." *Scientific American* 251 (December 1984): 98–104.

McNally, Karen. "Trapping an Earthquake." *Engineering & Science* 43, no. 2 (November–December 1979): 6–12.

INDEX

Italic numbers denote pages with maps.

281

JOHN TAGGART HINCKLEY LIBRARY
NORTHWEST COMMUNITY COLLEGE
POWELL, WYOMING 82435